Praise for

MEDIA LITERAC

and the

EMERGING CITIZEN

"A media literate culture is at the core of democracy. This is the simple and profound concept Paul Mihailidis illuminates in his fantastic new book. Through rich examples and analysis, he demonstrates how everyday actions of young people online are having a global civic impact. Youth media production, dissemination, alteration, and criticism are shaping everyday democracy for millions.

The tenets of media literacy, often associated with educational intervention, are boldly expanded beyond the classroom and into the civic realm. Mihailidis applies decades of media literacy scholarship and practice to his formulation of how and why youth are using media to influence social change in their communities and in the world. Through this lens, he argues that engaged citizenship is just as likely to happen on a mobile phone as it is in a voting booth. The book is a must-read for any scholar, practitioner, and educator invested in what civic engagement looks like in the 21st century."

— Eric Gordon, Ph.D., Fellow, Berkman Center for Internet and Society,
Harvard University; Director, Engagement Game Lab and
Associate Professor, Visual and Media Arts, Emerson College

"*Media Literacy and the Emerging Citizen* by Paul Mihailidis is a penetrating analysis of how the ever-beta digital tools and technologies of our age have become more than the armor of our individual and collective identities. In this important work, Mihailidis details how social media have become both the form around and the definition of public involvement and civic engagement. We are all Tony Stark—media are our exoskeletons. We have the power to do more than we ever could—and teachers and policy makers need to read Mihailidis's book to learn how we need to start."

—Susan Moeller, Professor, School of Journalism, University of Maryland

"At a time when frameworks for citizenship, engagement, and activism are being re-imagined in ever-more disruptive, proactive, and progressive ways, Paul Mihailidis's book places an emphasis on the media competencies young people need to be effective participants in digital culture. As new social tools and technologies are leading to new forms of engagement for youth across the Middle East, *Media Literacy and the Emerging Citizen* provides a theoretical and practical inquiry into the role of social and mobile technologies in the global civic landscape. This book is a must-read for anyone interested in the nexus of media, citizenship, and engagement in digital culture."

—Jad Melki, Director, Media Studies Program, American University of Beirut, Lebanon

MEDIA LITERACY
and the
EMERGING CITIZEN

This book is part of the Peter Lang Media and Communication list.
Every volume is peer reviewed and meets
the highest quality standards for content and production.

PETER LANG
New York • Washington, D.C./Baltimore • Bern
Frankfurt • Berlin • Brussels • Vienna • Oxford

PAUL MIHAILIDIS

MEDIA LITERACY
and the
EMERGING CITIZEN

Youth, Engagement and Participation in Digital Culture

PETER LANG
New York • Washington, D.C./Baltimore • Bern
Frankfurt • Berlin • Brussels • Vienna • Oxford

Library of Congress Cataloging-in-Publication Data
Mihailidis, Paul.
Media literacy and the emerging citizen: youth, engagement
and participation in digital culture / Paul Mihailidis.
pages cm
Includes bibliographical references and index.
1. Media literacy. 2. Mass media—Technological innovations.
3. Digital media. 4. Citizen journalism. I. Title.
P96.M4M54   302.23084'2—dc23   2013046515
ISBN 978-1-4331-2180-7 (hardcover)
ISBN 978-1-4331-2179-1 (paperback)
ISBN 978-1-4539-1293-5 (e-book)

Bibliographic information published by **Die Deutsche Nationalbibliothek**.
Die Deutsche Nationalbibliothek lists this publication in the "Deutsche
Nationalbibliografie"; detailed bibliographic data is available
on the Internet at http://dnb.d-nb.de/.

The paper in this book meets the guidelines for permanence and durability
of the Committee on Production Guidelines for Book Longevity
of the Council of Library Resources.

© 2014 Peter Lang Publishing, Inc., New York
29 Broadway, 18th floor, New York, NY 10006
www.peterlang.com

Printed in the United States of America

TABLE OF CONTENTS

DEDICATION

To Amy. Without her, this book would have not been possible.
To Emma and Mae. Who keep me working,
laughing and in constant amazement.

ACKNOWLEDGMENTS

This book would not have been possible without the help, support and guidance from a host of great friends, colleagues, mentors and students.

I'd first like to thank my colleagues at the universities that participated in the research for this book. Belinha De Abreu, Vanessa Domine, Chuck Fidler, Katherine Fry, Sherri Hope Culver, Susan Moeller, Moses Shumow, and Bu Zhong were all overly generous in both disseminating the surveys and allowing me to intrude on their classrooms to facilitate small group discussions.

I'm indebted to my colleagues and friends who read versions of this book along the way, from the initial chapters to the final product. Their eyes, ears, and constructive criticisms helped form the core arguments that I try to advance. In no particular order, I'm indebted to David Cooper Moore, Belinha De Abreu, Meg Fromm, and Eric Gordon for reading versions of this work and providing critical feedback. The theoretical developments early in this work, particularly in Chapter two, stem from some of discussions with Benjamin Thevenin, who I'm grateful to for being able to engage with in more substantial ways around critical media literacy and citizenship. I've sat many nights with Jad Melki, Moses Shumow, Roman Gerodimos, and Meg Fromm, talking about the ideas in this book, amongst many other things, that have all found a way to influence the work that follows. Many others contributed to the shaping of this book in formal and informal ways, too many to name here. A few I would like to offer thanks to specifically for their support. Angela Cooke Jackson for our work on media and health literacy with urban youth; Sanjeev Chatterjee, Jochen Fried, David Goldman, Manuel Guerrero, Andrea Lopez-Portillo, Stephen Reese, and especially Stephen Salyer, and Susan Moeller, whom I already mentioned above, founded, and helped build the Salzburg Academy on Media and Global Change, which largely shaped my thinking about the models I provide in this book. David Burns and I sat one night in an office in Salzburg in 2007 and played around with the 5A's model in its earliest stages. Without that night, I'm not sure I would have come to this point.

I wanted to extend thanks to the many students who helped develop the ideas found in this book. My media literacy students at Hofstra University, and later at Emerson College were crucial to my understanding of social media, young people, and civic life. Eivind Michaelsen, for the last two years at Emerson, has helped immensely in the transcription of this data, the creation of the figures and graphs in the book, in bringing the numerous examples you'll find in the appendices to my attention, and in being a fantastic friend and graduate assistant along the way.

I would also like to extend a warm thanks to my editor, Mary Savigar, at Peter Lang, whom I've now had the pleasure of working with on multiple projects. Mary has been supportive, flexible and responsive to all my inquiries throughout this process. Thanks also goes to the staff around Mary, as well as the reviewers of this book, who played a central role in shaping the ideas found in this book, and in the final product that you see here.

Finally, of course, none of this would be possible without the support of my family. Amy, Emma and Mae have given me the time and leeway to make this possible. I think I owe them a year of dinners, Saturdays, and ice cream. I can't wait to pay them back.

Paul Mihailidis, PhD
Emerson College, Boston, MA, USA
Salzburg Academy on Media and Global Change, Salzburg, Austria

FIGURES

· INTRODUCTION ·

CIVIC LIFE IN DIGITAL CULTURE

We exist today between worlds. At home, in school, and in public, our physical interactions are determined by the constraints of proximity. We speak to those around us; we socialize within our direct circles, and extend our interactions based on our willingness or need to communicate. The communities that we have historically formed were limited by physical surroundings. We help around the house, we support our neighbors and neighborhoods, and we participate in communities based on their closeness to us. Sharing stories with others has always been a central and necessary component of this existence.

In mediated spaces, a new landscape continues to emerge. Supported by the growth of mobile and social media technologies, new digital platforms now encompass large, diverse, collaborative, and interactive networked communities. They are not limited by demographic or physical boundaries. Interactions in these spaces are many-to-many, sporadic, unscripted, and lack the need for intimacy or a present audience. In these spaces our personal relationships merge together with loose acquaintances and distant family members. In these spaces, the lines between news and entertainment, facts and fiction, truth and hearsay are less distinguishable. In these spaces, our virtual identities are self-crafted around our ideals and extend outward into the networks "in which we participate, opt into and create.

The emerging landscape for dialog online is actively reshaping how we think about community and participation in the 21st century. From how we understand privacy, expression, and identity, to how we negotiate relationships, social media technologies have exposed a need to explore new codes, rules, and regulations for dialog, voice, and connectivity.

Digital media culture has become so central to civic society today; we see peer-to-peer information platforms playing ever-larger roles in contemporary issues. Joseph Kony and the Lord's Resistance Army becomes a global conversation for youth around the world, right alongside the most recent winner of *American Idol*, the death of Whitney Houston, and Kim Kardashian's latest relationship. We see millions come out opposed to "pink slime" condensed meat in our children's school cafeterias, and an entirely youth-run Harry Potter Alliance providing a communal home for many online, who have a say in the peripheral direction of the franchise and the causes they support.

From Barack Obama's use of social media to enable a new constituency in 2008, to Wikileaks publication of troves of information concerning a myriad of political topics and the use of social media for protest in support of the Nobel Prize-winning Chinese dissident Liu Xiaobo, social media platforms have enabled a flow of information with little regard for borders or boundaries. Generally referred to as the largest civic uprising supported by social media platforms and mobile technologies, the Arab Uprisings, instigated on December 19, 2010, in Tunisia, touched off a series of civic protests that eventually spread throughout the Middle East and North Africa. Citizens, who rarely had the communicative capacity to organize so fluidly in a mass media age, now had a host of connective networks to help organize and facilitate large-scale civic movements. Protestors and onlookers were able to document and share events with the entire world as they happened: exposing injustice, calling for resources, and garnering support.

Of course, it hasn't always been this way. The evolution of civic participation, voting, and what counts for political engagement, has changed dramatically over time. In the *Good Citizen*, Michael Schudson (1998b), traces the forms of civic participation since the founding of the United States: from a "politics of assent" where the wealthy land owning class represented citizens with power, to a political party system that arose with the growth of population, landmass and diverse views in the United States. The informed citizen evolved to include less emotion and more education in the U.S. political landscape. Parties vied for voters who had more representation through their ballot and who had more information at their disposal through a burgeoning mass communication industry.

Today, we are at a point of inflection for understanding "what counts" for engagement and participation in civic life. The growth of digital technologies has destabilized traditional media models, and therefore how citizens are informed about the issues they use to decide which party or politician to support. Beyond this, citizen-led social movements that are made possible by digital and social technologies are now dominant measures of social and civic progress. Walter Lippmann, back in 1962, noted, "Social movements are at once the symptoms and the instruments of progress. Ignore them and statesmanship is irrelevant; fail to use them and it is weak" (p. 144).

When I began writing this book, the Occupy Wall Street movement in New York City, Boston, Oakland, Washington, DC, San Francisco, and around the world was leveraging social media to organize meetings, participate in public protest, and express resistance to dominant financial and political systems that they opposed. As I sat down to write the final pages of this book, in the wake of the horrific bombings at the 2013 Boston Marathon, I followed the vast civic coordination to help runners to shelter and safety, and at the same time spread rumors, hearsay and misinformation.

Social media have also played a central role as civic watchdogs against aggressive and opaque business practices. Organizing through social media led to the reversal of arbitrary fee hikes by Bank of America and helped to refute unneeded new pay models implemented without warning by the online movie service Netflix. More examples of social media playing a larger role in the corporate, political, and economic arenas in the US and beyond appear by the day. These social spaces have empowered voices—largely those of everyday citizens—that are engaging a diverse flow of ideas and dialog across communities, across cultures, and across divides.

At the same time, this digital culture has given way to hackers, dissidents, and governments that are using the same new technologies to increasingly control populations, restrict information flow, and quell civic movements. Evgeny Morozov (2011) warns about "cyber-utopianism and Internet-centrism" (p. xvii) as disregarding the ways that digital technologies can extend oppressive regimes and further control marginalized publics. Morozov provides a lengthy account of ways that Internet freedom has marginalized citizens around the world, specifically in the transitioning former Soviet Bloc and Eastern European countries.

For better or worse (or maybe for better "and" worse), young people are relying more and more on peer-to-peer information platforms for local community issues, town planning, hyper-local news, and afterschool programs.

General research on Internet habits clearly reinforces the impetus for this shift. A 2010 Kaiser Family Foundation Study reported young adults spending upwards of 10 hours per day with media (Rideout et al. 2010). A Pew Center report (2013) found that young adults are now spending more time with news and information on social networks than ever before. Research conducted for this book, which we'll explore in chapters four and five, shows a clear shift towards social networks to facilitate a majority of information uses and needs. This large-scale change in information gathering and communication habits presents a myriad of opportunities and challenges to civic structures as they currently exist. How will these new spaces facilitate civic dialog? What types of information flow will they enable for personal and public needs? For advocacy and activism? For entertainment and leisure? What are young people being taught about these spaces? How do they conceive them as personal spaces? As public spaces?

Much new research, detailed throughout this book, has explored the behavioral dispositions of youth and young adults in these spaces, leading to almost as many diverse viewpoints as there are new research findings. This is largely a byproduct of the rapid growth and expansion of tools, spaces, platforms, and users. And while these inquiries help build a stronger understanding of the landscape for social media and civic society, there remains a great need to explore pedagogical models—both formal and informal—aimed at harnessing social media use for engaged citizenship in digital culture.

At the heart of this book are the opportunities that social media platforms and mobile technologies provide for communication, connectivity, and community. *Media Literacy and the Emerging Citizen* is about enhancing engagement in digital culture, and the models that educators, parents, and policy makers can utilize to place a media-savvy citizenry into positions of purpose, responsibility, and power.

Two specific challenges are at the core of this book's argument that *media literacy is the path towards more active and robust civic engagement in the 21st century.*

1. *How can media literacy enable core competencies for value-driven, diverse and robust digital media use?*
2. *How can media literacy enable a more civic-minded participatory culture?*

These challenges are indeed large, but need to be seen in their entirety for media literacy to begin to address the opportunities they present for democracy, participation, and discourse in a digital media age. By presenting information that places media literacy at the center of what it means to be an empowered citizen today, educators and policy makers will be able to see why media literacy must be integrated into formal and informal education systems before it's too late.

The call for more vigorous pedagogical responses to our current digital media landscape is arguably more important now than ever before. As long as educators continue to position social media outside the bounds of the class-room and detached from learning about community, democracy, and civic participation, our education systems will continue to fall well behind the expansive integration of social media platforms for daily civic functions.

Media Literacy and the Emerging Citizen is a manifesto for media literacy education that is at the center of how young people understand the influence social media have on their personal and public lives and use digital media for more inclusive lifestyles. The opportunity to reframe the debate on what an engaged citizen is and on how media literacy education can stand to em-power the next generation of leaders is apparent and glaring. This book is driven by the potential of networked communities to build new collaborative participation across all facets of society (Neal, 2012). Clay Shirky (2010) sees this as the true opportunity for collaboration today: "People want to do some-thing to make the world a better place. They will help when they are invited to" (p. 17). Media literacy can help activate that human element by harness-ing the true power each individual has to add value in society today. And we are not that far away.

Defining Terms

Throughout this book, terms appear repeatedly that are adopted in differing contexts and with different applications. Terminology is always a slippery slope when exploring large and broad concepts, and so I want to provide a primer for key terms that are used repeatedly in this text and that may slightly shift in shape and form as the book progresses.

- *Emerging citizen* – This concept is developed specifically to reframe how we look at young people and their daily civic lives. It stems from an understanding of citizenship as monitorial (Schudson, 1998; 1999), and new forms of engaged citizenship explored by Bennett (2008) and Dalton (2009), in addition to a host of work we'll visit in chapter one. The emerging citizen has integrated digital media culture fully into her life and understands public involvement not primarily by duties (taxes, voting, military service) but equally by engagement (expression, activism, sharing, dialog). These new voices are facilitated largely through digital media, where interactive platforms and social tools are largely replacing traditional avenues for information and communication needs.

- *Engaged citizenship* – This concept is used in this book in place of *informed citizenship*, or *civic participation*. It closely mirrors the idea of actualized citizenship developed as a new form of understanding civic efficacy, which is based largely on notions developed by Bennett (2011a; 2010), Dahlgren (2009; 2007), Schudson (1998), Jacobs et al. (2009), and Delli Carpini (2000). The destabilization of linear civic duties—voting, taxes, military service—and a linear media industry—TV, radio, newspapers—has shifted how young people receive information and contribute to civic dialog. As a result, Habermas's public sphere (1989), recreated in a digital age, becomes much less uniform and visible, and more multimodal. How young people participate in civic life becomes a more complex portrait: is voting alone the best metric for engagement? When does a citizen feel engaged? How does engagement work in digital spaces? Engaged citizenship embraces these complexities, and does not define parameters for participation, or make value judgments about which forms of engagement are more inclusive than others.

- *Media Literacy* – Media literacy historically has been used widely to fit into the pedagogical purview of many different disciplines. While many definitions exist—most broad and inclusive (explored in chapter two)—this book advocates media literacy education that has as its outcome the preparation of engaged citizens (Mihailidis & Thevenin, 2013):

  > ...for democratic participation by helping them analyze mediated *representations of* their communities, as well as address *issues within* their communities. And citizens who practice this critical thinking, will learn to deconstruct media texts, but perhaps more importantly, they will be engaged in "deconstructing injustices, expressing their own voices, and struggling to create a better society" (Kellner & Share, 2007a, 19–20) (5).

Media literacy takes different forms in early childhood education, K-12, and in the university. The civic focus here is deliberate. As students complete formal stages of education, and move towards adulthood, they must begin to make choices about communities, work, and school. Media literacy, on this level, should be predicated on helping to advance civic engagement and the continual goal of a more open, diverse and vibrant digital culture.

- *Social media* – Like media literacy, the term social media has come to encompass many different things. A landmark essay by boyd & Ellison (2007) deconstructs common terminology and unpacks some of the lineage from which the term "social networking" arises. In this book, social media is used to encompass an array of tools, platforms, and behaviors, that are *collaborative, peer-to-peer, and interactive*, to allow for user participation and control over content and presentation. The following chart by Kaplan & Haenlein (2010) is an accurate guide I have adopted for the use of the term social *media* throughout this book.

| | | Social presence/ Media richness | | |
		Low	Medium	High
Self-presentation/ Self-disclosure	High	Blogs	Social networking sites (e.g., Facebook)	Virtual social worlds (e.g., Second Life)
	Low	Collaborative projects (e.g., Wikipedia)	Content communities (e.g., YouTube)	Virtual game worlds (e.g., World of Warcraft)

Figure 1. Social Media Terminology Chart.
Source: Kaplan, A. M., & Haenlein, M. (2010). Users of the world, unite! The challenges and opportunities of Social Media. *Business Horizons*, 53(1), 59–68.

I chose to use social media inclusively here because this book is about media literacy, young people, and the future of engaged citizenship in a digital media age. It does not attempt to explore these topics through specific social media channels, but rather through more holistic understandings of the types of behaviors that exist in any popular, large scale collaborative spaces like Facebook, Twitter, Instagram, YouTube, Vine, Snapchat, and smaller more local spaces like community web sites, *blogs*, and alternative information spaces that incorporate the ideas, thoughts, and opinions of its constituents. Thus, at points in this book the conversation may be about Facebook specifically, while at other times it may be more broad and extensive. In Part Two of this book, which shows some exploratory research into social media and university students, I specify uses of social media—news, politics, entertainment, education, relationships, privacy, and expression—but do not uniformly differentiate platforms.

The Arc of This Book

To approach the questions posed above, *Media Literacy and the Emerging Citizen* is organized in three parts: *Emerging Landscapes, Listening to Emerging Citizens,* and *A Framework for Media Literacy and the Emerging Citizen.*

Before detailing how this book will progress, it's important at the outset to discuss what this book is *not* meant to do. This book is not a prescriptive curriculum guide. There are a host of books that do a thorough job looking specifically at curriculum for media literacy in the public school K-12 classroom (see De Abreu, 2011; Hobbs, 2007; Hobbs & Cooper Moore, 2013; Schiebe & Rogow, 2011; Share, 2009). Curricular and assessment guides for media literacy on the higher education level are less common, and rightfully so. One edited guide was distributed in 2006, including metrics for assessment across a range of communication disciplines in higher education (see Christ, 2006). This book will present a framework from which media literacy pedagogies can be developed, along with suggestions for developing media literacy competencies through formal and informal education. I chose this path for two reasons. First, media literacy is a multi-disciplinary movement that integrates into many different subject areas across higher education. Unlike the more linear approaches media literacy takes in K-12, on the university level it is difficult to implement top-down curricular mandates into university classrooms. This leads to the second reason this book does not offer specific curriculum: in higher education, curriculum is sacred and a valued space for faculty to explore, experiment, and develop ideas around their research and core concepts in their fields. To propose curriculum would be against the freedoms and innovative platforms that university educators enjoy. I hope the frameworks proposed in this book help to furnish new, exciting ideas and approaches to media literacy in the classroom.

This book does not offer specific commentary on how specific social media tools work in the context of media literacy. Because social media technologies evolve so quickly, with new tools constantly replacing old, focusing on specific platforms would self-defeat the larger argument that the book makes about digital media culture, and the competencies that young people need in order to succeed in this culture. This book is intended to explore the connections between media literacy, civic engagement, and digital media culture, as well as present frameworks and new models that extend these relationships into new workable spaces for parents, educators, and policy makers. This is beyond a single tool or platform.

What this book does do is try and push into new theoretical, conceptual and practical ideas about media literacy, young people and civic engagement in digital culture. The emerging citizen concept is developed to show the presence of media in the daily life of young people. I use the work of civic scholars to present various models, frameworks, and arguments for what it means to be an engaged citizen in the 21st century. I use this work to specifically expose some disconnects in thinking about civic engagement and the role of media literacy in civic education, which is where I attempt to break new ground.

...

Part One of this book lays out the foundations for the media literacy landscape in the context of young citizens today. Chapter one develops the concept of the emerging citizen in digital culture. It explores how notions of engaged citizenship have evolved in the context of digital media technologies, and investigates the connections between media and citizenship. These new connections set an important precedent for understanding why the actions of youth online—from 'likes' to signing petitions to sharing videos and posting personal projects online—can have an impact on traditional civic duties such as voting and volunteering. As scholars continue to explore changing metrics for civic involvement and engagement, educators need to follow suit in exploring different ways to think about teaching civic engagement and participation to the future generations, who will be voting for candidates, consuming information, and expressing ideas primarily online.

Chapter two complements the foundations of media and citizenship by offering an overview of the growth and current state of media literacy education. Media literacy, as the educational response to digital culture, is predicated on teaching and learning to critically think, analyze, evaluate, and create media and communication. This chapter explores some foundational frameworks for media education, along with the movement's traditional role as a protectionist outlet for youth and more recently as a means for empowering critical, independent and powerful voices across all ages. I argue in this chapter that media literacy, today, is the fundamental civic education for youth. If schools, homes, and policy arenas are slow to embrace media literacy, they run the risk of even greater pedagogical, and general, disconnect from the ways that people communicate and participate in contemporary civic society.

Chapter three builds from the theoretical explorations in chapters one and two to look specifically at the influences of digital culture on media literacy and the emerging citizen. This chapter presents a myriad of examples and cases showing how social media platforms and tools allow for organization, collaboration, interactivity, dialog, and expression that are inherently civically driven. The online behaviors of young people today have encouraged new approaches to how individuals, organizations, politicians, and marketers share information and engage in dialog. While it is easy to point out the obvious examples of activism within these spaces (Arab Spring, Obama Campaign, Occupy Wall Street), this chapter will show how civic behaviors are manifested on in daily life. This involves everything from the links that young people choose to share, to the types of dialog they engage in on a daily basis.

What happens when banks try to raise fees without first asking their customers? When a movie-streaming site tries to double its subscriber cost with no warning for its community? When governments try to impose their will without public approval? These questions, and the responses to them, hold great implications for what civic voice will mean as public dialog continues to shift into mediated spaces. These implications are not only important for policy makers, but also for an education system currently exploring not only how to incorporate social media into the classroom, but also how to teach about social media's use for adolescents today.

Part Two explores US university students' habits and dispositions around social media. In 2011, I went up and down the East Coast of the United States, surveying the social media habits of over 800 students, and talking in small groups to over 70 students about how they regard social media's role in their personal, public, and civic lives. What emerged was a rich and complex portrait of how university students perceive the shift in their daily habits because of the large amount of time they are spending on social media, and how they understand the growing centrality of these tools for social, civic, and political engagement. While using university students for my exploration skews my discussion to the (still) minority of young people in this country who will complete university, I do think the general ideas discussed can and will have relevance across many different population groups.

Chapter four explores the survey questionnaire, which asked university students about their social media habits across six categories: news, politics, relationships, entertainment, education, and privacy. The survey shows heavy social media use for all information habits—from news consumption to entertainment, shopping, personal and public communication, gossip, and so on. These results reinforce an "integrated" information lifestyle, where the boundaries for news, entertainment, personal and professional communication have disintegrated.

Chapter five summarizes the small group discussions conducted with study participants who took the survey and opted to speak about their social media habits thereafter. From these discussions an apparent disconnect emerged: students reported in their surveys using social media to facilitate a large majority of daily information and communication needs, but in the discussion sessions were unvaryingly negative towards mention of valuable or civic uses of social media platforms. A majority of the discussions centered on social media as personal time-wasting tools used mostly to stay in touch, gossip, and share personal information about their lives.

Part three of *Media Literacy and the Emerging Citizen* aims to bridge the emerging disconnect between social media use and perceived value through the development of a media literacy framework for engaged citizenship. If the students reported that most of their information habits now start through aggregated spaces and peer-to-peer information sharing, and are integrated within personal information spaces, how can we make the civic and community-based implications of their social media habits more transparent to them? What are the ways that educators can better connect time spent in social media spaces with thoughtful personal and civic contributions? What does a media literacy approach to digital culture look like?

In Chapter six, these questions are addressed in order to develop a case for more explicitly connecting social media habits and civic discourse. This chapter explores the digital media and learning movement to show specific parameters for education initiatives aimed at building competencies in young people for more inclusive and participatory lifestyles. A series of "connectors" are proposed to help to bridge the disconnect between social media's perceived use and value. These connectors are positioned to nudge the perception of social media into a more holistic and diverse lens. They can be adopted in formal and informal educational spaces. The chapter concludes by moving towards a normative model for media literacy and the emerging citizen that is premised on the lifelong development of skills and dispositions for digital culture.

Chapter seven proposes the *5A's of Media Literacy* model (see Figure 2). The 5A's offer a way for educators, professionals, parents, and policy makers to integrate a media literacy approach to teaching about the value of social media for a sense of place, community, expression, voice, and identity. The model is presented as a continuum, beginning with the notion of *Access* as a human right, and moving through *Awareness*, *Assessment*, and *Appreciation* towards *Action*, which is the default mindset for the media literate citizen.

This normative model provides a way to re-conceive what young people do in social media spaces, what their voice means, how they can take responsibility for the powerful voices they have, and the difference they can and will make for the future of participatory societies across the world.

ACCESS to media

AWARENESS of authority, context, credibility

ASSESSMENT of how media portray events and issues

APPRECIATION for the diversity of information, dialog, collaboration, and voices online

ACTION to become part of the dialog

Figure 2. The 5A's of Media Literacy Education.

What follows in this book is an exploration of the digital media realities and dispositions for youth today, and a passionate call for new approaches to teaching and learning about how social media can serve as a space for engaged and responsible dialog in information societies. Whether local or global, political, or personal, we live in an age where our daily lives are increasingly mediated. How we approach education about digital culture can and will determine how we utilize these new technologies for tolerance, diversity, transparency, and inclusiveness in the coming decades.

And while the education arena has been growing more effective in arming their classrooms with digital tools to elicit more dialog and communication among groups and with instructors, youth still struggle to transfer the diverse uses of digital tools to an understanding of their contributions to civic life. Fear of distraction, wasting time, fair use, and control over content all make the ability to teach about and with social media from a young age a challenge. This book provides a way to reconceive engagement starting with media literacy education.

Teachers, parents, policy makers, and public officials can all benefit from this newfound engagement with social platforms for community empowerment and civic engagement. I see these opportunities in my classrooms, in my home, and in my community happening all the time. I wonder what new and exciting forms of collaboration will come next. Building a media literacy approach that starts early and is a core part of lifelong learning can help bridge the divides, polarization, and general discord brought from the mass media industry. We are at the tip of an iceberg. I hope media literacy leads us to a more vibrant, diverse, inclusive, tolerant, and engaged future.

· PART ONE ·

EMERGING LANDSCAPES

· 1 ·

THE EMERGING CIVIC
LANDSCAPE

What does it look like to be civically engaged? Before the Internet, it often looked like reading the newspaper, watching local news on television, attending town hall meetings and rallies, and perhaps writing letters to representatives. But with the Internet, the terms and methods of being an informed and engaged citizen have changed.

— Eric Gordon (2013)

An engaged citizenry has always been a central, though not exclusive, prerequisite for democracy. From town meetings and community bulletin boards to the advent of social media, the expression of civic voices has always been a precondition for a democratic public.

Michael Schudson traced the evolution of citizenship in the United States to arrive at what he termed the monitorial citizen—a gatherer, monitor, and surveyor of information, who "swings into public action only when directly threatened" (Leman, 1998). Schudson argued that the "good" citizen-an active participant in his or her community who votes, volunteers, participates, and believes in the public service of the government-no longer exists. Rather, Schudson understood citizenship as a combination of the attributes that comprise *valuable* contributions to society, and this obligation, in an information age, was not only about being informed. "Citizens can be "monitorial" rather than "informed," wrote Schudson (1998), "A monitorial citizen scans (rather than reads) the informational environment in a way so that he or she may be alerted on a very wide variety of issues for a very wide variety of ends and may be mobilized around those issues in a large variety of ways."

No longer, Schudson argued, is citizenship solely based on politicians, parties, and partisanship. Instead, new understanding of civic participation must also include new modes of thinking about expression, engagement, and activism. In Schudson's argument, the monitorial citizen is "not an absentee citizen but watchful, even while he or she is doing something else. ... In this world, monitoring is a plausible model of citizenship" (Schudson, 1998).

This world that Schudson describes is one in which media are at the center of formulations of civic efficacy and conduits for civic voice. Schudson (1999) asks, "Where do the media fit with all of this? The press is not the focal point of civic life. It never was. It is a tool of civic life. It is a necessary tool. The media's main task is critique, monitoring, a watchdog over authority." When Schudson wrote this, over a decade ago, the argument could have been made that media were not a central conduit for civic life. Today, however, in an age of ubiquitous digital media, that argument is harder to justify.

Today, digital media platforms and mobile technologies have integrated seamlessly into the daily routines of citizens around the world, to the point that young citizens no longer organize their lives around information but instead organize information around their lives. The results of this shift point to a new civic culture that is dependent on media for daily functions, knowledge about local issues, and communication with friends, family, and acquaintances. Schudson (1998) argues that in the context of this shift, "If the new digital media are to be integrated into a new political democracy, they must be linked to a serious understanding of citizenship, and this cannot happen if we simply recycle the old notion of the informed citizen" (p. 1). The informed citizen, born from an age of mass communication industries and a growth in education systems for all of society, posited that citizens could be educated to have full information about politics, and vote with secret ballots for their candidates. This model, while still relevant for citizens who use mainstream media (television, newspapers, etc.) to learn about civic issues, is less relevant to younger digital generations.

Henry Jenkins expands on the concept of the monitorial citizen by focusing on the ways in which digital media have shifted what it means to be a participatory citizen. In *Convergence Culture*, Jenkins (2006a) uses Pierre Levy's (1997) knowledge culture—"knowledgeable in some areas, somewhat aware in others, operating in a context of mutual trust and shared resources" (p. 226)—to advance the monitorial citizen as one who "develop[s] new critical skills in assessing information—a process that occurs both on an individual level within the home or the workplace, and on a more collaborative level through the work of various knowledge communities (p. 227). Jenkins advocates for seeing citizens as surveyors of information rather than gatherers. Armed with a variety of social communication tools, the ability to express ideas, and monitor topics, citizens stand ready to respond and spread messages when they feel it is right to do so. The monitorial citizen, as a verifier of information, can debunk political propaganda, participate in dialog about relevant political topics, and contribute to critical discourse about civic and social life outside the bounds of the mainstream mass media industry.

Zizi Papacharissi (2010) argues, like Schudson, that "the monitorial citizen is neither a better nor worse servant of democracy than past citizens were" (102). She notes that while citizens now receive more information than those in the past, in no way does this equal a more informed disposition. A convergence of technologies, new landscapes for public-civic communication, and a shifting perception of civic duty, however, have reframed the relationships citizens have with their immediate constituents and their surrounding communities. A converged media landscape provides a new way to understand the citizen of today as monitorial, where, according to Papacharissi (2010) they are afforded: "(a) a wider scope of issue and coverage to monitor, (b) guidance on issues based on standards that resemble their own, and (c) a direct route for mobilization and exerting influence" (p. 152).

Such new developments are reshaping what participation means in digital media culture. While monitorial citizenship may be more isolating, it is predicated on a rich information diet, and accelerated and exacerbated by digital media technologies that allow for many-to-many sharing and collaborative expression. The monitorial citizen is not concerned with institutional structures (Bimber, 1998; 2000; 2001), but uses social platforms to share content, express ideas, and collaborate around issues that are personally relevant.

This evokes new questions about what it means to be an engaged citizen and participate in modern society. In a converged and digital media culture, how do we understand what constitutes an engaged citizen? What are the metrics with which engagement can be measured? And how does this relate to digital technologies and civic voice? Before exploring some of these questions in more detail, I first want to unpack the engaged citizenship concept as it has evolved within digital culture.

Engaged Citizenship

In *The Good Citizen*, Russell Dalton presents a framework for what he calls "The Changing American Public." In this framework Dalton (2009) advocates a new norm for what it means to be a participating citizen, moving "from Citizen Duty—Citizens vote, pay taxes, obey the law—to Engaged Citizenship—Independent, assertive citizens concerned with others" (p. 4). Writes Dalton (2009):

> Most definitions of citizenship typically focus on the traditional norms of American citizenship—voting, paying taxes, belonging to a political party—and how these are changing. I call this duty-based citizenship because these norms reflect formal obligations, responsibilities, and rights of citizenship as they have been defined in the past. However, it is just as important to examine new norms that make up what I call engaged citizenship. These norms are emerging among the American public with increasing prominence. Engaged citizenship emphasizes a more assertive role for the citizen and a broader definition of the elements of citizenship to include social concerns and the welfare of others. (p. 5)

To facilitate this shift, Dalton cites a host of changing social conditions that are reorganizing what it means to be a good citizen. These include *generation shifts* (to Gen X), *living standards* (more affluence), *education* (more college degrees), *work experience* (more knowledge-based), *gender roles* (more women in workforce), and *social diversity* (more opportunities for minorities) as the main predictors for changing norms of citizenship in the United States today. Dalton (2009) summarizes the outcomes of this shifting landscape in the form of political consequences, highlighting *participation patterns* (from voting to protest), *political tolerance* (accepting various viewpoints), *role of government* (more active), *social policy* (increased support for social programs), *trust in government* (decreasing), and *democratic ideals* (pressuring democracy to meet its ideals), as primary factors in the shift from an obligation-based citizenry to a citizenry that is concern-based.

Dalton reinforces his premise with troves of valuable data that show how younger citizens place more importance on values such as making the United States and the world better, and understanding how they can personally affect change. From the emergence of a more diverse and inclusive workforce, to debunking the myth of the disengaged American citizen, Dalton paints a convincing picture of a younger generation that is civically active, more tolerant of others' political views, and more critical of traditional government behavior than generations before.

This is in direct opposition to what Dalton calls *duty-based citizenship* where emphasis lies in voting, the military, taxes, and obeying the law. This aging demographic, according to Dalton (2009), is far more patriotic and nationalistic, and less likely to participate in a domestic protest. The generational gap that accompanies this division is large and widening by the year.

Media scholar W. Lance Bennett explores the similarities and differences between the *Actualizing Citizen*—a loosely networked individual who reflects civic ideas through a personal lens—and the *Dutiful Citizen*—one still adhering to the traditional norms for civic engagement. Bennett (2007), like Dalton, questions the efficacy of evaluating the participation of today's youth population with metrics of past societies, and ponders whether family, private and public entities are "willing to allow young citizens to more fully explore, experience, and expand democracy, or will they continue to force them to try to fit into an earlier model that is ill suited to the networked societies of the digital age?" (8).

At the center of these changing norms of citizenship are the ways in which people identify with issues, ascribe to viewpoints, and find information to assert or refute their beliefs. While a general rise in education levels will expose individuals to more ideas, viewpoints, causes, and events—leading to more thoughtful consideration about the world—today's younger generations are not only finding their voices in traditional education spaces, but more so in the social spaces that have integrated deeply into their lives. The concept of the *emerging citizen* grows from young citizens' dependence on new social media platforms and mobile technologies to fulfill the new norms of Dalton's engaged citizen and Bennett's actualizing citizen.

Scholars have explored how social networks are impacting social capital (see Ellison et al., 2010, 2007; Steinfeld et al., 2008), a concept brought to prominence by Granovetter's (1973) landmark study that argued for the potential strength of linking members of different small groups around relevant causes or issues. Granovetter's work set the course for explorations in weak tie connectivity and potential that was again thrust into the spotlight at the turn of the 21st century by sociologist Robert Putnam. Putnam (1995; 2000) posited that the rise of the mass communication industries was causing a decline in ties that bind communities and the civic virtues that these communities uphold. Recent findings by Ellison et al. (2010) show that "the social and technical affordances of Facebook support the conversion of latent ties to weak ties, in that the site provides identity information, enables communication between parties, and helps bring together those with shared interests" (p. 887).

The weak tie phenomenon, alternatively known as "slacktivism" has reemerged in an age of ubiquitous social media platforms, large-scale civic organizing, and disintegrating barriers for public expression.[1] Shirky builds on this phenomenon in his book *Cognitive Surplus*, where he explores how social media technologies can enable collaboration, sharing, and collective action on scales never seen before. To preface this new collaborative landscape, Shirky (2010) makes the simple but powerful observation "...when we use a network, the most important asset we get is access to one another" (14). We are entering an age of a re-engaged emphasis on community values that, as evidenced by local food movements, online town forums, and local, national and global political organizing suggests, is at the heart of engaged citizenship in participatory democracies.

How will young citizens incorporate civic agency into their digitally mediated identities? Peter Dahlgren (2012) develops a "cautious optimism for young citizens, digital media and participation" around a core of what he calls "six dimensions of mutual reciprocity" (19)—knowledge, values, trust, spaces, practices, and identities—that together form a fluid but structured context for understanding the changing realities for youth and participation in the context of their digital habits. Dahlgren prefaces these dimensions by acknowledging the indisputable centrality of digital media for civic life, and presents his framework as a way to "help[s] us to analytically grasp the notion of citizenship in a manner that can mediate between specific political contexts and larger perspectives of situated human agency and subjectivity" (p. 25). Dahlgren urges his readers to expand how we think of civic culture in light of the expansive penetration of digital media into all facets of society. This allows us to explore the implications of new technologies on how citizens connect to serve needs outside of the duties traditionally reserved for civic participation. Allan (2012) notes that "efforts to rethink civic engagement, I would suggest, need to better understand how personal experience gives shape to the ways young people relate to their communities beyond 'citizenship' narrowly defined" (36). Broadening the connotations of citizenship cannot happen without the inclusion of online media, specifically the digital technologies that are connecting citizens in new and dynamic ways.

Evolving Norms for Civic Contributions

In 2008, W. Lance Bennett noted the barriers that continue to exist for young people to engage in civic affairs, even in digital culture: "It is clear that many young citizens of this digital and global age have demonstrated interests in making contributions to society. Yet the challenge of engaging effectively with politics that are linked to spheres of government remains, for most, a daunting prospect" (1). Indeed if civic contributions are located in the context of government there may be difficulty in locating where and how those contributions manifest themselves. However, outside of the confines of government, we see civic activity growing in scope, form, and reach.

When I first sat down to write this book in 2012, my social networks were inundated with dialog around Trayvon Martin, the 17-year-old Florida youth who was shot senselessly during a confrontation while walking home from a convenience store one spring evening. As the events of the case began to unfold, the mainstream media were nowhere to be found. Almost two weeks lapsed before national coverage materialized.[2] On social media, however, an entirely different story emerged. Dozens of Facebook groups were created, amassing millions of gestures of support. The hashtag "IamTrayvon" elicited thousands of tweets per hour. So-called weak tie activism raised awareness of the case, facilitated national media coverage, helped to organize public protest, and engaged numerous constituents in dialog about civic, social, political, and cultural injustices.

In Trayvon's case social media facilitated exposure of the tragic events and led to national dialog around issues of racial profiling, local law enforcement, and the legal system in Florida. Citizens engaged in in-depth conversation around what these issues meant to the case, and to the U.S. democratic system writ large. This type of self-organization is reorienting how people think about their voice, their ability to participate in local and national dialog, and what power they have to effect change. In his 2010 *New Yorker* article "Small Change: Why the Revolution Will not be Tweeted," Malcolm Gladwell (2010) writes:

> Our acquaintances—not our friends—are our greatest source of new ideas and information. The Internet lets us exploit the power of these kinds of distant connections with marvelous efficiency. It's terrific at the diffusion of innovation, interdisciplinary collaboration, seamlessly matching up buyers and sellers, and the logistical functions of the dating world.

Gladwell (2010) follows this by writing, "But weak ties seldom lead to high-risk activism." While his point has been true in the past, numerous examples now exist that show how distant connections are enabling dialog and collective coordination that have stimulated—to steal a term of Gladwell's—a tipping point into real high-risk activism. This has caused public officials and governments to respond, reform, or take action. Of course, this type of activism is not always embraced with such positive dialog and support.

The tragic bombings at the 2013 Boston Marathon exposed the collective power citizens have to help uncover information and organize effective responses in the wake of tragedy. While the hunt for the bombers ensued in Boston, citizens took it upon themselves to both offer safe places for marathon runners to rest, find family and get help if needed. Citizens also offered thousands upon thousands of images and videos to help point to the scene where the bombs were detonated, and also used their collective power to help provide as much diverse information to help the investigation as possible.

At the same time, citizens crowded social media channels with hearsay and rumors, clouding the ability to discern what information was important from what was misleading. The social news aggregator *Reddit* hosted forums where users were posting so many different stories it became difficult to distinguish fact from fiction. There were many shallow and lewd public comments disparaging certain ethnicities. The open nature of networks comes with certain drawbacks, namely that the unfiltered flow of content in real time offers little to no ability to discern truth from rumors, or to verify information before it spreads far and wide. This poses many challenges for local governments, and for the public as they try to follow and make sense of events.

Examples of civic engagement may be a bit clearer when they are seen in response to corporations or governments who attempt to impose policy without transparency or open dialog. In 2011, Netflix founder and CEO, Reed Hastings, decided to create a new business model that amounted to a fee raise of nearly 100% and a split in terms of how customers were billed and received physical and streaming content. Hastings delivered this news in a self-indulgent one-off letter to his customer base, without any real regard for their preferences or opinion. As a result, not only did Netflix lose thousands of customers, but also those who valued the service took to social media to create a groundswell of protest, and demands to repeal the charge. Under buckling pressure Netflix reverted to their old model with slight alterations to their delivery model and pay structure.

Around the same time, the Bank of America corporation, still repairing its image in the wake of the 2008 financial collapse, and servicing customers who were hard hit by the economic crisis that befell the global economy, in response to new federal regulations on retail bank revenue, chose to increase revenue with a small five-dollar monthly fee for debit card use in the United States. As word spread about this choice, customer disdain grew. The social media sphere exploded in condemning dialog, heated debates harkening back to the 2008 financial collapse, and proposed responses to the fee hike. One patron, 22-year-old Molly Katchpole, who we'll read about in more detail later, gathered over 300,000 signatures in an online grassroots campaign, which led to the halting of the fee charge altogether. How did she do it? A social petition web site called *Change.org*.

What do these examples tell us about the emerging citizen in the 21st century? For one, the new landscape for civic engagement is not a temporary fad. As citizens find more convenient ways to voice opinions and support causes, they are proving to be more vocal and responsive to government and corporate behavior. The more citizens learn to harness new social media platforms for mass movements of support and protest, it's increasingly clear that the fundamentals of how citizens choose to participate in contemporary society are changing.

One noticeable result is that companies are now implementing socially responsible initiatives. Reebok's Witness program, the Pepsi Refresh initiative, and Stonyfield's support of organic causes all signal a more transparent corporate landscape. Tom's Shoes has amassed a large and loyal following based on its humanitarian agenda, and Walmart has integrated organic products and LEED certified mandates for its stores. These small shifts show that citizens are paying more attention, responding faster, and engaging in dialog where possible. In their book, *What's Mine Is Yours*, Rachel Botsman and Roo Rodgers (2010) highlight the increase in sharing and reproducing value in goods, largely facilitated by new media technologies. They stress three specific evolutions—"the convergence of social networks, a renewed belief in the importance of community, pressing environmental concerns, and cost consciousness"— that are collectively "moving us away from the old top-heavy, centralized, and controlled forms of consumerism toward one of sharing, aggregation, openness, and cooperation" (p. xx). Botsman and Rodgers emphasize new collaborative communities that are facilitated largely from social networks. With populations moving more into urban spaces to accommodate a post-industrial age, a need for ownership of goods is being replaced by unique community services that create efficiencies and do not promote hyper-consumption. And citizen voices now play a more central role in demanding new standards and accountability for business and government.

Humanitarian campaigns have also found new life and dynamism through new media technologies predicated on heightened sharing, aggregation, openness, and cooperation (Botsman & Rodgers, 2010). Citizens from around the world used social media to help raise support for disaster relief in Haiti after a devastating earthquake struck in 2010. Citizens shared links photos, stories, and updates to help humanitarian organizations navigate their way around conflict torn countries in the wake of civic uprisings in North Africa and the Middle East. In the 2008 China earthquake, social media tools were helping to organize relief efforts days before government responses. Examples as such are increasingly seen on more local levels as well, from campaigns to raise support for health causes and local parent groups fundraising for school support to environmental awareness and community cleanups. And while there was some abuse among these initiatives—fake donation sites for example—these new mechanisms for humanitarian and community outreach are generally adding to civic engagement and participation in new and profound ways.

Digital Culture's Role in Citizenship

Contemporary discussions about citizenship can no longer exist outside of the discussion of digital media. The facilitation of civic participation and engagement through digital media spaces has opened up new opportunities for connectivity in public, social, and cultural spaces. The evolution of "networked social movements" (Castells, 2012), organized largely around digital tools and social media platforms, has stimulated a rich and active debate that emerges when citizens now have the digital tools to become active and engaged storytellers along side more traditional forms of media storytelling (Allan, 2013).

Scholars have commended the new possibilities that social technologies have provided for increased collaborative production (Benkler, 2005; Benkler & Nissenbaum, 2006; Lessig, 2008), for crowd-sourced participative potential in civic activities (Brabham, 2008; Surwowiecki, 2005; Howe, 2008) and for the increased value provided in peer-to-peer participatory models for engagement in daily life (Jenkins, 2012, 2006a; Jenkins & Thorburn, 2004; Deuze, 2006; Shirky, 2010). From organizing protests to facilitating global awareness about issues of justice and civic rights, digitally-savvy young citizens are capitalizing on social tools to engage with public bodies in new and unique ways (see Chadwick & Howard, 2010; Garret, 2006; Mercea, 2013; Siegel, 2009). One of the most clear ways to see the influence of digital culture on civic engagement is to analyze the robust activity that social and digital technologies facilitate in the face of civic injustices, oppression, or marginalization of the public. A host of recent studies have shown how platforms, specifically Twitter, Facebook, and blogs, have been used as effective organizational tools to help citizens engage in collective action around the world (see Earl et al., 2013; Thorson et al., 2013; Tufekci & Wilson, 2012; Valenzuela et al., 2012).

Of course, the challenges to engaged citizenship are as great as the opportunities. In his book, *The Shallows*, Nicholas Carr paints a picture of a distracted, fragmented society in which the Internet has mitigated our ability to concentrate, and explore ideas in detail and depth. He makes the case that "we willingly accept the loss of concentration and focus, the division of our attention and the fragmentation of our thoughts, in return for the wealth of compelling or at least diverting information we receive" (Carr, 2011, p. 134). Evgeny Morozov, in *The Net Delusion* (2011), details how, while the open dialog and exchange of information has been wonderful for civic dialog and expression, we have lost sight of "how useful it would prove for propaganda purposes, how masterfully dictators would learn to use it for surveillance, and how sophisticated modern systems of Internet censorship would become" (xiv). Complexities in the digital mediasphere in the form of "communication-effects gaps" (Coleman & Price, 2012, 38) and "participation gaps" (Jenkins, 2006a, 257), have brought into question the extent to which digital technologies create avenues for valuable civic engagement and social impact (Dean, 2005; Gladwell, 2010; Morozov, 2013).

The introduction of any new technologies into society will always be accompanied by numerous implications, both helpful and harmful, depending on how they are adopted. While it is true that the youth of today are rewiring their cognitive processes around digital tools built for multitasking and short attention spans—just look at any college classroom today to notice this phenomenon—the opportunities to engage in more dynamic social and civic interaction are also ripe for exploration. Instead of fitting today's new realities of students, media use, and concentration into a model of the past, this book looks at the new participatory avenues for engagement that allow for more vibrant communities to grow, flourish, and act as social change agents for issues of local and global consequence.

And at the same time, while the Internet and social media technologies have allowed for more systematic control, propaganda, and surveillance—you don't have to look outside of the United States to see this rising practice—these tools also allow for more organized resistance, protest, and grassroots activism. A 2012 article by Kurlantzick and Leader, "How democracies clamped down on the Internet," detailed the tactical measures of control and surveillance that even so-called democratic nations have been implementing with regards to Internet freedoms. All the while we see more protest, action, and advocacy for better health standards, more political transparency, tolerance, and vigilance in society writ large.

These struggles are—above all—indicative of change. They point to a burgeoning new structure for civic society. They point to new relationships between citizens and public institutions. And they point to new ways society is learning to think about voice, participation, and citizenship within an age of distraction. What this means for the future of democracy, we are still figuring out.

Media Education & Engaged Citizenship

Where does education come into this new conception for engaged citizenship today?

Dalton (2009) notes that "education is more strongly related to support for engaged citizenship" (40), than it is for duty-based citizenship:

> …this evidence suggests that social modernization—rising educational levels and improving living standards—during the latter half of the twentieth century probably contributed to a shift in citizenship norms. These traits encourage a more engaged form of citizenship that goes beyond the deferential, subject-like role of duty-based citizenship. Participating in politics beyond voting and deliberating with others is more demanding than voting based only on a sense of duty. As more Americans possess these skills and resources, their norms of citizenship also change. (40–41)

As participatory forms of democracy continue to evolve, media education is positioned to be the movement that builds the skills and dispositions needed to effectively navigate digital media, and that instills an understanding of the opportunity they possess for engaged citizenship in information societies. To date, however, educational responses have been somewhat slow and staggered. Bennett and Wells (2009) note the struggle that scholars have to capture and understand notions of citizenship that are fast evolving and with no clear definition from which to work. As a result, they posit that, "in reality, two broad clusters of citizen ideals are in play and that different demographic groups (meaning, especially, different age groups) experience them differently" (7).

Increasing attention has been given to measures for assessing civic engagement in learning contexts (Bennett & Segerberg, 2012; Walgrave et al., 2011; Buckingham, 2007, 2008; Kahne et al., 2011, 2010; Zukin et al., 2006). Scholars have explored the opportunities for political involvement fostered by digital technologies (Lasica, 2008; Rheingold, 2008a; 2008b), and the connectedness that can manifest in online communities (Ellison et al., 2010; Gil de Zúñiga, 2012; Haythornthwaite, 2005; Fowler & Christakis, 2010; Romer et al., 2009; Shah et al., 2009; Steinfeld et al., 2008; Valenzuela et al., 2009; Watkins et al., 2009; Zhang et al., 2010). These pathways for education and engagement are not simply a result of digital tools. From learning to navigate large and vast information landscapes to critically discern among the multitude of voices, facts, opinions, and ideas that stream endlessly and with little structure online, young citizens of tomorrow will need to think of participation in a new way (Dahlgren, 2003).

Eric Gordon (2013) advocates for the development of a civic web that allows us to think "beyond participation, or the efficient citizen transactions that take place on most municipal websites, like pay taxes and parking tickets, and moving towards engagement, or creating or harnessing platforms for collaboration, learning, and social connection." Gordon (2013) offers six principles—*tools solve problems, audience matters, networks are composed of people, scale matters, the civic web is on- and offline,* and *design for distraction*—that are bound by a need to build core competencies in future generations that will be immersed in digital spaces and tools for a vast majority of information and communication needs. While Gordon approaches the civic web from the point of design, his shift in thinking, like Dalton's, moves us towards new formative ways to imagine the role of digital media culture in the civic realm.

I want to propose another core competency needed to address the place of the citizen in the information age: *the role of media literacy.* Young citizens today are awash in an array of digital tools and technologies, and they are quite savvy in adapting and using these technologies in a number of different ways. However, technological savvy does not necessarily correlate with core competencies in understanding how digital technologies can encourage engagement across all facets of daily life. Alongside new models for civic engagement that deal with measurement and design, we need to think about new formal and informal pedagogies that can better connect digital media culture with more inclusive engagement in daily social and civic life.

The next chapter explores the emerging media literacy landscape with the aim to develop the connection between media literacy and new models of engaged citizenship. I believe that without making more explicit the connections between critical inquiry and critical citizenship, young people will continue to be technologically savvy but perhaps not as media literate as digital culture necessitates. I position the role of media literacy as a *connector* for smart consumption and smart citizenship in an information age. Media literacy teaches:

- Critical Inquiry: The ability to access, analyze, evaluate, express, share, and produce media communications across platforms.
- Critical Expression: The ability to harness media for engaged, responsible, and inclusive and active participation in daily civic life.

These connections are predicated on core competencies in media analysis and media use. They entail critical inquiry as the base for which young people can see the personal and public value of the information they interact with on a daily basis. At the outset of her white paper, *Digital and Media Literacy: A Plan of Action*, Hobbs (2010) notes that, "to fulfill the promise of digital citizenship Americans must acquire multimedia communication skills and know how to use these skills to engage in the civic life of their communities" (vii).

How do young people acquire multimedia communication skills? And how do they translate those skills to their role as private and public citizens? These questions are fundamental for understanding the potential of digital media contemporary citizenship. They are also questions that we will continue to revisit throughout this book. But first, we need to define what media literacy looks like to really see how it can connect to the digitally fluent, emerging citizen.

· 2 ·

THE EMERGING MEDIA
LITERACY LANDSCAPE

In 1993, thirty leading media educators and scholars from around the United States gathered for a retreat sponsored by the Aspen Institute to discuss the current status and future of media literacy education. Out of this conference materialized a report titled, "The Aspen Institute Report of the National Leadership Conference on Media Literacy," which proved to be the "birth-certificate" (Center for Media Literacy) of the U.S. media literacy movement. From this meeting emerged the founding definition for media literacy in the United States, "the ability to access, analyze, evaluate and produce both print and electronic media" (Aufderheide & Firestone, 1993), and five general concepts recognized as central to any media literacy educational experience:

- media are constructed, and construct reality
- media have commercial implications
- media have ideological and political implications
- form and content are related in each medium, each of which has a unique aesthetic, codes and conventions
- receivers negotiate meaning in media (Aufderheide & Firestone, 1993).

These concepts, broad and encompassing, signify a strong theoretical foundation for media literacy in general, absent of attention to any specific educational level, discipline, or learning outcome. The Center for Media Literacy described the outcomes of the Aspen Institute Report and their influence on the media literacy movement in the United States:

> Consisting of three interrelated documents, including an extensive background paper sketching important developments and contributions in the early years of the movement, the report was distributed widely to the worlds of education, media and philanthropy. With the highly respected Aspen Institute name attached, doors opened, calls were returned and funding proposals began to be approved. Many will attest that although media literacy was actually born in the U.S. years before, it was this report that served as the official birth certificate.

The concepts born over two decades ago, while still largely driving the media literacy movement in the United States today, are by no means the first. In the 1930s pamphlets on film viewing and radio listening were developed for English teachers to help their students find "good" programming (Heins & Cho, 2003). In the 60s, educators began developing curriculum for television viewing, and in 1969, "the National Education Association passed a resolution recommending critical viewing curricula to counter the presumed ill effects of media violence" (Heins & Cho, 2003, 7). Since, media literacy has evolved in fits and starts across the United States, and has generally lagged behind in media literacy efforts in Australia, Canada, and the United Kingdom (Kubey & Baker, 1999; Mihailidis, 2006).

While this book does not have the space to detail the history and evolution of media literacy education, a series of works provide thorough explorations into the development of the field. Heins & Cho (2003) provide a nice working history of the media literacy movement in the United States and incorporate viewpoints from abroad. Scholars have written extensively about the evolution of media literacy definitions, applications, and contexts as a pedagogical movement across primary, secondary and higher education, and as a fundamental teacher-training field (De Abreu, 2007; Leaning, 2009; Scull & Kupersmidt, 2011; Stein & Prewett, 2009). The *Journal of Communication* (1998), *American Behavioral Scientist* (2004), and *Action in Teacher Education* (2011) dedicated entire issues to explore definitions and applications of media literacy education across a host of topics. Renee Hobbs's (1998) seminal paper, "The Seven Great Debates in the Media Literacy Movement," remains a foundational work in the media education field. Works by Rosenbaum (2003), Koltay (2011), and Oxstrand (2009) have developed extensive looks at the various definitions, uses, and approaches to media literacy. Past inquiries I have conducted explore the origins of media literacy in the United States and abroad on the higher education level (Mihailidis, 2009; 2008). Still further, new works (De Abreu, 2011; Hobbs, 2011 2011a, 2011b; Hoechsmann & Poyntz, 2012; Jenkins et al., 2009; Lankshear & Knobel, 2006; Knobel & Lankshear, 2010) have pushed the boundaries and scope of media literacy into new fields of inquiry and application. There are too many studies too ma.

New explorations continue to move media literacy education in new directions and encompass an increasingly wider scope. This chapter will build from these foundations to develop the emerging media literacy landscape in the context of (1) its development as a normative field of inquiry, (2) predominant contemporary models and methods used regardless of education level or discipline, and (3) in the context of young people and civic engagement.

Where Media Literacy Sits Today

As media grow increasingly central to civic and political functions of contemporary society, models for teaching and learning about media have emerged both within and outside of education circles. Media literacy, the term most commonly associated with the media education movement, is premised on promoting critical thinking skills through the ability to access, evaluate, analyze, and produce information (Aufderheide & Firestone, 1993; Ofcom, 2005; Potter, 2010; Silverblatt, 2001; Thoman & Jolls, 2005). Media literacy's overarching goal for teaching and learning outcomes oscillates between and among informed decision-making, individual and social agency, critical analysis of mediated messages, savvy consumption and production skills, and participation in local, national and global dialog (Frechette, 2002; Gaines, 2010; Hobbs, 2010, 2011a; Livingstone, 2004b; Tisdell, 2008). Media literacy scholar David Buckingham (2003) succinctly aggregates the myriad of approaches to conceptualize media literacy as:

> A critical literacy that involves analysis, evaluation, and critical reflection, that is possible only through the 'acquisition of a metalanguage—that is, a means of describing the forms and structures of different modes of communication; and it involves a broader understanding of the social, economic and institutional contexts of communication, and how these affect people's experiences and practices. (Luke, 2000) (38)

Buckingham positions media literacy as holistic in scope and immersed in a ubiquitous media landscape today. He sees media as an ecosystem embedded in the larger discourses and experiences of our daily lives, and positions media as extensions of our beliefs, attitudes, and dispositions. Buckingham (2003) also believes that media literacy is an outcome of the media education process: "Media *education*, then, is the process of teaching and learning about media; media *literacy* is the outcome—the knowledge and skills learners acquire" (p. 4).

The emerging media literacy landscape is one that is more fully integrated into the competencies needed for future participants in information societies. Research in this book, and elsewhere, shows that youth today primarily use aggregated and curated digital spaces for information consumption, sharing, and production. They no longer think of news in terms of specific outlets, but instead, in the context of their social information feeds. The convergence of media platforms and the advance of mobile technologies have fostered an immersive media landscape. In *Media Literacy and Semiotics* Eliot Gaines notes that as more of our daily lives become inundated with interpreting signals and messages, there is a larger systematic shift underway. Gaines (2010) writes: "And while we are busy interpreting necessary information, the processes of communication and the media are in the background. Those processes have significant effects on the interpretation of meanings and the messages they convey" (p. 5). In light of the picture that Gaines portrays, media literacy education is about more than simply the interpretation and analysis of messages. It must also incorporate the larger environments and landscapes that are part of digital culture.

Frameworks for Media Literacy

New efforts are growing around the aim to develop media literacy outcomes that build critical competencies for a digital world. In the United States, *The National Association of Media Literacy Education* (NAMLE) has developed a set of core principles for media literacy education that provides a broad framework around critical thinking, cultural indicators, and personal voice. Like Buckingham's approach, the core principles (see Figure 2.1) represent a macro-level methodology for understanding media's role in our lives. NAMLE places this approach in the context of a working outline for educators, parents, policy makers, and citizens writ large.

1. Media Literacy Education requires **active inquiry and critical thinking** about the messages we receive and create.
2. Media Literacy Education **expands the concept of literacy** to include all forms of media (i.e., reading and writing).
3. Media Literacy Education **builds and reinforces skills for learners of all ages.** Like print literacy, those skills necessitate integrated, interactive, and repeated practice.
4. Media Literacy Education **develops informed, reflective and engaged participants** essential for a democratic society.
5. Media Literacy Education recognizes that media are a **part of culture and function as agents of socialization.**
6. Media Literacy Education affirms that **people use their individual skills, beliefs and experiences to construct their own meanings** from media messages.

Figure 2.1. NAMLE Core Principles of Media Literacy Education.
Source: National Association for Media Literacy Education (NAMLE) http://namle.net/publications/core-principles/

The *Center for Media Literacy* (CML) advances its own core concepts that position media literacy education on a continuum between authorship and purpose see Figure 2.2 (Jolls & Thoman, 2005).

1. **Authorship** - All media messages are constructed
2. **Format** - Media messages are constructed using a creative language with its own rules
3. **Audience** – Different people experience the same media messages differently
4. **Content** – Media have embedded values and points of view
5. **Purpose** – Most media messages are organized to gain profit and/or power

Figure 2.2. CML Five Core Concepts for Media Literacy Education.
Source: Center for Media Literacy (CML) www.medialit.org

These two models are widely adopted for media literacy education in the United States, and provide some of the grounding in which the field has grown over the past decades. Despite this growth, media literacy's wide and broad framework has left it susceptible to some growing pains across primary, secondary and higher education. Until recently, a majority of media literacy education initiatives were reserved for understanding how to effectively consume messages, with little exploration into the ways that social media technologies have shifted conventional producer-receiver information structures (Potter, 2010; Adams & Hamm, 2001). Media literacy education, weary of prohibiting adoption and appeal for K-12 educators, strayed from developing outcomes that were tied to any singular civic or political ideology (Kellner & Share, 2005). As a result, the field positioned itself as protectionist (Buckingham, 2005)—teaching students how best to navigate and shield themselves from advertisements, spin, propaganda, and manipulation.

Spotlight: Media Literacy & the Protectionist Debate[3]

In 2005, David Buckingham delivered a keynote speech at the National Media Education Conference in San Francisco, titled: "Will Media Education Ever Escape the Effects Debate?" Buckingham's speech addressed a key dispute in media literacy education: whether media literacy education is better suited to protect youth from violent and aggressive media content, or to empower them to make smart choices in an open media system.

In his speech, Buckingham differentiated teaching media effects to *protect* students from teaching about media effects to make students *aware*. His speech attempted to show that media education should ultimately not be about protecting youth *from* media effects, but about engaging students *with* media. Buckingham argues that the effects debate may distort or oversimplify a complex landscape:

> [The effects debate] puts kids in a false position, because it presumes that they are incompetent—that they are somehow passive dupes or victims of the media. And then it marks out a place for teachers as their saviors, as the people who will rescue them from media influence and show them the error of their ways. I think this mistakes what kids already know about media; and it oversimplifies how they learn. (2005, p. 20)

Buckingham argues that placing media education within the effects debate assumes that the audience is powerless and that the media are all-powerful. Buckingham premised the above statement with an example of violence portrayed in American media. He asks if the media are the root of violence and aggression in society, or rather a microcosm of cultural, ethnic, class, religious, and societal ideologies and dispositions that already exist.

Teaching about media's *effects* is central to media literacy education. However, couching media literacy in *cause and effect* frameworks avoids the key complexities involved in the civic roles of media. Buckingham (2005) elaborated on this idea by noting that "...we can only understand the role of the media in the context of other social, historical and cultural forces, and that seeing this in terms of simple notions of 'cause and effect' often leads us to ignore the complexity of what we are concerned about (p. 19). The purview of media literacy is to embrace the effects debate and utilize its theories to teach about media's relationship to society, democracy, and culture. Media literacy that teaches media effects with the aim to only provide students the means to protect themselves from the influences of media will not deliver the holistic and embedded education needed for digital culture.

Nevertheless, as media literacy evolved it incorporated more subdisciplines (news, advertising, politics, science, etc.), technologies (social, mobile, cms, etc.), and more inclusive approaches that evolved from a *message-based model* to a *citizen-based model*.

In her white paper *Digital and Media Literacy: A Plan of Action*, Hobbs (2010) doesn't see the core of media literacy education needing to reinvent itself to face the new digital dispositions of youth; rather, she finds it ever more necessary for youth to harness human curiosity, seek diverse knowledge, and build habits of inquiry. These dispositions give young people the competencies to navigate abundant information spaces, constant sharing, public identities, and low barriers to production (Hobbs, 2011a). This, Hobbs (2011a) believes, "can turn people from passive spectators to active citizens, where people generate ideas that are relevant to their own communities. Technologically speaking, every person can be a pamphleteer" (p. 154). This approach is rooted not in technological change but rather in the core competencies needed to build powerful voices within mediated digital spaces. Hobbs sees these proficiencies as essential for youth to take full advantage of the opportunity digital technologies provide for health, confidence, inclusion, tolerance, diversity, and community.

Jenkins's (2009) exploration of participatory culture highlights the prospective power of media literacy to promote active, inquiry-based, and collaborative social and online behaviors. Jenkins sees this new phenomenon as a growing response to digital technologies and spaces that allow for "average consumers to archive, annotate, appropriate, and recirculate media content in powerful new ways" (p. 8). This newfound presence of the active audience in the producer-consumer relationship brings with it an opportunity—and responsibility—for audiences to help shape the media ecosystem to better suit their wants and needs. This necessitates, Jenkins believes, a need to "...foster the skills and cultural knowledge necessary to deploy those tools toward our own ends (p. 8). Whether for popular television shows, books, games, or hobbies, Jenkins points out the potential for large-scale, dynamic, and purpose-driven organization in participatory media spaces. In these platforms the media literate citizen stands at the forefront of leading participatory democracy and social change.

Building on the foundations of media literacy education, Jenkins "identified a set of core social skills and cultural competencies that young people should acquire if they are to be full, active, creative, and ethical participants in this emerging participatory culture" (Jenkins, 2006b).

1. **Play** — the capacity to experiment with your surroundings as a form of problem-solving
2. **Performance** — the ability to adopt alternative identities for the purpose of improvisation and discovery
3. **Simulation** — the ability to interpret and construct dynamic models of real world processes
4. **Appropriation** — the ability to meaningfully sample and remix media content
5. **Multitasking** — the ability to scan one's environment and shift focus as needed to salient details
6. **Distributed Cognition** — the ability to interact meaningfully with tools that expand mental capacities
7. **Collective Intelligence** — the ability to pool knowledge and compare notes with others toward a common goal
8. **Judgment** — the ability to evaluate the reliability and credibility of different information sources
9. **Transmedia Navigation** — the ability to follow the flow of stories and information across multiple modalities
10. **Networking** — the ability to search for, synthesize, and disseminate information
11. **Negotiation** — the ability to travel across diverse communities, discerning and respecting multiple perspectives, and grasping and following alternative norms.

Figure 2.3. Jenkins Core Media Literacy Skills.
Source: http://henryjenkins.org/2006/10/confronting_the_challenges_of_6.html

The goal of presenting these skills, according to Jenkins (2006b), is to "encourage greater reflection and public discussion on how we might incorporate these core principles systematically across curricula and across the divide between in-school and out-of-school activities." This set of skills reflects a forward-looking framework for how collaborative platforms and digital tools are changing basic learning behaviors in youth today. Jenkins places participation and engagement at the center of the media literacy education experience and stresses the need for media literacy education to connect learning to active experience; a primary need for media literacy in a more dynamic media ecosystem.

...

The case of the nonprofit organization *Invisible Children* and the viral video sensation *Kony 2012* exemplifies the important role media literacy plays in Jenkins' vision of participatory culture. *Kony 2012* was the fastest growing online viral sensation of all time after its release, amassing over 80 million views in approximately six days. It caused a groundswell of activism from the local grassroots level all the way up to political actions taken by the United States government. As a result significant public "weak tie" support surfaced around the movement. All over the world, people shared the link to the video; told friends, family and colleagues about the story through social networks; and supported *Invisible Children* in their pursuit of the capture of Kony. At the same time, a counter-narrative emerged, one that was extremely critical of the video, of *Invisible Children*, and of the overall intention to dumb down a complex and complicated issue.

What ensued was public dialog that did not expose more information about the issue itself, or about the public response, but about the validity of the video's intent, aim, and purpose. There is no doubt that the video itself also exposed an issue in the world that many in the U.S. (and beyond) had never heard of, or even discussed for that matter. But while the world debated the merits of the video, media educators wondered if those who chose to promote, publicize, and share the video to large online communities understood the implications of their actions. And were the people who saw the video pop up in their news feeds and Twitter lists ready to ask the important questions about the *content* and *context* of the video? How did they receive this video? What did the video say about the issue? How did it portray its message? What did the video omit? What were the implications of sharing the video? Who was being affected by sharing this content?

Kony 2012 exemplifies the increasing centrality of social media in civic life. The ability to share information and engage in active online dialog is fundamentally changing what it means to participate in discourse and dialog around all types of information and media: from reality television and documentaries to children's programming, online advertising, documentaries, and news programming. The responsive modes of inquiry, dialog, debate and expression are at the heart of media literacy education today.

Media Literacy's Role in Engaged Citizenship[4]

In 1985, British media scholar Len Masterman emphasized the potential of media education for participatory democracy:

> Media education is an essential step in the long march towards a truly participatory democracy, and the democratization of our institutions. Widespread media literacy is essential if all citizens are to wield power, make rational decisions, become effective change-agents, and have an effective involvement with the media. It is in this much wider sense of "education for democracy" that media education can play the most significant role of all. (p. 13)[5]

Masterman posited that citizens, if educated about media, would not only increase their ability to intelligently use media for personal gains, but also strengthen their engagement with and participation in civic society. Through media education, Masterman believe, dialog about political, social, economic, and cultural issues would be knowledgeable, diverse, and progressive. Masterman (1998) understood the core role of media educators as "to ensure the continued evolution of that critical public" (p. xi).

While much has changed in the last three decades, Masterman's argument remains just as (and arguably more) valid as when he penned it. And while approaches to media literacy remain diverse, "there is growing consensus among scholars and educators that media literacy is a promising means of "develop[ing] informed, reflective and engaged participants essential for a democratic society (NAMLE Core Principles)" (Mihailidis & Thevenin, 2013).

So what does Masterman's critical public look like? Is it a public who knows how to make their voices heard? Who engage in vibrant communities online? Who are skeptical about the messages they see? Or who embrace the vibrancy and diversity of digital media culture? Media literacy education, is all of these things together. According to Masterman, media literacy education builds competencies in citizens to be both engaging and skeptical, both critical and creative. It shows how media build identity, facilitate worldviews, and reproduce both positive and negative impressions of humans

in the world. It teaches skills but also the larger ideological and cultural relationships embedded in information and society.

Masterman's ideas also reaffirm the codependency between media and citizenship that we see more and more evident today. In the present day, media
increasingly provide people membership into groups (programs, chat rooms,
products), stabilize daily life (news outlets, TV daily programs, email), and
function as a large educational tool (TV, Internet, entertainment) (Silverblatt, 2004). Buckingham (2003) argues that in the context of media's ubiquitous position in cultural expression and socialization—"The media, it is often
argued, have now taken the place of the family, the church and the school
as the major socializing influence in contemporary society" (p. 5)—citizens
must become active participations and media users to effectively engage with
daily life.

While mass media organizations still play a large role in disseminating
information to citizens, but more and more we see peer media platforms facilitating the dissemination, sharing, and appropriating of messages. Parallel to
their socializing functions, media have adopted a civic role: that of preserving
and maintaining an engaged, active, and participatory public.

To be active civic participants, individuals must have access to information that explains how, why, and to what end certain decisions are made.
How this information is interpreted is a personal question, and one that media literacy helps to develop in people (Christ, 2004; Christ & Potter, 1998).
Seeing more details, viewpoints, arguments, opinions, facts, and data can all
help to diversify the wealth of information used to build positions on issues.
Of course, research also shows that people's tendencies are predetermined
(see Lakoff 2008, 2004; Lakoff & Wehling, 2012; Manjoo, 2008). Nevertheless, access to information provides a palette from which citizens can make
the decisions they believe will better themselves, their community, and their
country.

One of the main aims of media literacy education is to enable in individuals
the ability to effectively use media to exercise democratic rights (Brownell &
Brownell, 2003). The increasing centrality of media in the facilitation of daily
information and communication needs "calls for the implementation of curricular and cocurricular pedagogical practices that develop *media literacy*—the
ability to critically analyze and decode messages embedded in various media
productions" (Carducci & Rhoads, 2005, p. 3). Silverblatt (2004) advocated
for media literacy as a response to society's increasing dependence on media
for all facets of daily life:

...audiences have come to expect the media to serve the functions of traditional social institutions—functions that they were never designed to fulfill, looking for answers when the media presentation is simply focused on attracting a large audience by any means possible. The public's reliance on Western media for guidance and support can therefore be problematic unless media messages are examined critically and put into meaningful perspectives. (p. 38)

Silverblatt highlights the long standing dilemma in the relationship between media producers and audiences: while producers of mass media have one primary goal—viewers and ratings—citizens use media to facilitate a range of social and civic needs. If indeed media *guide and support* citizens in their daily endeavors, media literacy must facilitate more critical, engaged, and active dispositions towards the role of media in everyday life (see Barber, 2007; Jerit et al., 2006; Dahlgren, 2006; Lewis, 2006). Of course, this is a complex proposition because of the multifaceted ways that people use media and because of the abundance of messages that exist in the present day. Nevertheless, if media literacy cannot reach the critical connections between inquiry and expression, the relevance of being critically engaged with media will be compromised.

The following three arguments position media literacy as a core competency for engaged citizenship through preparing citizens to become *critical thinkers*, *creators* and *communicators*, and *agents of social change* (Mihailidis & Thevenin, 2013).

1. Media Literate Citizens as Critical Thinkers[6]

Common to the skills of engaged citizens is the ability to act as *critical thinkers*— able to access and analyze information on which to base democratic participation. In an age when an increasing percentage of the public is able to access troves of information via cable news channels, social media, and online publications (not to mention traditional media sources), citizens must be able to critically read this copious stream of media messages. Traditionally, much of media education has emphasized the analysis of media texts—introducing students to issues of representation, authorial intent, aesthetic presentation, etc. However, especially in the last few decades—as the interpenetration of media consumption and civic participation has become increasingly apparent— scholars and educators have begun to discuss media literacy as the ability not just to read texts but also to situate them in relation to broader social, cultural, and political contexts. For example, in Renee Hobbs' "Seven Great Debates in the Media Literacy Movement" (1998), she emphasizes that media literacy "invites students to identify the cultural codes that structure an author's work, understand how these codes function as part of a social system, and disrupt the text through alternative interpretations" (p. 22). In learning to critically read media messages, citizens can develop the ability to gather accurate, relevant information about their society *and* to question authority (both textual and, by implication, institutional).

This is especially important considering the critical pedagogical traditions from which much of media literacy education stems. This discussion of citizens as critical thinkers deliberately recalls Paulo Freire's concept of *conscientizacao*—or 'critical consciousness'—in which individuals develop the ability to perceive their social reality "not as a closed world from which there is no exit, but as a limiting situation which they can transform" (1970, p. 49). Media literacy education, then, prepares citizens for democratic participation by helping them analyze mediated *representations of* their communities, as well as address *issues within* their communities. And citizens who practice this critical thinking will learn to deconstruct media texts, but perhaps more importantly, they will be engaged in "deconstructing injustices, expressing their own voices, and struggling to create a better society" (Kellner & Share, 2007a, pp. 19–20).

2. Media Literate Citizens as Effective Creators and Communicators

Proposed definitions of 'good citizenship' also rely on individuals' ability to act as effective *creators* and *communicators*. Descriptions of today's citizen as *actualizing* and *engaged* imply a type of civic participation that goes beyond affiliating with a political party or casting a vote on Election Day. Rather, a truly participatory democracy relies on citizens' efforts to develop and share their unique perspectives on societal issues, as well as developing new approaches to creating and circulating these perspectives. Examples of how digital media has been utilized in such efforts are plenty—from Shepard Fairey's Obama image in the 2008 election to the use of social media in the *It Gets Better Project*.

But this link between political participation and media participation is not limited to the appropriation of social media for campaigning or advocacy efforts. It is worth noting that this emerging definition of *engaged citizen* bears some resemblance to the concept of the *active audience* forwarded by scholars of media and culture in the late twentieth century (see Clarke et al., 1976; Hall, 1980; Hall & Whannel, 1964; Hoggart, 1959). Rather than understanding media audiences as passive consumers, this approach understands television viewers, filmgoers, book readers, etc. as cocreators of meaning that always reinterpret and often remix media texts and share these creations with communities. And studies, for example, that explore the practices of fan communities have even greater relevance to our interest in engaged citizenship when we consider the increasing conflation of popular cultural practices and political participation. Today, supporting a candidate or cause may mean writing a check or hitting the street; it certainly involves viewing (and 'liking') the online video. Jenkins (2006a) suggests that increased attention to this convergence of consumption and citizenship, especially in the classroom, can be the means of preparing new generations for engaged citizenship and even revitalizing our political system:

> ...we may also want to look at the structures of fan communities as showing us new ways of thinking about citizenship and collaboration. The political effects of these fan communities come not simply through the production and circulation of new ideas (the critical reading of favorite texts) but also through access to new social structures (collective intelligence) and new models of cultural participation (participatory culture). (p. 246)

These spaces of online communication, collaboration, creation, and circulation of popular cultural products can potentially prepare individuals (and especially young people) for more active participation in democracy, and perhaps even introduce new processes and practices into political culture (Beer & Burrows, 2010). This budding relationship among media creation and communication and political participation is admittedly tenuous—Jenkins (2006a) follows the previous quote asking, "Am I granting too much power here to these consumption communities? Perhaps"—but still potentially productive (pp. 246–47). In the end, the interpenetration of media participation and political practice is inevitable, but media literacy education provides an opportunity for citizens to better recognize and ultimately embrace the productive possibilities of this convergence, and express their enthusiastic support of not just Harry Potter, but maybe also Harry Reid, through the creation and communication of alternative media.

3. Media Literate Citizens as Agents of Social Change

Lastly, an engaged citizen recognizes his or her role as an *agent of social change*. As discussed previously, today's citizen must be able to gather and analyze information, develop informed opinions, and share these perspectives with others. Ultimately though, these efforts are most significant when this engagement leads to the organization of political movements, the creation of new political practices and processes, and the institution of new legislative policies. After all, Max Horkheimer, father of critical studies of media and culture (and arguably the godfather to critical media literacy education) described this project as "not simply the theory of emancipation; it is the practice of it as well" (1937, p. 233). However, as demonstrated previously, any effort to promote social change in contemporary society always already involves the consumption and production of digital media.

And while the role of "political or social change objectives" in media education has historically been a site of struggle within the media literacy community (see Hobbs, 1998; Jhally & Lewis, 1998; Kellner & Share, 2005), scholars and practitioners of all stripes are beginning to recognize the promise of "reposition[ing] media literacy as the core of new civic education" (Mihailidis, 2009, p. 9). For example, the media literacy community's commitment to democratic education and critical pedagogy encourages the creation of classroom cultures and teacher-student relations that prepare students for self-directed learning (and hopefully engaged citizenship). It is not incidental that classrooms in which media literacy is being taught often resemble workshops. Traditional, hierarchical relations between teacher and students are avoided in order to facilitate sites of co-learning. Students are encouraged to collaborate with one another to identify challenges facing their communities, research these issues through critical analysis of media and other sources of evidence, and cooperate on creating and circulating alternative media that raises awareness about these issues and prompts political action.

In media literacy classrooms, students are not only encouraged to examine media and society and their roles as consumers and citizens, they also practice critique and collaboration in preparation to become political agents in a participatory democracy. "Communication alone can create the Great Community," wrote John Dewey (1927, p. 142). Today, we are still awaiting the arrival of that society of which Dewey dreamed, but in order for that dream to be realized, the public must recognize its role in this end, and the potential for our critical, creative use of digital media to achieve it.

Towards a Media Literacy Framework for Engaged Citizenship

The emerging media literate citizen is born from a convergence of the tools and platforms that now occupy the divide that once existed *between* the media industry and the individual. This formerly divided space is now filled with vibrant voices and cluttered information, and with no clear or distinct borders and silos. For younger generations, older models of "mass" media—television, radio, newspaper—are less relevant to them as separate silos of information. Rather, their media landscape is one that starts at the level of peers, and that extends through a mazelike network of sources, formats, and messages, constantly moving and shifting at rates far faster and wider than ever before.

The Figure 2.4 represents a concentric framework for the new realities of media and the citizen. It is premised on the increasing disintegration between mass media and the audience, and recognizes the new spaces that citizens, and media organizations, need to negotiate in a digital media age.

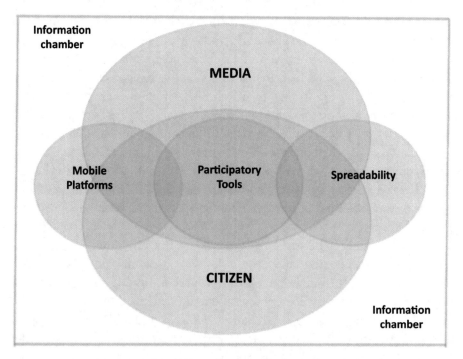

Figure 2.4. The Nexus of Digital Media Culture and Citizenship.
Source: Mihailidis, P. (2012): *News Literacy*: Global Perspectives for the Newsroom and the Classroom. NY: Peter Lang.

The framework begins with the acknowledgement that the boundaries between the media—conceived as the message producers—and the citizen are disintegrating. While media practitioners will continue to play influential roles in providing the stories needed for public dialog and civic inclusion, they will no longer be doing this separate from the public, or as an act of sim-ply gathering, producing, and disseminating information. In a participatory culture, the emerging convergence media landscape has been accelerated by three specific factors.

In the first concentric circle that connects the media and citizen are *mobile platforms*. Mobile platforms—smart phones, e-readers, tablets—are fast replacing desktops, televisions, and even to an extent laptops as the main space for information gathering, sharing, and producing. As a result, a so-cial shift towards mobility in all facets of information habits has emerged. In *Convergence Culture*, Jenkins (2006a) notes two principal trends that dictate this: first is "the tendency of modern media creations to attract a much greater degree of audience participation than ever before," and second is the "the phenomenon of a single franchise being distributed through and impacting a range of media delivery methods" (p. xx). The rise of mobile technologies has coincided with an explosion of *participatory tools*, the second concentric circle. These new tools allow for users, absent of location, to share information with large, disaggregated groups with few physical constraints. When we see civic protests, or natural disasters strike around the globe, details and stories first emerge not from the media organizations but largely from citizens contribut-ing narratives through different participatory tools, with different angles and perspectives.

The third new reality of the information sphere that is working to dis-integrate the divide between the media and the citizen is that of *spreadabil-ity*.[7] It is well established that the borders for information flow have largely disintegrated. As a result, the sheer reach of information has now been hy-pothetically equalized between the media industry and the citizen. What does spreadability look like? Take Occupy Wall Street. A small-scale protest movement at its outset, the Occupy movement grew locally, nationally, and globally, largely facilitated by spreading images and messages about what was happening on the ground and highlighting the people, issues, and events that were propelling an expanding movement. The borders of information have eroded to the point where they exist only in terms of the limits of access to tools and technologies. This has enabled information sharing on scales never before seen.

The framework above offers a new way to approach the relationship between media and citizenship today. Media literacy education is the move-ment that can help empower young citizens to use these newfound opportuni-ties for greater engagement, dialog, and inclusiveness in daily life. It is and can be the education space that cultivates purpose, value, transparency, responsibility, and a self-awareness of the reach and impact of expression online.

Creating value for one another is at the core of engaged citizenship, and at the heart of communities in a participatory democracy. Media literacy integrated in formal and nonformal educational spaces can help build a concrete approach to enabling the civic voices of tomorrow to be more active, collaborative, and united towards a more full and inclusive democratic vision for an increasingly interconnected world. The next chapter details some of the networks, crowds, and collaborative technologies that demand a media literate citizenry.

DIGITAL MEDIA CULTURE AND THE CIVIC POTENTIAL OF MEDIA LITERACY

The Power of the Media Literate "Crowd"

In October of 2011, Molly Katchpole, a 22-year-old Rhode Island native, living and working in Washington, DC, heard that Bank of America was implementing a new $5/month banking fee. With little explanation behind the increased fees and on the heels of a hefty government bailout, which technically involved the American taxpayer keeping Bank of America afloat, Katchpole, like most Americans, wasn't too pleased. Instead of simply closing her account, and moving on to another bank, Katchpole decided to respond.

Using the nonprofit, nonpartisan, Change.org, Katchpole mounted a participatory campaign urging Bank of America to cease its new fees. Her petition letter, posted on the site, read:

```
To:
Brian T. Moynihan, President and CEO, Bank of America


I'm writing to express my deep concern over Bank of
America's decision to charge customers $5 a month to use
their debit cards when making purchases.
```

The American people bailed out Bank of America during a
financial crisis the banks helped create. You paid zero
dollars in federal income tax last year. And now your bank
is profiting, raking in $2 billion in profits last quarter
alone. How can you justify squeezing another $60 a year
from your debit card customers? This is despicable.

American consumers can't afford these additional fees. We
reject any claims by BofA that this latest fee is somehow
necessary.

Please, do the right thing. Reverse your decision to
charge customers $5 each month for using their debit cards
to make purchases.

Sincerely,
[Your name]

Figure 3.1. Katchpole Petition Letter to Bank of America.
Source: http://www.change.org/petitions/tell-bank-of-america-no-5-debit-card-fees

This simple, concise, and direct letter was published to the change.org
community. Change.org boasts of having 25 million users in over 196 countries, all who contribute to causes and petitions to help "transform their
communities-locally, nationally, and globally."[8] Change.org's mission is to
use new digital media tools and social platforms to help citizens advance their
civic voices for causes small and large. They recognize, in their mission statement, that "technology has made us more connected than ever," and aim to
provide a space for individuals to work towards leading and supporting change
through collective action.

...

New social tools have led to more vibrant forms of collective action. Clay
Shirky writes in *Here Comes Everybody* (2008), "collective action, where a
group acts as a whole, is even more complex than collaborative production, but
here again new tools give life to new forms of action. This in turn challenges
existing institutions, by eroding the institutional monopoly on large-scale coordination" (p. 143). Citizens now have the capacity to organize, express, and
participate to degrees rarely seen in the mass media age. However, tools are
only half of the equation.

Katchpole's petition launched at a time when public animosity against large financial institutions was at an all time high. In the wake of the 2008 housing collapse and large bank bailouts, citizens were weary of banks taking liberties with their finances. In a short period of time, Katchpole's petition amassed over 300,000 signatures. This was followed by calls from Bank of America to Katchpole—alas too little too late—and national media attention that put her plight, and her 300,000 fellow concerned citizens, at the center of a battle between citizens and corporations. Less than one month later, Bank of America announced it was dropping its new fee proposals, and a host of other national banks followed suit by dropping fees they had already or were planning to implement themselves. Dozens of similar and smaller-scale "copy cat" campaigns followed Katchpole's, and mainstream press lauded her work as a victory for consumer rights against corporations.

The Katchpole story offers a great example for the potential of social media technologies to support participatory culture. Jenkins (2006a) outlines the core attributes of participatory culture:

> A participatory culture has relatively low barriers to artistic expression and civic engagement, strong support for creating and sharing one's creations, and some type of informal mentorship whereby what is known by the most experienced is passed along to novices. It is also one in which members believe their contributions matter, and feel some degree of social connection with one another. (p. 3)

For a participatory culture to engage around an issue, cause, or hobby, the technologies that allow people to collectively share their voices must be readily available. There also must exist some driving problem, challenge, or want for communities to gather around. At the same time, these tools, spaces, and campaigns depend on citizens that know how to critically engage with information in collaborative and digital spaces. A participatory public must be active in seeking dialog, be conscious of the diversity of voices in any public discourse, and be willing to use media, information, and communication to collaborate, communicate and act. Understanding how to find, evaluate, analyze, share, collaborate, and create information and communication in digital spaces is fundamental to media literacy education. These outcomes are also essential for the types of activism exemplified by the coordination we see in protest, campaigning, and advocacy by Molly Katchpole, Change.org, and a host of other organizations and groups.

While Molly Katchpole may have been fortunate in the timing of her campaign, she knew when, where, and how to act. She found a platform that garnered the attention of fellow concerned citizens, and she understood how to responsibly use media to help publicize her goals. Very few campaigns may have the impact that Molly Katchpole's did—her follow up campaign to stop Verizon's extra fees, impressive in its own right, netted her 175,000 supporters. The success of acts like Katchpole's result from a combination of timing and luck. But the more media literate the crowd of concerned citizens is, the more likely they are to find, understand, and actively engage with the causes they start, support, or care about. Media literate crowds have the potential to push engaged citizenship to new frontiers of active engagement and inclusive activism.

The [Media Literate] Crowd Is Always Right

To open his book *The Wisdom of Crowds,* James Surowiecki tells the story of British scientist Francis Galton's encounter at a weight-judging competition at a county fair in Plymouth, England. As the story goes, in watching contestants submit guesses about the weight of an ox, Galton wondered about the average guess of the crowd. After borrowing the submitted cards at the conclusion of the competition, Galton found that the collective average of voters was within .001 pounds of the actual weight, closer than any individual guess. Surowiecki (2005) extrapolates from this feat of crowd wisdom:

> We generally have less information than we'd like. We have limited foresight into the future. Most of us lack the ability—and the desire—to make sophisticated cost-benefit calculations. Instead of insisting on finding the best possible decision, we will often accept one that seems good enough...yet despite all these limitations, when our imperfect judgments are aggregated in the right way, our collective intelligence is often excellent. (p. xiv)

In Surowiecki's example, the crowd at the fair did have limitations—they couldn't examine the animal, they had no information on the animal's diet, or most had no idea about that specific breed of ox. Nevertheless, their collective judgment proved to be near perfect.

The ability to organize through collaborative platforms is resulting in large-scale coordinated engagement to extents rarely seen before. Much of this has to do with "the rise of participatory networks" (Howe, 2008, p. x) that are disrupting the top-down practices and patterns for information and communication that until recently dominated the media landscape. From the launch of crowdsourced platforms like Wikipedia and Linux to collaborative sites like

Flickr, Airbnb, iStock Photo, and RelayRides, we are seeing crowds leverage participatory technologies to share ideas and solve problems. In *Crowdsourcing*, Jeff Howe (2008) writes about the growth of the "active" crowd: "Over the past several years people from around the world have begun exhibiting an almost totally unprecedented social behavior: they are coming together to perform tasks, usually for little or no money, that were once the sole province of employees" (p. 8). Motivated less by financial means, and more by solving problems or combating injustice, these crowds are increasingly sophisticated, agile, and media savvy.

And as avenues for online collaboration continue to expand, along with crowd-based civic activism, the ability to participate in civic life will require greater media literacy skills, competencies, and knowledge.

Collective Crowd Intelligence

The concept of collective intelligence traces back more than a century but has found renewed rigor in its application to the online crowd. Jenkins (2006a) defines collective intelligence as: "...the ability of virtual communities to leverage the combined expertise of their members. What we cannot know or do on our own, we may now be able to do collectively" (p. 27). More importantly, Jenkins (2006a) differentiates the production of knowledge from activism that incorporates the crowd online: "What holds a collective intelligence together is not the possession of knowledge—which is relatively static, but the social process of acquiring knowledge—which is dynamic and participatory" (p. 54).

Howe identifies three core forms of collective intelligence that crowds normally excel in. The first is that of *prediction*—the ability for the crowd to engage in large-scale information sharing to help determine outcomes, trends, and solutions to problems. Nate Silver, renowned prediction expert formerly of the *New York Times* blog FiveThirtyEight.com and now at ESPN,[9] routinely analyzes social media spaces, information repositories, and online civic dialog to make accurate predictions about who will be in certain political offices well before elections are held and decisions are made. Using crowds to make popular predictions or to help make certain ideas known is a trend that the web has enabled for some time now.

Reddit the social news aggregator, is an early example of leveraging the collective intelligence of a crowd to bring as issue to the public's attention. Reddit functions in a very simple way: its users post stories of interest across a range of categories, and the crowd votes their popularity up or down. In the end, the most popular stories get the lead space on the website, while those deemed less interesting fall victim to the Internet's abyss.

The second form of collective intelligence Howe mentions is that of *problem solving*. Here, groups of interested people come together to find ways to address an issue, challenge, or problem that they want to see solved. Unlike prediction, problem solving is predicated on a crowd gathered to address a specific issue or challenge they are invested in solving. In 2007, Reddit users posted a story about Greenpeace's mission to stop illegal whaling in Japan. Greenpeace, an environmental activist organization, had a plan to insert a tracking chip into a whale as a means to see if illegal whalers were going beyond their legal means to catch and harm whales. Soon after the story was posted, it was voted as the most popular story on the Reddit front page. Greenpeace launched a contest to help name the campaign, and one of the choices, less popular to Greenpeace themselves, was "Mr. Splashy Pants." Nevertheless, the Reddit community was so pleased with the name and the cause that they easily voted it to the top of the list, and as a result Greenpeace created an entire marketing and advocacy campaigns around the concept. In the end, the campaign led to mainstream press coverage, which exposed the illegal whaling practices. This was started by a crowd who showed that they care, not specifically about whales or illegal whaling per se, but about the general cause to the point that they spent time to participate in the movement.

Lastly, Howe advocates for the notion of *idea jams*, which he sees as "essentially just a massive, online brainstorming session…[that] are used to generate new ideas of any stripe" (p. 134). Idea jams are spaces for people to help bring more efficiency, fluency, and innovation to any social, civic, or personal cause. Starbucks launched its *My Starbucks Ideas* website to encourage the open and unfiltered posting of new ideas to help make the Starbucks experience better for its customers. Data.gov is a public information movement where citizens of the United States can find and share information on any public topics with the rest of the country. The effort was launched to provide an open hub for all types of communities looking to extend their networks and interests online.

These types of collective intelligence all depend on media literate crowds to facilitate real, actionable outcomes. The engaged citizen stands a better chance to make valuable contributions to civic society if armed with the core competencies to participate, collaborate, express, and critique. The better prepared, or media literate, citizens are, the more mindful and engaged they can be. In their introduction to *The International Clearinghouse on Children, Youth and Media's Yearbook*, Tufte and Enghel (2009) advocate for media literacy to "provide citizens with the skills they need to make sense of the sometimes overwhelming flow of daily media and in particular new media and information dissemination through new communication technologies."

But this is not something that we should assume happens naturally, but rather a disposition that media literacy education can help to foster in young citizens from an early age. As we will see in Part Two of this book, occasionally the transfer between young citizens' participation on social and mobile spaces, and their understanding of civic contributions is broken. And as I will argue, This is something literacy can fix.

Crowds Depend on Networks

In *Connected: How Your Friends' Friends' Friends Affect Everything You Feel, Think and Do*, Nicholas Christakis and James Fowler (2011) note that "Our connections affect every aspect of our daily lives. How we feel, what we know, whom we marry, whether we fall ill, how much money we make, and whether we vote all depend on the ties that bind us" (p. 7). Christakis and Fowler open their book by offering some very foundational rules for life in a network— (1) We Shape Our Network, (2) Our Network Shapes Us, (3) Our Friends Affect Us, (4) Our Friends' Friends' Friends Affect Us, and (5) The Network Has a Life of Its Own—and preface the importance of members to maintain and reinforce a network's strength. They liken a social network to "a commonly owned forest: we all stand to benefit from it, but we also must work together to ensure it remains healthy and productive...while social networks are fundamentally and distinctively human, and ubiquitous, they should not be taken for granted" (p. 31).

How are networks maintained? And who is responsible for this maintenance? Christakis and Fowler note that individuals are responsible for advancing new ideas; advocating for new causes; supporting local, national and global initiatives; and promoting more civic dialog in their networks, whether family-based, friend-based, or public. And the technologies now exist to make this possible. Christakis and Fowler (2011) offer four distinct modifications to social networks made possible by the Internet—*Enormity, Communality, Specificity,* and *Virtuality*—that together offer the potential for wider use of networks for collaborative efforts. This, of course, depends on the individuals who make up these spaces. Whether advocating for a new brand of socially responsible shoes, a new electric car, or the growing income disparity around the world, individuals that have the capacity to engage, participate and actively contribute will define the true vibrancy of that network. Christakis and Fowler (2011) write:

> Our interactions, fostered and supported by new technologies, but existing even with them, create new social phenomena that transcend individual experience by enriching and enlarging it, and this has significant implications for the collective good. Networks help make the whole of humanity much greater than the sum of its parts, and the invention of new ways to connect promises to increase our power to achieve what nature has foreordained. (p. 286)

The potential of a network also depends on the level of trust that people have in that network and the expected reciprocity they will find in return for their efforts. Like Jenkins's framework for participatory culture, "...social networks and norms of reciprocity can facilitate cooperation for mutual benefit" (Putnam, 2000, p. 21).

In *Bowling Alone,* Putnam presented two ways to think about social capital. *Bonding social capital* refers to strong ties that groups form, which do not extend outward to bring others into their network. While bonding social capital is good for reinforcing friendships, it is not as helpful in maintaining strong networks. *Bridging social capital,* on the other hand, allows for the creation of weak tie relationships in which loosely affiliated groups organize around an event, issue, or cause.

Bonding and bridging social capital do not exist separately but symbiotically. Some social networks show strong bonding social capital, but still exert behaviors of bridging social capital, depending on the capabilities of the members of the network. Barabási (2003) found that in social networks some individuals inherit a strong capability of being able to connect people with each other through bridging social capital. These people are defined as *connectors,* and they are fundamental to networks because they can connect people of different, races, levels of education, interests, and so on. Barabási's (2003) work positions connectors as individuals who "create trends and fashions, make important deals, spread fads, or help launch a restaurant" (p. 56).

Today, with young citizens moving increasingly into mediated spaces to help promote all types of activism, like Molly Katchpole, there is some due optimism that real contributions to every day civic issues and causes can be handled online and with real outcomes. Of course, this all depends on people's ability to effectively access, analyze, share, and cooperate online. Media literate populations stand to contribute meaningful dialog to issues as a default action within networks.

The More Media Literate a Network Is, The More Engaged It Will Be

As mediated networks become ever more common in the facilitation of everyday participation, how citizens find and adapt to online spaces plays an increasingly central role in the efficacy of the crowd. This is premised on citizens being able to see themselves as core participants in the media process, not simply passive consumers of content who occasionally share a thought or idea in their social network.

If it were not for over 300,000 active citizens with an online presence who were ready to act, Molly Katchpole's campaign would not have flourished to the extent that it did. If not for millions of concerned citizens who knew how and where to navigate their support for natural disasters in Haiti, New Orleans, and most recently along the coasts of New York and New Jersey, the amount of support would have not reached the levels that it did. In this day and age, media literate citizens are at the foundation of engaged participatory citizenship.

In *Mediacology*, Antonio Lopez writes about media literacy as a conduit for helping people find a *sense of place*. Lopez's arguments are grounded in concrete critiques of media literacy education as a linear pedagogy that teaches citizens to critically respond to media texts that they consume. Lopez sees this approach as both shortsighted and misguided. Instead, he offers a critical approach to media literacy that is grounded in what he calls a mediacology—a holistic approach to exploring media as at the center of our sense of place, affinity to culture, and to the social ecosystems within which we function. Writes Lopez (2008): "By focusing on media as a kind of "conduit" that transports information objects, we are failing to grasp how deeply our perception influences the manner by which we frame information, communication, and the world" (p. 3). Lopez places the individual's self-perception of engagement and sense of purpose at the heart of understanding how our actions engage and influence communities. This starts not from a linear response to media texts, but rather from a point of seeing the value and purpose of our situated place and voice online.

How do citizens find their "sense of place" in networked communities? How do citizens perceive efficacy and expressive competency in social networks? In *Here Comes Everybody* Shirky offers a model for engaged, active, and outcome-oriented community initiatives in the digital age. While Shirky's model looks at the organizational side of networked-community building, here I want to apply his community engagement metric work to the digital citizen, and explore what role media literacy can play in this process.

Shirky (2008) believes that the group-forming capacity of social tools are engaging a human instinct lost in the mass media age: "Ridiculously easy group-forming matters because the desire to be part of a group that shares, cooperates, or acts in concert is a basic human instinct that has always been constrained by transaction costs" (Shirky, p. 54). Transaction costs, or the barriers to engagement with media, have hindered communities' ability to extend and engaged beyond spatial distance. As Fowler and Christakis develop in their exploration of networks in digital spaces, Shirky (2008) extols the value of new dynamic and nimble communication tools for civic engagement. "It isn't just that our communication tools are cheaper," notes Shirky, "they are also better. In particular, they are more favorable to innovative uses, because they are considered more flexible than our old ones" (p. 77). All communities, Shirky believes, exist in the context of a *promise*, what binds the community; a *tool*, what the community will use to communicate and organize; and a *bargain*, what processes communities use to share and cooperate. Once such parameters are defined, to build effective community action and reach goals Shirky develops what he calls the *engagement ladder*. The engagement ladder encompasses a progression of collaborative behaviors towards a goal or outcome. The ladder consists of three steps: *sharing, cooperation*, and *action*.

Sharing is the initial basic step of any crowd, as it demands very little from its members. Individuals can choose to share and not actively participate. This type of behavior is quite common in Internet culture. Community members may advocate, post, or express support for issues or causes of interest, which help define the boundaries of the crowd. These actions also build entryways for further dialog, conversation, and cooperation.

Cooperation signals a behavioral shift in the mentality of the crowd or community. In this case, the members of an active community must move beyond sharing content to directly engage with one another—either in physical or networked proximity—towards a shared goal. Linux, Last.fm, Groupon, and Craigslist, exist entirely on the cooperative engagement of their users.

This part of Shirky's ladder is not entirely determined by active coordination but must encompass clear and direct behaviors towards a shared outcome or goal.

The final step in Shirky's ladder is collective *action*. This is the most difficult step in the process, because unlike cooperation, it requires coordinated steps to reach the intended outcome. This is where, in the case of the Occupy Wall Street movement, the crowd physically gathered to show solidarity in their goal (vague as it was purported to be). Collective action was also evident in the physical gathering coordinated by *Invisible Children* to reach their goal to spur real political action against Joseph Kony. Barack Obama's campaigns in 2008 and 2012 were both predicated on the collective action of the many youth who voted to support change they believed in. There are a number of examples of collective action facilitated by expanding network connectivity and crowds who are now, as Shirky (2008) mentions, "inherently cooperative and are beautifully supported by social tools, because that is exactly the kind of community whose members can recruit one another or allow themselves to be found by interested searchers" (p. 101).

Of course, collective action is more active when "it expresses group emotions such as anger, moral outrage, or guilt, affirms the group's distinctiveness, directly expresses the group identity, or affirms the illegitimacy of an intergroup relationship" (Louis, 2009, p. 729). Collective action in crowds is normally more vibrant, as in the case of Molly Katchpole, when its members feel emotionally charged on a personal level.

The ability for individuals to engage and move through the engagement ladder necessitates a level of media literacy. Individuals invested in issues on very local and personal levels need to know how to seek out, join, and participate in the communities that share their concerns. They must have the confidence to join and climb engagement ladders around issues of local, national, and global importance. They must see their acts of sharing not as the end goal of participation but as a starting point to cooperative and actionable outcomes.

To get to this point, citizens need to be fully aware of how to locate the spaces, information, and platforms that help them think critically and actively about the issue, and then activate their voice to constructively and critically contribute to dialog (Buckingham, 2003; Luke, 2000; De Abreu, 2011). If we reposition Shirky's engagement ladder from the point of the organized community to that of the media literate citizen, we can see how the steps towards engaged citizenship may be enhanced by the development of media literate competencies in individuals.

- *Media Literate Sharing* – While sharing is identified as the initial and "easiest" step in the engagement ladder, it is vital in deciding which issues gain traction and coalesce into community movements and which issues fall by the wayside. How we share, what we choose to share, and who we think of as our audience all dictate what we make public and extend to our networks. Media literate approaches to sharing include a series of internal evaluations based on access, audience, value, purpose, and exposure. A set of checkpoints for what is being shared, who will see the shared content, who will be affected, and how this act affects their identity, all stand to make the type of sharing that happens online more thoughtful. I am not advocating that every time people share content or express something in social spaces they stop and pull a checklist out of their pockets to ask a series of questions. But the more they are made to consider such questions around sharing, the more they become critically reflective to make certain thoughtful valuations.

- *Media Literate Cooperation* – Cooperative acts necessitate, as Shirky mentions, a behavioral shift in the community dynamic. Members must actively carve out space and time to work towards shared outcomes or goals. Thanks to the organizational power of the web, people are very good at self-managing in online spaces. Media literacy can serve two purposes in cooperative contexts. First, by cultivating more awareness of the capacity people have to be part of supportive landscapes, media literacy education can help build effective engagement and participation in a community. This entails the ability to assess trust in communities, explore what cooperation means in mediated spaces, and understand who benefits from it. Second, media literacy can facilitate a more critical content approach to cooperation. If crowds are able to access, analyze and critically evaluate the content they are sharing, they will be better positioned to critique existing content and provide relevant content needed to cooperate and engage around an aim or cause.

- *Media Literate Action* – Action is something that we normally know when we see it but often find hard to identify in the abstract. We do know that civic actions are more easily predicted when they are responsive. If we personally feel oppressed, taken advantage of, or in stark disagreement with something, it's much easier to be able to cultivate the gusto to be part of the response. Media literate action would try to re-purpose action as proactive. Because we now have the tools to build activity into the context of our daily lives, media literacy can teach about collective action as a default part of our media use.

Engagement ladders, in the context of large-scale organizational movements, will always require yeoman's work by a few connectors that lead movements to resist, change, advocate, and mobilize. But what if engagement ladders were also applied to the small, daily community- and crowd-based activities needed to sustain local health, neighborhood safety, environmental awareness, and respect for diversity? Could we see social platforms used for everyday civic life in smart, efficient, and inclusive ways? We already are in some cases (see Appendix A for my list of exemplary cases). Shirky (2010) emphasizes the potential that networks provide for coordinating effective organization and action, based on human connectivity that social networks encourage: "We want to be connected to one another, a desire that the social surrogate of television deflects, but one that our use of social media actually engages" (p. 14).

For a media literate crowd to flourish in Shirky's engagement ladder, or in the context of any collaborative movement, they must have basic competencies that allow them to opt-in. I have identified five competencies that I think are central to media literate collaborative efforts in networked culture.

Competencies for Media Literate Crowds

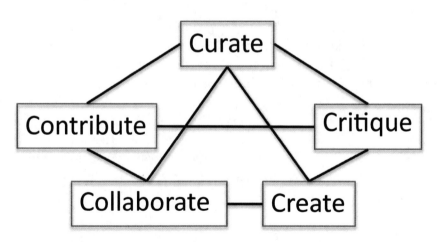

Figure 3.2. The C's of Media Literacy Networks.

1. **CURATE** – To curate, historically, has meant to organize, to pull together, sift through, select for presentation, to heal, and *to preserve*.

Traditionally reserved for those who worked within museum or library settings, curation today has evolved to apply to what we are all doing online. The preservation and organization of content in digital culture is now largely the responsibility of the individual (Mihailidis & Cohen, 2013).

As the Internet continues to develop technologically, so have organizational tools for civic engagement. From mobile apps to help cities track infrastructure problems to government data aggregators, citizens today have access to a multitude of platforms and spaces where we can curate information. We share links, re-tweet ideas, and express comments in spaces that are open, accessible, and curated by a multitude of diverse participants. The web now mandates curation as a default for users navigating its exponential content. The ability to curate information is central to media literate competences in collaborative spaces.

2. **CRITIQUE** – Media literacy rests on the foundations of critical thinking (see Alvermann & Hagood, 2000; De Abreu & Mihailidis, 2014; Kellner & Share, 2005; 2007a; Livingstone, 2004b). The abundance of information online has made available more valuable, balanced, critical, and independent information. It has also brought the possibility for the uncritical consumer to collect mistakes, mistruths, and misinformation (Bartlett & Miller, 2011). To help mitigate uncritical consumption on the web, Kellner and Share (2005) developed a framework for critical media literacy predicated on *non-transparency, codes* and *conventions, audience decoding, content* and *message*, and *motivation* (pp. 374–77). Helping young citizens become critical thinkers can facilitate the transfer of power from distributers to receivers, expanding the reach of citizens into new participatory and collaborative spaces.

3. **CONTRIBUTE** – Youth primarily use social networks, aggregators, and mobile apps for information needs today. In turn, social networks have provided new functions that help users share information in meaningful and productive ways. Social networks, writes Shirky (2008),

> ...operate as both amplifiers and filters of information. Because information in the system is passed along by friends and friends and friends (or at least contacts and contacts of contacts), people tend to get information that is also of interest to their friends. The more friends you have who care about a particular piece of information—whether gossip or a job opening or a new song they like—the likelier you are to hear about it as well. (p. 221)

Research shows how individuals are disposed to sharing, expressing, re-posting, and commenting in social networks (see Ligon & Schechter, 2012; Kumar et al., 2010; Sharma et al., 2010; Wasko & Faraj, 2005). Media literacy, in this context, must approach the act of contributing as a self-reflective, audience-based experience, where individuals are able to "produce effective and responsible media messages" (Silverblatt, 2001, p. 120). In the digital age, producing messages is as simple as a tweet, post, or share.

For the networked crowd, contribution is a default. For without contributions, the network will dissipate. Media literate crowds understand their contributions to public spaces as helping to define narratives, dialog, and topics of interest for a large group. They see the value of their contributions—whether humor, insight, or escape—as adding to a dynamic and eclectic group of voices collectively fueling the group's position, connectivity, and vibrancy.[10]

3. **COLLABORATE** – Collaboration, closely tied to cooperation in Shirky's engagement ladder, involves the behavioral shift from simply contributing meaningful and valuable content, to an *active* form of collaboration. Participatory approaches to media literacy can be seen in the rich examples of collaborative spaces that exist today. Kickstarter, Groupon, Carrotmob, Charity Water, and Ushahidi are only a few of the platforms that exist entirely around the collaborative capacities of citizens. Supporting great ideas, finding ways to benefit local organizations or to voice opinions and track violence all take coordinated and collaborative effort between members of the network. Media literacy competencies must advocate for the "collaborationists," a term Jenkins coins,[11] to find ways to extend into certain causes or issues in which they have a stake. Like Greenpeace's Mr. Splashy Pants campaign, networks form and collaborate around issues they generally care about because they have the access and collaborative possibilities to extend their voices into these spaces. Media literacy can extend this competency into the context of daily networks.

4. **CREATE** – In *Living and Learning with New Media*, Mimi Ito writes of the friction between participatory youth and traditional pedagogical models. Ito (2008) understands participation in digital culture as "more than being able to access serious online information and culture. Youth could benefit from educators being more open to forms of experimentation and social exploration that are generally not characteristic of educational institutions" (p. 2). We have to look no

further than YouTube to see the creative capacities of young citizens today. Over 100 hours of video are uploaded to this space every minute. Citizens can now compete with networks for creativity, creation, and appropriation. Uploading diverse content—some original, some remixed—shows the development of an ecosystem of civic creations that provide a collective narrative about any range of searchable issues. In *Remix*, Lawrence Lessig explores how creating in digital spaces has perhaps become a more dominant form of writing. Lessig believes that using "...even the simplest tools, bundled into the most innovative modern operating systems—anyone can begin to 'write' using images, or music, or video. And using the facilities of a free digital network, anyone can share that writing with anyone else" (p. 69).

Creation, in the context of media literacy, is about the capacity that youth have to produce, share, and appropriate "media" content in public spaces. Creation does not necessitate starting from scratch—as it may have been deemed in a pre-digital age—but includes the new ways in which media and information are repackaged, appropriated, and distributed. Creation also allows youth to take ownership of their capacity to produce and to understand foundations in critical message construction, distribution, and reception. "By creating their own productions," writes media literacy scholar Belinha De Abreu (2011), "[students] must now learn to conceptualize and critically think while being reflective of how audiences view texts" (p. 37). Creation is what fuels the collaborative production of networks today. From memes to remixing, media literate citizens take advantage of their ability to create and share contributions, and recognize the power that such relationships have for civic voices online (Erstad et al., 2007).

Why Media Literacy Matters for the Emerging Citizen

The Molly Katchpole story is but one of dozens of examples of individuals and communities using digital tools and technologies to gather likeminded individuals around causes. Of course, tools are less than half of the story. If not for those who enter collaborative spaces and create value out of the tools they adopt, there would be no real value to begin with. The abundance of new platforms and spaces that now exist foster more collaborative production, social advocacy, and interactive dialog necessitates a new look at the ways in which young citizens today socialize.

In developing his notion of a networked information economy, Yochai Benkler (2005) advances the notion of a virtual public sphere where citizens are seen as public participants, and not private individuals:

> The Internet allows individuals to abandon the idea of the public sphere as primarily constructed of finished statements uttered by a small set of actors socially understood to be "the media" (whether state owned or commercial) and separated from society, and to move toward a set of social practices that see individuals as participating in a debate. Statements in the public sphere can now be seen as invitations for a conversation, not as finished goods. (p. 180)

Young citizens today enter this new knowledge culture with a certain level of familiarity with digital tools and platforms (Prensky, 2001; Ofcom, 2010; Rosen, 2010). And while these digital technologies open new avenues for thinking about discourse in public spaces, citizens are not necessarily being trained or educated to excel in these spaces (Hargittai, 2005; Jones et al., 2010; Kennedy et al., 2008). Jenkins (2006a) acknowledges this general disconnect, noting that how we educate youth today "contrast[s] sharply with the kinds of learning that are needed as students are entering the new knowledge culture" (p. 183). Investigations into youth and digital competencies have shown that proper pedagogical methods that approach critical inquiry online, knowledge construction, reliability, and savvy web navigation can increase digital and media literacy (Kuiper & Volman, 2008; Sanchez et al., 2006; Taboada & Guthrie, 2006).

New approaches to community engagement must "make sure that digital citizens are well-informed citizens in both understanding information and in their ability to evaluate and analyze what they are seeing (Swiggum, 2008, p. 16). I would also extend this idea to include competencies to express, share, and actively cooperate in digital spaces.

The success of collaborative platforms largely depends on the ability for networks to be interactive knowledgeable, critical, trusting, and transparent. From those supporting interesting design and art, to those helping to build environmental policy, networks are dependent on accurate, relevant, timely, and detailed information to move forward. This includes not only the sharing of timely information and knowledge, but also being able to assess the accuracy of that shared information. Without knowledge about how to become an active participant in social and collaborative platforms, it would be difficult if not impossible to harness the true participatory nature of the web to strengthen community dialog, collaboration, and action.

This is where media literacy comes in. As I wrote in chapter one, studies have shown that increased levels of Internet savvy, digital competence and goal-oriented online learning can lead to more quality time spent online (Kahne et al., 2012; Rheingold, 2008a). Measuring media literacy outcomes in the classroom has been less common, but studies do exist that have correlated the attainment of media literacy skills with more critical analysis, evaluation, and comprehension of media texts (see Arke, 2005; Mihailidis, 2009a; Hobbs & Frost, 2003; Feuerstein, 1999).

Not only will youth and young adults need to understand how to effectively analyze and critique media messages, but also they are going to rely on participatory, expressive, and collaborative competencies for their online lives (Hobbs, 2011a; Hobbs & Cooper Moore, 2013; Share, 2009; Schiebe & Rogow, 2011). These competencies are just now emerging. However, most of our attention and energy focuses on the implications of the tools, platforms, and spaces, and less on the people that inhabit and contribute to them. This could lead to shortsightedness and a lack of real engagement around the civic potential that such tools empower in *people*. Gordon (2013) cautions us not to see digital tools as saviors in and of themselves, noting "Digital tools are a means to an end. If they are treated as an end in themselves, they threaten to subvert the community engagement process, sublimating the potential human connections and learning to the flashy functionality of a digital billboard."

To better understand the frameworks that may approach media literacy competencies for the emerging citizen, my exploration into the social and mobile media lives of young citizens in the United States was guided by two fundamental questions:

- How much are young people relying on social platforms and mobile tools for daily information and communication needs?
- How do young people understand and perceive these tools as vital conduits for engagement in civic life?

The college students I surveyed and spoke to were dependent on social media for a majority of their information and communication needs. They were agile and savvy in their use of social media platforms for connecting with friends, exploring trends, sharing humor, and reading about current affairs. The survey responses show a reliance on social networks and peer-to-peer platforms for a significant majority of their social and civic information. At the same time, they were reticent to admit to social networks as being more than time-wasting outlets. They repeatedly saw little value in the role of social media outlets for daily civic value, instead relying on networks for what they perceived as personal and unproductive communication. The young people I spoke to consistently fell back on seeing social media as a way to check out, stalk friends, and waste away an afternoon. When pressed to discuss more diverse platforms for information consumption, sharing, expression, and participation, the dialog was met with dissent.

The lack of transfer from use to perception may be the result of social media displacing time spent in engaging in social and civic life. The perceptions here illuminate the need for real reform in how youth and young citizens see social networks as holistic social and civic tools for engagement in daily life. The opportunity exists for dynamic civic networks to emerge, driven by citizens for issues large and small: local, national, and global. Developing these new competencies in young citizens must start in the classroom, in the home, and from a young age. The tools will only extend as far as we develop them for social and civic causes. To do that, we must develop the core competencies in citizens to harness social media technologies and platforms for real civic use.

What do these new tools and platforms do for how youth consume, share, and create information? How do they negotiate the personal and public communication avenues that these social platforms provide? Talking with groups of students gives some keen insight in these phenomena, and moves closer to making a concrete case for media literacy as the core civic competency of our digital culture.

· PART TWO ·

LISTENING TO EMERGING CITIZENS

· 4 ·

YOUNG CITIZENS AND PERCEPTIONS OF SOCIAL MEDIA USE — INTEGRATED INFORMATION LANDSCAPES

So far I've presented some background on the evolving frameworks for citizenship, the field of media literacy, and some of the ways that they are connected in digital culture. The connections between media and citizenship are, of course, as old as Gutenberg's printing press. But they are taking on a new codependence in a society that relies on media for more and more of its basic infrastructure. The sheer growth of time spent with digital media, social networks, and increasingly mobile "smart phones" (see Lenhart et al., 2010, 2010b, 2010c), is facilitating new ways to communicate with friends, family, and our communities. Young people are now seen as *always on*, connected and expressive throughout their daily lives (Ito, 2009). They are using social networks to find out about current events (Monk, 2011), to engage in the sharing of content, and to extend the walls of the classroom (Junco & Cotten, 2010; Junco, 2012a).

A host of studies have explored how collaborative technologies are enhancing sociability, hobbies, personal and professional connectivity, collaboration, and professional networking (Anderson, 2011; Hartley-Brewer, 2009; Watkins, 2009). At the same time, studies have found that multitasking students are distracted to the tune of switching between media devices every 14 seconds, or 120 times in 27.5 minutes (Brasel & Gips, 2011). This multitasking has taken a toll on short-term memory (Clapp et al., 2011). Heavy technology use has also been associated with weakened face-to-face communication (Small & Vorgan, 2008), anti-social behavior (Stout, 2010), and a lack of focus and engagement in the classroom (Berman et al., 2008; Richtel, 2010).

Searching for the effects of social media will lead to somewhere in between *they are good for you* and *they are not good for you*. These studies, however, are helpful for exploring ways to develop new uses of digital tools and technologies and their place in society. And just as important as studying the effects of technologies, the perceptions of a technology's value can help us understand its various uses.

The following exploration is about young people's perceptions of social media, to try and make sense of how young people see this complex and messy landscape of tools, platforms, and technologies as facilitating information and communication needs in daily life.[12] Making sense of this space, or as much sense as I am able to, can lead to the development of core approaches to helping young people use these tools for more expansive, diverse, and fulfilling purposes. If we are going to prepare young people with the necessary skills and dispositions to be thoughtful citizens in a digital media culture, we must first explore how they are using these technologies, and how they perceive them in the context of daily life. Only then can we begin to design and develop core media literacy approaches that accurately address the digital competencies needed for young people to effectively participate in civic life online.

Exploring Social Media Dispositions: A Survey of Six Spaces

In 2011, I spent the better part of the year talking with university students about how they envision social media in their daily lives. I wanted to specifically find out how they understood these spaces as facilitators of information and communication needs, social and familial relationships, and civic contributions.

Before speaking with students, I set out to conduct a survey[13] of perceived social media habits across six spaces: news, politics, relationships, education, entertainment, and privacy. The survey was distributed to nine US universities[14] and contained over 70 multiple-choice questions spread across the six categories. The survey was divided into categories that reflect a broad framework for social media and information uses: (1) *news* questions asked about news consumption habits through social media; (2) *politics* inquired about following local and national politics through social networks; (3) *relationships* explored personal communication through social networks; (4) *education* posed questions about social media use in class, and the effectiveness of social media for educational purposes; (5) *entertainment* explored social network use for games, shopping, music, movies, and leisure; and (6) *privacy* asked about trust and the willingness to share personal information in social media spaces.

In total 873 students completed the survey.[15] The participants comprised 63% females and 37% males. The majority of participants were seniors (33%), followed by juniors (29%), sophomores (28%), and freshmen (9%). Approximately 40% of the participating students were enrolled in a communication-related major, with the remaining participants spread across disciplines, and 8% had yet to declare a major course of study. Of the entire sample, 75% were Caucasian, 10% Hispanic/Latino, 4% African/black American, and the remaining participants split among Native American, Asian American, Arab American, and other.

The participants showed media use averages in line with Pew (Mitchell & Rosenstiel, 2012) and Kaiser (Rideout et al., 2010) studies on youth and media use. Less than half (42%) of the students claimed to spend 3–4 hours per day on the Internet, while 29% reported 5–6 hours per day online, and 16% reported spending more than 7 hours per day online. When asked to estimate their *social media* use, the data trended down a bit, with 49% spending 0–2 hours per day, 33% spending 3–4 hours per day, and 12% spending 5–6 hours per day. Of course, such figures are a tenuous measure at best, considering both self-reporting bias and the fact that estimating time spent online is increasingly difficult with the emergence of mobile technologies. But they do help provide context for exploring detailed perceptions of social media.

Surveys cannot provide the richness of speaking to people directly. They can't bring about complexities, variations in opinion and thought, and the messiness with which we think about topics like friends, family, news, community, and digital media. This makes it difficult to isolate and develop behavioral traits in people's information habits that can account for a full range of views and opinions. Nevertheless, this survey was essential for creating a baseline for the rich dialog I was able to have with over 70 university students in the months following the survey dissemination, which is the topic of chapter five.

The survey results reinforce existing data that show social media platforms providing spaces for both bonding and bridging social capital in young adults (Burke et al., 2010; Steinfeld et al., 2008; Valenzuela et al., 2009). Information and communication habits across all categories are migrating to social platforms, specifically in the areas of personal relationships, news, and entertainment. By exploring each category in this survey I hope to provide a rich portrait of young peoples' perceptions of social media use today. This data will be used to support the rich dialog that emerged from the small group discussions, which exposed a disconnect in the perceived use and purpose of social media.

Space #1 – News

In his 2005 text, *Tuned Out: Why Americans Under 40 Don't Read the News*, David Mindich explored the lack of attention paid to news by the under-40 population in the United States. Mindich found that, not surprisingly, students devoted more time to pop culture and entertainment than to hard news. This was the result of a myriad of factors: a population that is complacent, less trustworthy of mass media, with low levels of social capital, who watch more television, and have retreated to the cozy confines of isolating suburbia. The obvious culprits, television and entertainment, have eroded the public sphere and proportionately reversed social capital. Mindich (2005) expresses his concern for the current state of declining interest in news:

> The evidence for the long-term decline in news interest is overwhelming. In order to prove that young people are following the news less than their elders do, and less than young people once did, I have devoted an entire chapter to this argument. I urge you to join me in wading through the many statistics because I am convinced, and believe that you will be too, that our democracy is in big, big trouble. (p. 19)

Mindich's argument is reinforced by data that show a decline in the ability of the under-40 population to recall specific information about local politicians, current events in the press, and political issues. Using polling data and market research, the picture is convincing indeed. The argument goes that students are less interested in news; affiliate less with parties; have less knowledge than their elders about political candidates, political processes in the United States and abroad; and are lowest on the totem pole when it comes to newspaper readership, television news viewing, and overall media consumption for news purposes (Mindich, 2005).

These arguments are collectively worrisome, and as Mindich (2005) appropriately notes, we are in the midst of "a marked and steady decline in political engagement and news consumption. While there are anecdotal accounts of increased news interest among preteens and young teens, there is no statistical evidence yet to suggest a rebound" (p. 26). Mindich is correct that we have no statistics that show a resurgence of news interest by youth. Measurements for engagement with news have historically focused on mass media industries and deal with knowledge retention. This has merit, of course, but may not longer be as relevant for digital media systems that integrate both platforms and information types into single aggregated spaces online. Young people today rarely compartmentalize information into silos or through separate mediums. Nor do they feel a need to recall general political news and information because they carry this information with them in their pockets on a daily basis. I want to problematize Mindich's and others arguments of a tuned-out youth population (see Delli Carpini, 2000; Tewksbury, 2003; Wattenberg, 2007).

In this digital age, much of the research around eroding social capital has been challenged, in some cases by the authors of the original research (Putnam et al., 2004) and by a host of others who are finding new forms of engagement in digital spaces (see Ellison et al., 2010; Papacharissi & Mendelson, 2008; Valenzuela et al., 2009; Steinfield et al., 2008).

I want to focus on two emerging phenomena that can show engagement with news beyond reported recall of issues, politicians, and current events. First, in an age of ubiquitous "smart" phones that can deliver full web capabilities in real time, there is less need to recall candidate names or positions on issues, particularly when that information is available at the tip of our fingers. If we measure civic engagement on recall alone, most of us today would fall well short of our perceived level of engagement with our community and country. Dalton's *The Good Citizen* develops new parameters for engagement based on volunteering, voting, signing petitions, and helping those less fortunate—which portray a different picture of engagement than laid out by Mindich. Further, the amount of information that we can access today is so much wider and vaster than in the past, that needing to navigate these spaces is almost as important, if not more, than recall.

Second, in a digital information age, separating news from other content is problematic. Part of the difficulty in surveying student's news consumption habits lies in how the term news is presented. In today's digital information landscape, news is not something that can be limited to certain outlets or spaces on the web. Rather it is integrated heavily into aggregators, feeds, and social networks (Mitchell, 2010; Tewksbury & Wittenberg, 2012).

One of the key arguments made by Mindich (2005) is that "people who choose entertainment over news are less likely to participate in community projects" (p. 11). In an age where news is increasingly integrated into social spaces, the overlap between news and entertainment is inevitable. Entertainment, be it films, sports, or reality television, has always been more attractive to young people because it's fun, interesting, and offers a pleasant escape from the world. Today, it's more difficult to isolate news content from personal or entertainment content, thus making it harder to know when and how news is consumed. In the news portion of the survey conducted for this book, 59% of students reported spending less than one hour per day consuming news, while 34% reported spending 1–2 hours per day with news. These numbers are typical of the 18–24 age demographic, where the term "news" is often conceived as something parents watch, or which matters to older demographics.

However, 40% of respondents reported primarily reading/watching news online. Not surprisingly, Facebook (65%) and Twitter (33%) were the predominant outlets for online news consumption. Almost one-third of students (29%) see *blogs* as credible spaces for news, with half of those students visiting two or more *blogs* daily. In the survey, when students were asked about searching out news on a story, the most common reported way to do so was to "Google it" (76% ranked it their top choice), followed by visiting a specific website (67%), watching television (51%), picking up a newspaper (30%) and then calling friends or family (22%) and using Facebook (20%) and Twitter (12%). Of the participants, 29% reported having a news app on their mobile phone. Visiting an online news site was reported by half of the student participants. Traditional media outlets are facing growing competition from digital and social tools for news consumption.

When looking for news do you (select all that apply):

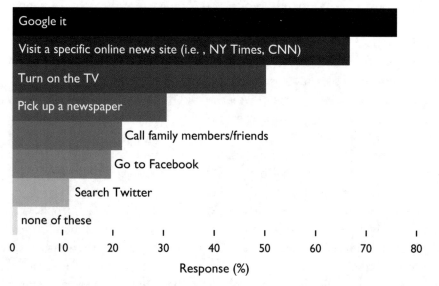

Figure 4.1. Social Media and News Habits.

Collectively, these numbers signify a shift from news consumption as a separate act towards it being part of an integrated information platform in which news is a component. On an average day, 40% of the students sought out news and current affairs online with a majority using social media to do so. While students reported consuming a relatively small amount of news, they showed a growing reliance on social media for news consumption. When students hear the word news, as we will explore in the next chapter, they immediately think of news as it exists in a mass media space. They talk about not reading newspapers, not having the time to sit in front of the television at a certain time in the evening, and not caring about all the cynical politicians and deaths that exist on a daily basis.

This leads to a few implications for how we think about news in social spaces. As Google, Facebook, Twitter and aggregators increasingly serve as primary facilitators for information, student news habits will increasingly be integrated into their online news feeds and general Internet use. So when personal missives integrate with shared links to news stories and direct tweets from news organizations, how we understand engagement with news goes beyond where they read or watch programming on a regular basis. It now involves an increasingly fluid and complex set of digital and social competencies.

Space #2 – Politics

Like news, questions about politics and citizenship often elicit negative and disinterested responses in students. Rarely do they embrace politicians or political agendas. In *Is Voting for Young People?* Martin Wattenberg provides a convincing argument for the declining involvement of the young voter in the United States today. Wattenberg cites the familiar downward trajectory of information consumption via mass media channels and the lack of ability to recall knowledge about current political figures and issues. To substantiate his argument, Wattenberg cites the decline in newspaper readership, television viewing, and the general increasing apathy of those under 30. Using conventional measures—voting, contacting local political officials, and tuning into political conventions—Wattenberg (2007) makes a strong argument for the waning interest of youth in politics in the United States:

> People under 30 have consistently scored lower than other age groups on each and every factual question in recent surveys. Regardless of whether the question concerned basic civics facts, identification of current political leaders, information

about the presidential candidates, or knowledge of partisan control of the Congress, the result was the same: young people were clearly less well-informed than the elderly. (p. 79)

Again we see detailed attention paid to a linear model for political engagement, measured by traditional metrics that existed in a pre-Internet, pre-digital information age. It is true that in the mass media environment, "If politicians know that young people are far less likely to vote than the elderly, why should they care about young people?" (Wattenberg, 2007, p. 140).

This book is not about arguing for a right or wrong way to understand political engagement, but it does advocate for widening the measures and approaches to assessing political engagement. It also advocates for a vision of political and civic participation that focuses on *engagement* in addition to *duties*. It is clear that the 2008 presidential election signified a shift from predominantly mass media-based political engagement to more social media driven grassroots politicking (Harfoush, 2009). Zukin et al. (2006) focus their text, *A New Engagement: Political Participation, Civic Life and the Changing American Citizen,* on widening the view of political engagement and civic participation that has emerged through activism, outreach, and campaigns propelled largely through social media and mobile technologies.

In his concluding chapter, Wattenberg offers a host of suggestions for re-engaging youth in the political process. He mentions compulsory voting as a key policy reform in this area, but also lists friendlier mechanisms for voter registration, less exposure of political candidates, voting on leisure days, and improving civics education (Wattenberg, 2007). Improving civics education is essential to broaden not only how young people think of political and civic engagement, but also how educators develop pedagogical pathways to more dynamic and current outcomes for youth in a digital information age.

Accordingly, the survey respondents, half of whom voted before, reported sparse consumption of information about politicians, or political issues. Those who did, mentioned the Internet (55%), the television (54%) and word of mouth (44%) as the most common ways to get political information. Social media, however, found a new and growing place in students' political lives, and 40% reported using Facebook as a way to find political information, while approximately 25% used Twitter for the same purposes. Only 18% reported following political figures on Twitter. Online news aggregators were very common (88%) for hearing political information, while *blogs* faired less so (29%).

However, when asked about social media and political communication, a different picture emerges: 44% of the sample claimed social media to be the primary way they communicated about politics. Over 55% of the sample claimed to use social media to "actively" voice their political opinions, and 34% of the sample belongs to at least one political or civic advocacy group on Facebook. The final question dealing with citizenship and politics asked how social media had influenced political awareness in the students: 48% of the students agreed that social media had made them more aware of politics, while over 85% disagreed with the statement that social media had lessened their political awareness, or dissuaded them from politics in general.

While it is clear that students do not see themselves using social media to consume political information in the traditional sense, they are using social media spaces to voice political opinions, share ideas, and circulate content. This bodes well for more diversity and dialog in the public sphere as social networks and peer-to-peer platforms for online interactivity continue to grow.

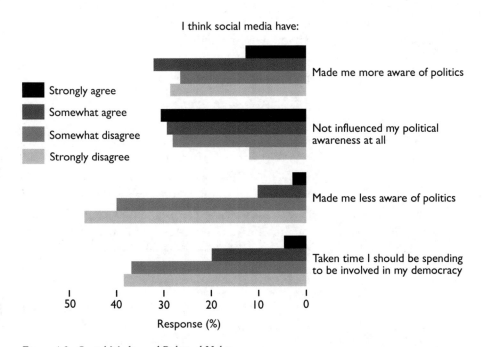

Figure 4.2. Social Media and Political Habits.

Space #3 – Relationships

"Are they Facebook official" is a question I hear a lot when students talk about the role of social media in relationships. I also hear students detail their conflicted struggles about whether or not they "friend" their parents online, and what they choose to share with them if they do. Creeping, following the adventures and journeys of peers, sending notes of encouragement, and wasting away lonely and boring afternoons in classrooms are all common social media activities of students today. Fowler & Christakis (2010) found in a recent study that actions of public good increase in the context of witnessing peer actions in social networks. This cascading effect increases the more individuals are exposed to such public goods. Other studies show a complex landscape for understanding the types of relationships that are maintained in social networking spaces, in which most of the results are not positive (see Dunne, 2011; Tong et al., 2008; Walther et al., 2008).

Our relationships are now facilitated not only by our direct circle of friends and acquaintances, but also to a large degree by our friends' friends, and their friends, who contribute to the information and content that we see. Christakis and Fowler (2011), to this end, point out that social networks don't do much to extend or enhance our close tie networks, but they do facilitate more expansive latent or weak tie communications that expand the scope of information and dialog we encounter on a daily basis:

> Social network sites can expand and redefine what counts as a friend, while at the same time facilitating the maintenance of ties within this broader group of people. Social-network sites are used to keep tabs on real friends, of course, but most people have online connections to others whose phone numbers, for example, they might not have, whom they might not be able to recognize on the street, and, frankly, whom they might not feel comfortable chatting with in a bar. (p. 276)

This connectivity opens up a host of possibilities for how we access news and information. And this type of extended network offline simply could not exist. Of course, we are left to the whims of fancy algorithms put in place by the programmers who design the network, which clouds the picture a bit, but overall the centrality of our social graphs have expanded.

Still, "our ability to get along emerges spontaneously from the decentralized actions of people who form groups with connected fates and a common purpose" (Christakis & Fowler, 2011, p. 280). It is not clear how this type of connected activity will transform daily civic life. This seems to be a perception issue. How people envision the role and place of social networks for extending and enriching their connectivity, information flow, and communication network will dictate the value of the networks themselves. "The evidence from real-world networks suggests," Christakis and Fowler (2011) write, "that online networks can be used to enhance what flows between real-world friends and family, but we do not yet know whether the Internet will increase the speed or scope of social contagions in general" (p. 286).

Part of the answer to this lies in people's ability to recognize the connectivity provided by social networks and the opportunity for engagement that extends from friends, to acquaintances, and family. In the survey conducted for this book, we asked students about the influence of social networks on their personal relationships. The aim was to see how much or little they acknowledged social media's place in their daily relationships with family, friends, and significant others, and the extent to which they perceived this engagement as valuable or not.

The data reveal a population, like Christakis and Fowler note, who see social media as enhancing their real life friendships and family communication, but not as a surrogate for them. When asked about the effect of social media on friendships, 48% believed that social media had no influence on their friends, while 40% reported feeling closer to their friends because of social media, and 26% felt that they had "more friends" because of social media, while less than 3% actually saw social media as taking away from time with friends or making friends.

While students recognized the value of social media for communicating with friends, it was seen as a secondary avenue for maintaining friendships; 48% of the students reported spending more time talking with friends in person than online, which may be a slightly self-inflated statistic, considering how much time they reported actually spending on social networks per day. However, 16% did report spending more time communicating with friends online than in person. At the same time, 63% of the sample had never met a friend online that turned into a face-to-face friendship.

The data from this portion of the survey reinforces the idea that students today do not like to see social networks as infringing upon their friendships that exist in real time and space. They resisted seeing social media, particularly Facebook, as having a real influence or impact on their friends. Friends were, to them, sacred ground, while Facebook seemed simply a space to either enhance the consistent dialog with their friends and to ogle at acquaintances. The communication aspect was for the strong tie community, and the social information flow extended to the weak tie community.

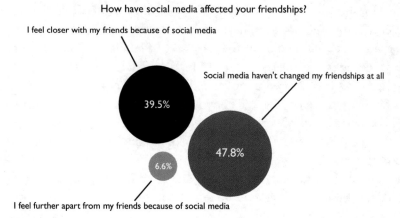

Figure 4.3. Social Media and Perceptions of Friends.

Social media, on the other hand, seem to be playing a more central role in how students communicate with their families, particularly their parents. Half of the students who took the survey reported being friends with their parents on Facebook, albeit begrudgingly. Talking on the phone was still the most common form of family communication (33%, m=2.79), followed by text messaging (24%, m=3.15) and then Facebook (21%, m=3.98). While many students reported closer relationships with cousins and siblings who are not always in proximity, negotiating communication with parents and older relatives was somewhat more complex. As the focus group data will show, students were torn over how much information their parents should see about them on social networks, and how to negotiate allowing parents into a space that they see as primarily social and friend-based.

It seems that as social media become more prevalent in the lives of youth today, they remain cognizant of the importance of face-to-face relationships that transcend mediated spaces. At the same time, while they look negatively upon the time they spend on social networks in general, the data here shows that these networks are generally used to enhance their relationships with friends and family. Still, over 75% of the sample reported preferring face-to-face communication above all else.

And in contrast to a very detailed chapter by Christakis and Fowler in *Connected* on why social networks increase the chances of finding a significant other, 88% of these students have never dated online, with no plans to in the future. Perhaps online dating is more common with older populations that have graduated from universities, but these students may indeed be missing out.

Space #4 – Education

In *Rewired: Understanding the iGeneration and the Way They Learn*, psychology Professor Larry Rosen details the current disconnect between the wired lives of youth and the rote teaching practices still predominant in the K-12 classroom. Rosen (2010) notes that our approaches to teaching future generations are increasingly disconnected from the reality of their everyday lives. "Book learning, classroom teaching, paper-and-pencil homework, research reports, and creative writing activities have always been fine ways to accomplish these tasks…[however] These kids are not like those of previous generations, and they learn through technologies that didn't exist just a decade ago" (p. 5).

The argument goes, then, that if our schools are not firstly accepting that new social technologies have a place in learning and the classroom, and secondly, do not utilize these new tools and platforms in their learning plans, then those tools will be deemed less serious than what they do in school. Students then have a tendency to visualize social media as something trivial, for personal and social use, and with little educational purpose.

In Rosen's investigation, he shows a youth corps of content creators, multitaskers, and media savvy explorers. He offers a host of approaches to learning that involve mobile platforms, social networks, user-generated content, and spaces that enable creativity and curiosity in youth. Rosen (2010) and his coauthors fear that youth will tune out education delivered in ways that are increasingly less relevant to their lives. If they do, they will both lag in their educational trajectory and also underutilize the social media tools that they can handle very well, and that can be used to enhance many if not all facets of their lives:

> The longer educators wait to appreciate and integrate iGeners cyberworlds, the more students will be bored with traditional classroom learning, and the more we will miss out on opportunities to reach them within environments where they have already shown us that they are happy to reside and learn. (p. 16)

In the university classroom, applications of technology have mostly been reserved for helping to make classes organized (smart boards, learning management systems, Blackboard and WebCT) and streamline communication between faculty and students (Wiki's, Facebook Groups, etc.). There have been initiatives to help supply classrooms with transformative technologies (iPads, laptops) to help move away from traditional linear formats to more fluid, dynamic, and efficient ways to handle content, class work, and communication.

Social media in the classroom has often been seen, across all levels, as something of a taboo. Schools regularly block or restrict video sharing sites like YouTube, and popular social networking sites. Most classrooms on the K-12 and higher education level have a no cell phone policy, and more still enact no technology rules. Because of the fast changing social media landscape, and the distracting tendencies of digital technologies, most teachers find the easiest route for classroom facilitation is to ban social media outright.

Junco et al. (2012, 2011) have found that designing learning with social media tools, particularly Twitter, can in some cases enhance the learning experience of college students, by means of more structured dialog, interactivity within the classroom, and coexploration. If students are not embracing social and mobile technologies to enhance their learning experiences, it will be hard for them to envision these tools as much more than time wasters or gadgets for socializing.

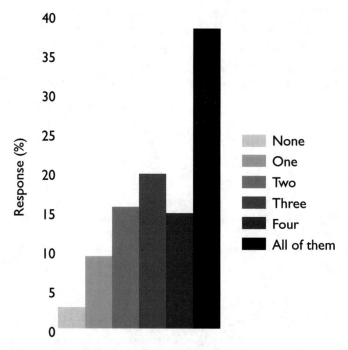

How many of your teachers use blackboard or similar classroom technology to post syllabi and assignments online?

Figure 4.4. Technology and Classroom Organization.

The student answers to survey questions exploring social media and education reinforced Rosen's point. There was little use of social media tools for learning in the classroom; 30% of the sample reported no social media use in any of their college classes, while another 42% reported only 1–2 classes using social media. Only 10% of students reported using social media in four or more courses per semester.

In terms of technology to organize classrooms, 74% of the sample reported classroom technology used to post syllabi, assignments, and updates in four or more classes. However, few college classrooms (14%) used technology for students to turn in their assignments online. Almost no classes that the students in this study were enrolled in allowed the use of Facebook, Twitter, Wikipedia, Google, or other social media spaces for classroom activities.

This was in sharp contrast to how students use social media for educational purposes: 71% of the sample reported always or most always using Wikipedia to conduct research for class work, and 96% of the sample reported using Google to conduct primary research for class assignments. Over 60% of the sample reported being on Facebook during class time, and over 70% used Facebook to connect with classmates on group projects, for assignments and to obtain notes from the course.

The division between teachers' and students' views of social media in the classroom has created a small chasm in the relationships among students, teachers, and learning. When asked about the overall influence of social media on the classroom, a majority of the sample (39%) strongly agreed that it was "easier to waste time" in the class; 21% strongly agreed that it made classes easier. Students did agree that when utilized appropriately social media has made classes more interesting (47%), and learning fun (45%). Social media's role in the classroom seems to be benefitting students in their self-organization and studying outside of the classroom, but not so much in terms of its place within the formal learning setting. Nor does it seem to be enhancing or engaging the learning experience for the students in this study.

This is not entirely surprising, for the fast-paced evolution of social media technologies and their generally distracting tendencies seem to inhibit how the traditional classroom is structured. Until this changes, the tension will likely exist. But if the solution is to turn off technology in the classroom, we create a situation where the tools and platforms that students are using to engage in daily life become forbidden fruits in a sense. They drift into a realm of social outlets, not accepted by formal socializing institutions, and seen as little more than distractors and deterrents. If education doesn't shift towards more inclusivity and acceptance, it will fail to embrace the opportunities these tools provide for engaged, inclusive, and applied learning.

Space # 5 – Entertainment

In *Cognitive Surplus*, Clay Shirky details the rise of *free time* in the developed world. Citing a myriad of conflating factors, Shirky (2010) notes that "Since the Second World War, increases in GDP, educational attainment, and life span have forced the industrialized world to grapple with something we'd never had to deal with on a national scale: free time" (p. 4). With a population that was more educated, living longer, and working less, the amount of "free" hours in a day increased significantly. What did we do with this extra time? According to Shirky (2010), we simply "watched TV" (p. 5).

From soap operas and sitcoms to nightly news, television became the surrogate for a nation. It provided an outlet for information, commercials for products, and an escape from everyday life. As television grew, it displaced time spent with family and friends, community socializing, human contact and even sleep. As we spent more of our free time in front of the television, the argument goes, we became less trusting, reliable, and social. As a result, people spent more time alone, isolated, and not engaged in the daily routines that created social cohesion.

According to Shirky (2010), Americans now watch up to 200 billion hours of TV per year. However, younger generations are reversing course: "… for the first time in the history of television, some cohorts of young people are watching TV less then their elders." Shirky notes studies that collectively reinforce the trend that "young populations with access to fast, interactive media are shifting their behavior away from media that presupposes pure consumption" (p. 11). The transition from mass media to interactive media is providing more diverse avenues for leisure activities. It is what people do with this free time, Shirky muses, that will define how productive, cooperative, and efficient societies can become.

The tension that exists between media consumption and use for personal entertainment and public engagement resurfaces in the social media sphere. While youth are very adept at sharing personal missives, photos, and experiences online, and finding time to appreciate cute kittens, funny babies, and spectacular double rainbows, how they see their civic agency in these interactive spaces is somewhat more complex. Shirky (2010) notes that "creating a participatory culture with wider benefits for society is harder than sharing amusing photos" (p. 185).

The entertainment portion of the survey asked students how much of their general free time was spent on social networks, and what type of activities and hobbies they were engaged with during leisure time. The results show that students are increasingly using digital and social media for shopping, watching television and movies, hanging out with friends and family—activities traditionally associated with leisure time. While mobile phones have yet to find their place as shopping tools—75% never use their phones to shop— 72% shop online more than visiting stores, and 88% reported "always/often" watching television programming online for free, while 66% of participants download music for free online. Interestingly, watching movies online for free is still rare for students, as the downloading process is still onerous and well protected by the industry. Renting movies is declining fast, and purchasing music is increasingly rare. Students also reported relying on peer reviews when deciding what to watch or listen to online, and 54% of students often read online comments and peer reviews before choosing a program to watch.

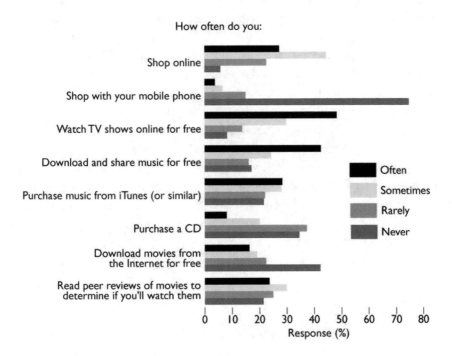

Figure 4.5. Social Media and Leisure Activities.

From sharing music with friends and swapping online programming to sharing what they've recently shopped for, social media spaces have increasingly facilitated the exchange of information about leisurely hobbies and activities. Perhaps students want to share fun experiences because they are personal, entertaining, interesting, and express the more exciting side of life. They admit to shopping less in stores and placing more trust into online exchanges with retailers. Almost the entire sample reported sharing credit card details with online retailers that they were not familiar with. Leisure activities have incorporated into the online world.

When asked how they spend their free time, a majority of students (71%, m=1.35) reported very likely to be with friends, which is not surprising. After that, however, social networks and the Internet took precedent: 47% (m=1.77) were very likely to be on social media sites, while 45% (m=1.71) were very likely to be online browsing. Reading (m=2.54), watching television (m=1.96) or movies (m=2.40), were all less common leisure-time activities. Spending time away from media altogether (m=3.33) was the least likely of activities for the students.

When leisure activities become in part subsumed in social media platforms, it is harder to separate entertainment from other types of information. As content types continue to merge in interactive and participatory spaces online, we will have more opportunities to be informed, entertained, and expressive at the same time and in the same spaces. Of course, how we understand these spaces will dictate the vibrancy and diversity of their uses. Writes Shirky (2010): "The opportunity before us, individually and collectively, is enormous; what we do with it will be determined largely by how well we are able to imagine and reward public creativity, participation, and sharing" (p. 212).

While the opportunities do exist, one thing is clear: we have moved beyond the point of discerning entertainment vs. news as far as social networks, and even the Internet, are concerned. We know when we are watching a show online, and we know when we are listening to music, but it's harder to tell when our news feeds, aggregators, and home pages are sending us hard news, soft news, or personally tailored information. This complicates the discussion on what it means to be engaged and informed, and more importantly how to navigate online information, discern types of information, and critically analyze the content we consume.

Space #6 – Privacy

Trust is a significant predictor of social capital. Strong communities are bound by a sense of trust within their surroundings. In the context of mass media, privacy and trust are secondary concerns for young people. Parents can easily monitor what children listen to on the radio or watch on TV and youth have little ability to use mass media to express ideas to large and disaggregated groups. The Internet's open information landscape brings forth numerous concerns for how young people perceive their online identities. De Abreu (2011) traces this growing fear to an open, and less regulated World Wide Web, where "no restrictions are in place, and in fact, there seems to be an 'anything goes' attitude when dealing with the Internet. It is the greatest of resources, but it is also one that needs careful guidance, especially when it comes to the young" (p. 95).

First, clearly, is the content they choose to post and share. Studies show that youth are not overly concerned with the final destination of what they make public online (Acquisti & Gross, 2006; Barnes, 2006; Lewis et al., 2008). When we can't see where or how companies use our information, it's difficult to see the implications for where this information may go and who is using it. Second, the dizzying array of social media platforms and the ease with which we sign up for them, keeps us consistently opting into new platforms with little hesitation. This makes it nearly impossible to keep track of where our identities go and with whom we've shared passwords, credit card account numbers, personal emails, addresses, and phone numbers. Third, it's close to impossible to navigate the privacy settings and binding legal terminology of these spaces we willfully opt into. Nick Bilton (2010) wrote in the *New York Times* that Facebook's privacy policy was 5,830 words long–longer than the United States Constitution. Opting out of certain information-sharing options, according to Bilton, would involve clicking into 50 privacy settings with over 170 options in total. It's not only Facebook that clouds the privacy settings for its users. Google's algorithm is notoriously secretive, and the data we submit through Internet search, viewing YouTube clips, and the like, allows them to gather reams of data about our daily Internet habits.

danah boyd (2010) notes the difficult position students face with their decisions about public content online: "Over and over again, I find that people's mental model of who can see what doesn't match up with reality." This is a complicated terrain to navigate, and beyond the premise of this book. However, if we readily accept and opt into agreements with social networks, without checking into our rights and protections, then logically that would denote a level of trust in the systems or platforms we engage with.

In the privacy part of the survey, participants reported a lack of general trust in the spaces online, but also reflected little ability to inquire about privacy rights in the spaces they use; 86% of the sample reported being somewhat or very concerned about their privacy online. At the same time, 53% of participants reported rarely or never reading the privacy policies of the social networks they belong to. A little over half of the sample (53%) believed that social media sites do a "fairly" good job of protecting their privacy, but over 20% had no idea about how well their privacy was maintained; 17% of students thought that social networks were only out to collect and use their data, but that prevented none of them from opting out of social networks.

Meanwhile 79% of respondents believed they have control "for the most part" over their online identities, while the remaining 21% believed they had no control over their online identities. Despite their general lack of precaution concerning their privacy online, over 75% of the sample voiced concern over the influence of social network identities on their career prospects.

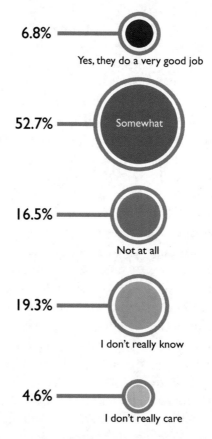

Do you feel that the social media sites you use do a good job of protecting your privacy?

6.8% — Yes, they do a very good job

52.7% — Somewhat

16.5% — Not at all

19.3% — I don't really know

4.6% — I don't really care

Figure 4.6. Social Media and Perceptions of Privacy.

The trust that students have in social media sites to protect their identities can be seen as healthy for trusting online platforms with our information. But having some markers of balance and scrutiny helps maintain accountability and transparency in the networks themselves. As students continue to share all types of personal information, they will be volunteering more of their personal narratives to companies who use this information in a myriad of ways. Additionally, over 80% of the students who took the survey make some (66%) or most (21%) of their Facebook profiles available to the general public. When using tools such as Facebook and Twitter, students also claimed to use their real identity a large majority of the time. The only place where they protected their identities was in chat rooms.

Perhaps the lack of self-policing of online identity comes from the fact that threats to privacy are somewhat distant. Only 20% of the sample knew of acquaintances that had experienced a privacy or safety issue within their social networks. Students seem very aware of the possible implications of sharing so much of their personal information in social networking sites. Regardless, they feel protected—or distant enough—from the consequences that it does little to dissuade them from opting in and using these platforms carte blanche. Privacy and trust go a long way towards utilizing media spaces for information and communication needs. Practicing some constraint and diligence is a learned habit, one that can help put pressure on these networks to increase transparency, and lessen the complexity of their privacy settings.

What the Survey Suggests...

The results of the survey reinforce the idea that social media platforms are providing spaces for new types of social and civic engagement in young people. Survey responses show that information habits across all categories are migrating to social platforms. This is not a clean picture, or an inclusive one. But it supports the notion that students think of information and communication habits primarily through aggregated, peer-to-peer, and social spaces. It's difficult, in this context, to judge their civic engagement by whether or not they tune into traditional channels for information and how much knowledge they can retain about any certain issue. Rather, the data reinforce the need for new approaches to prepare young citizens for engagement in daily civic life that starts with their social networks.

At the outset of *Digital and Media Literacy Education: A Plan of Action* Hobbs (2010) positions media literacy as "strengthening the capacity of individuals to participate as both producers and consumers in public conversations about events and issues that matter. Media and digital literacy education is now fundamentally implicated in the practice of citizenship" (p. 16). The survey suggests that an abundance of "information and entertainment choices" are made available to young people primarily through peer recommendations, in social networks, and online. To recap, five key points emerged from the survey that can elaborate on the state of social media and young citizens today.

1. The information and communication needs for students' daily lives are merging into social networks.
2. Students are consuming, and more importantly sharing, news and information about issues, events, and affairs increasingly through their social networks.
3. Leisure time is increasingly mediated by social platforms; this includes shopping, viewing, and hanging out.
4. A real divide exists between how educators are (not) using social media for learning, and how students learn with social media.
5. Students are throwing themselves online, with little real regard for what that means for their identities or the images and information they share.

The survey results in the categories above are only the beginning of this story. While they provide an overview of how young people conceptualize media types and spaces to facilitate daily information and communication needs, surveys alone cannot explain the *why* behind the reported uses and behaviors.

To build a more complete picture of how young people perceive the role of social media in their lives, I spoke with over 80 college students in a series of small group discussions elaborating on the emerging results of this survey. I wanted to find out, through rich dialog and open conversation, how young people see social media as facilitating knowledge of the world, communication with friends and family, leisure activities, and in the school and home.

These discussions exposed a disconnect in how young people report their social media habits and how they perceive the role of social media in their lives. We can observe and build many different hypotheses about how young people today use social media for a myriad of daily needs, but if they perceive these tools as little more than personal outlets outside of any serious social and civic engagement, we may not fare well in fully utilizing the opportunities these tools present. Chapter five details these discussions to help complete the picture of emerging citizens and social media and to solidify the case for a real need to develop effective pedagogical models for media literacy in formal and informal settings as core competencies for engaged citizenship in a digital media age.

· 5 ·

YOUNG CITIZENS AND PERCEPTIONS OF SOCIAL MEDIA'S VALUE – A DISCONNECT EMERGES

> But in addition to mass media and popular culture leisure activities, many people are discovering the pleasures of participating in digital media culture, being able to stay connected to friends and family, share photos, learn about virtually anything, and exercise their creativity by contributing user-generated content on topics from cooking to politics to health, science, relationships, the arts and more.
>
> — Renee Hobbs, *Digital and Media Literacy: A Plan of Action*, 2010, p. 15

While the survey results provide a snapshot of behavioral trends in young people's social media use, they don't unpack causality: the reason behind adopting a new technology, behaving a certain way, or opting in or out of certain networks. This chapter examines conversations with over 70 students in eight small group discussions, which amassed almost 15 hours of open, vibrant, and occasionally humorous dialog about the role of social media in daily life. What do students see as the major impacts of social media in their lives? What about relationships with their friends and family? And how do they view social media's impact on news, politics and democracy?

These questions guided spirited discussions that uncovered a rich, messy, and complex landscape for social media in the lives of students today. They also teased out some emerging disconnects between the migrating habits that students reported in the survey and perceptions of social media in their daily lives. If young people are using social media for more diverse purposes, but only see these networks as simple tools to check in on friends and waste time, then to what extent will social networks be utilized for diverse purposes? Will young people harness the diverse capabilities of social media for a range of social and civic pursuits? And how will collaborative technologies influence public debate, dialog, and discourse? These wide ranging discussions provide keen insight into the perspective of social media for young people today and also a foundation for my argument for *media literacy as the new civic education for digital culture*. To establish the grounds for that argument in Part Three of this book, let's first explore what their conversations unveiled.

Exploring Causality – Talking Social Media and Daily Life

The small group discussions encouraged open dialog and free exchange of opinions and thoughts about the role of social media in family and personal relationships, consumer behavior, and political identities. Because these platforms integrate all facets of communication but originated as "social" spaces, students were hesitant to admit the purposeful uses of such spaces as reflected in the survey results. They struggled, for example, to understand Facebook as anything but a waste of time. Likewise, YouTube was just a place to procrastinate while watching "stupid" videos and Twitter was where you find out dumb stuff about famous people. At the same time, students were somewhat critical and reactive to parts of the focus group discussions that explored common perceptions of youth as tuned out, distracted, and less engaged than prior generations. These parts of the discussions elicited mention of numerous examples and instances of sharing relevant news, supporting causes and organizations, and helping friends.

These sessions show that perhaps youth today are not less knowledgeable or engaged with civic and political issues, but rather it is an issue of perception. If students understand social media tools as social outlets with little greater value, their behavior will follow suit. If they see them as more vibrant spaces for expression, collaboration and dialog, then the tools can and will take on new meaning. The discussions below attempt to tease out perceptions of young people towards social media to see where, if at all, they saw value in networks.

A Note on Student Voices

Before exploring the student dialog below, it is important to recognize the discourse here as elaborative but not evidential. Discourse, writes Buckingham (1993) "should not be seen as straightforward evidence of what individuals think or know, but as a form of social action" (p. 202). In the conversation below, students are engaging in dialog that involves posturing, status conferral, and social-value statements that need to be justified in the group context. This results in what Buckingham terms "cynical chic" which he builds from research on adult dialog (Eliasoph, 1990; Gamson, 1992), to explain the phenomenon of student posturing. Writes Buckingham (1993):

> According to this argument, such expressions of cynicism serve as a valuable – and indeed pleasurable – way of rationalizing one's own sense of powerlessness, and even of claiming a degree of superiority and control. Certainly, there is a sense in which the students' expressions of apathy or disinterest (as distinct perhaps from cynicism) should be seen as superficial. (p. 213)

Such posturing was evident throughout the small group discussions. Students were routinely claiming to use social media for little more than checking in on friends and wasting time. When the dialog shifted to topics like news and politics, the students were resistant to those terms, as was anticipated.

Nevertheless, Buckingham, in his work with US and UK youth and political engagement notes that cynical chic is more than superficial and surface level. He argues that cynicism stems from a certain engagement with content in the first place. Therefore it must imply some assessment of terms or concepts, even if they are not acted upon or realized in the discussion. In this study, I align with Buckingham and Gamson (1992: from Buckingham), who write that, "in their engagement with politic, people (in this case young people) are by no means as stupid or passive as they are frequently made out to be" (p. 203).

Students did recognize the potential of social networks to build inclusive participation in news, politics, and daily civic life, but those recognitions were fleeting and quickly replaced by the generally negative dialog that permeated a majority of the conversations. These conversations should not be seen simply as "cynical chic" but more as a reflection of a generation that are early adopters—even trend setters—of complex and messy technologies. Their ideas reflect the new tensions that develop as young people negotiate new integrated platforms for communication, dialog, and information consumption with little guidance in the home or the classroom. They also expose the growing divide between perceived use and perceived value of these spaces, which is the crux of this book's call for media literacy education.

As we move through this exploration, I claim that these perceptions of social media are: (1) born from a socialization of these tools as simply entertainment, (2) a lack of acknowledgment of these networks in the home, family, or school, and (3) a reluctance to acknowledge civic engagement in the context of peer-to-peer platforms.

Talking Points[16]

The small group discussions were designed to begin on a personal level—social media in your life—move to a social level—social media and communication with friends and family—and finally end on a civic level—social media for public information, news, and social outreach. This design was meant to move the dialog from exploratory and personal to critical and expansive, and to build comfort in the session before moving to more weighty topics.

Defining Social Media through Their Eyes

Before diving into the discussion, I want to give context to the commentary below by highlighting a few general trends that emerged from how the discussion participants defined social media. First, social media was an online communication platform that allowed for commenting and peer-to-peer interaction where people could share ideas and express freely to large audiences. Second, social media was about "wide groups of people that can interact and talk back to each other," said one student. Third, students thought of social media as "forums for people to come together and learn about information and interact," where people could "participate" and have ownership over their personal expression, dialog, and interactions.

This centered on large social networks—Facebook, Twitter, YouTube— but also included sites, apps, and platforms that "get people talking to each other," like places for commenting on news sites, and forums for public dialog. When we defined social media as a group to start these discussions, we centered on the notion of peer-to-peer communities, participation in dialog, and many-to-many voices. As we will see below, these discussions used social media freely and openly at points, and pinpointed certain tools, platforms, and sites at other times.

1. Talking Daily Life

The general entry point for the discussions was the comprehensive integration of social networks in the lives of university students. Throughout the focus group sessions students mentioned the central role of social media in communication with peers. They highlighted closing physical distance gaps, maintaining bonds with old friends, and a general enhancement of personal communication. "I think it's definitely made me closer with friends," said one student, "My friends are in schools all over the country and it's helped keep us together." Echoed another, "I think it's great for keeping in touch. I graduated last year and it's like I haven't been apart from any of my other friends. Even my grade school friends, I talk to them through [social media]. It's keeping us close." Most students reported having Facebook and/or Twitter "open on their computer throughout the day," but not being on the programs the entire time. Many mentioned using social media to talk with peers being the "first thing I do when I wake up," and "the last thing I do before I go to sleep."

"Chatting with friends" was another central function of social media for students. They often chatted while performing other tasks online, like reading, doing homework, watching television shows or movies, or shopping. Exposure was a central part of their need to be "in" with peers, as one student mentioned: "Two other people could be posting on each other's walls and I can see it. Someone might contact me this way too."

The students' were primarily focused on "keeping in contact," and constantly looking for new information that their peers post. "I like to look at pictures from people who I was with in high school. Just to see what they are up to," said one participant. "I look at things that people post," stated another, "I start on news feeds and see what videos or things people are posting on someone's wall...I'll see what they are saying, to keep up with things." Peer reviews, status updates, "creeping" and "stalking" were all prevalent descriptors of what students are doing on social networks.

This need to know what's going on—sometimes 20 miles away and sometimes 2000 miles away—was at the center of the consistent presence of social media in the students' lives. "Seeing what this person's up to," "Seeing their pictures," and "Oh I haven't seen that person in a while" were all mechanisms that triggered the urge to dive into a social network and search for information on people in random and unstructured ways. "You want to check in and see what's going on with them," was a sentiment echoed early and often throughout the small group discussions. The students found the need to be *in the know* so strong at times that they admitted getting lost in the streaming content. That included stumbling upon meaningless videos, scrolling through Twitter feeds, and forgetting why they logged in, in the first place. "I don't even know one thing [I look for] specifically," mentioned one student, "I have a lot of people who I need to know what they're doing."

This need to connect with peers also perpetuated the phenomenon of wandering—where students become lost in the act of communicating and peering into the lives of friends. "I'll look at someone's pictures or wall post [or tweets] or blog and that will take me to someone else, and somewhere else. I get lost in that," mentioned one student. What the students perceived as connectivity quickly turned into a form of gazing into the spaces of people they have or had no inherent interest in before they logged on. "I start on my news feed and click someone," said one student, "and then go to somebody else. Somebody else. Somebody else. Somebody else. I do [the same thing] on Wikipedia, I read something that has a link, and go there, and to the next thing. It's the same concept."

This need to connect, so present in the student dialog, must be questioned. Are students really connecting to something or someone? Are they engaging in meaningful communication? Are they finding valuable information? Are they really keeping in touch with friends, family, and acquaintance? Or are they simply using others as a way to feel a sense of belonging? One student remarked:

> I'll see a mutual friend and then I'll realize I do know that person. I haven't checked up on them in a while. Then I look at their friends. Things start getting connected after a while. You look at somebody's wall and you know someone else that's written on their wall. You see they have a new profile up and you think, 'oh that's so cool, or fun, or whatever.' The next thing you know things start getting connected and connected [and connected]…

This perceived connectivity by students brings into question how they understand the term *connected*. Is peering in on random acquaintances and exploring their self-manicured profiles connecting? Or are we seeing the equivalent of the need to gaze into other's lives, to justify our own? These questions are complex and messy. But the discussions show how important social media are for forming a sense of self-worth. And perceptions do matter: "Even my grade school friends and I talk to through that. We may not have been closer from the beginning, but [social media] are keeping us closer."

Daily Information and Communication Needs

At a point in the discussions of social media in daily life, the conversations shifted to the types of information that social media facilitate for students. Students talked about local and campus news, about finding out what's going on in their hometowns, and about when events happen in the world.[17] Social media, it seemed, were helping to diversify the students' information consumption, and primarily through word-of-mouth. "Mostly I just hear about things through my friends—word-of-mouth—on Facebook," stated one participant. "I get information from word-of-mouth," said another. Others wrote: "I rely on my friends to provide information with their updates," and "I guess I see most of my information through my friends' feeds on Facebook." It is no surprise that social media have created a vacuum for information. The participants in the focus groups revealed, in their conversations, how much they rely on *friends* for much of their information diet and vice versa.

"I often want to voice my opinion," said one student, who then explained how social media were the vehicle to do so. Another spoke about the role of social media in facilitating the spread of information to peers, "If I see stories and I think they are pertinent, or would be overlooked normally, I post them. Just sort of spread the information." Because of the strong social connectivity that students perceive in social media, these networks begin to facilitate a majority of their information needs, as we saw in the survey results.

The value of this newfound connectivity, however, did not translate in the context of the discussions. The idea that they could *access* information from friends was valuable, but the *content* of that information was not acknowledged in any positive or beneficial light. "I don't even know one thing [I look at] specifically," answered one participant. When asked about how a tool like Twitter could be used as a beneficial information resource, one student remarked, "I don't care about what a lot of people say," followed by another student, who said, "I don't think everyone needs to know what I'm doing all day," and, "all the information is distracting." The students, after mentioning how much they were using social media and peer-to-peer platforms to keep informed about daily events, turned around and criticized this space as little more than "looking at people" and "getting connected" with no real inflection on what it means and why. Stated one student, "The fact that we are willing to dedicate a significant portion of our day reading what other people are doing instead of doing something tangible...I think that is a significant change."

This need to connect, as I'll explore below, can be seen as vibrant social connectivity or as self-interested social tethering. The students clearly acknowledged social media platforms as central to their daily information and communication needs, but they saw this connectivity as primarily personal, time wasting, social, and shallow. This is in contrast, also, to the survey data, which showed a clear and growing reliance on social media platforms facilitating more daily information and communication needs. As long as students continue to value social connectivity but experience it as simply a shallow form of communication, the less it will be perceived as a holistic and vibrant tool for engagement in daily life.

~ Talking Friends & Family

After discussing the integration of social media in students' lives, the conversation shifted towards the ways in which social networks had affected communication with friends and family. Students across the discussions didn't have many positive things to say about the content and depth of communication with friends via social networks. And more so, they thought their family interactions were superficial, heavily filtered, and annoying. Some went as far as creating fake profiles that they shared with their families only. Many found the idea of being Facebook friends with parents akin to parents sitting around the cafeteria at their university—awkward and intrusive. While some contested this idea, the majority believed their social network profiles were for friends and not family.

Friends

In the portion of the focus groups that discussed how friendships (and without prompts, personal relationships) functioned on social networks, students began by listing how many "friends" they had online (the range fell roughly between 400–1300). In a majority of the groups, this conversation turned self-deprecating—"Everyone's on Facebook. No one wants to go outside," "I think [having Facebook friends] distances everyone from each other," "it has made us less active." Students briefly touched upon the definition of a friend, i.e., "Can you be friends with someone you have never seen?" but did not think it necessary to get bogged down in this discussion.

On the other hand, students were eager to speak of different ways they negotiated relationships and communication in these spaces. Students across discussion groups used the term "Facebook cleaning" to discuss methods they used to monitor their connections online. Students mentioned "going through once in a while" and un-friending "people I don't talk to or who don't really use Facebook." One student's story of monitoring friends was particularly receptive: "[my friend] uses the filter method…when it's someone's birthday and it pops up in the corner, if you don't feel comfortable saying happy birthday to them, then she deletes them as a friend."

Students were also quick to note that Facebook had not made them closer to friends, but almost the opposite. This was contrary to the survey data, which showed that networks were either neutral or enhancing existing friendships. To students, social networks "hinder social relationships…my friends don't really know how to talk to people face-to-face. After the conversation is done they feel awkward," and "Social networks distance everyone from each other. You're saying you're friends with everyone but really just pushing them away."

The general sentiment in this portion of the discussion was that social networks can have an antisocial effect. Spending time updating Facebook profiles, tweeting, watching YouTube videos, are all under the umbrella "social" but they refer more to the tethering phenomenon. This, to the students in the discussion, also encroached on their face-to-face communications with friends, causing what one student termed "face-to-face disconnect:"

> It's also caused a face-to-face disconnect. Just this past weekend I went to the bar with a couple friends. A good portion of the time they'll go on their phones on Facebook or whatever and try to talk to someone else. I just sit there like, we were having a good conversation, but now I'm not good enough for you?

I think overall it is positive that the students recognized differing levels of quality of communication on social media versus face-to-face communication. I also don't think it's that hard to differentiate between hanging out in person and typing communication into a keyboard. I would even argue having a phone conversation places more emphasis on interactivity than social media. Despite this acknowledgement in the groups, there was no real discussion on why social media have become so pervasive, if they don't do anything to enhance the communication or relationship, but in fact do the opposite. After prodding this question, students were comfortable thinking about their relationships on social networks as "secondary," "shallow," and "pretty much killing time."

Family

When the other "f" word was brought up, the conversation turned animated. Students were uniformly against most familial and personal relationships online. In a simple sense, the negotiations students mentioned often mirrored those that young people experience in the physical realm of familial relationships. Because social media, and Facebook in particular, began as student-centered and social, many early adopters see family as impeding on what was once a sacred space, "It's something for friends," commented one student, "I just don't feel comfortable with my mom on [Facebook]. It just seems like something for kids. When I got it a few years ago that's what it was." This encroachment on "their" space manifested itself in a negative tone. "I just don't want them commenting, talking, touching. I live this far away from them. I live in New Jersey. When I go home, that's when I talk to them," commented one student. "I blocked my dad from everything, but I'm friends with him. He can't see my wall, pictures, or status updates," echoed another. Few students mentioned having positive relationships with their parents on Facebook. On the other hand, some offered interesting possible solutions, "My cousin created two Facebook profiles, one for his family and one for everyone else."

With family communication expanding fast into social networks, young people are feeling new demands for family communication that infringe into online spaces they once considered strictly for social purposes. As a result, they were resistant to Facebook as a space where multiple types of relationships can and should be maintained. "I act different around my friends than I do my parents," said one student. "I have things on there that I'm not proud of…I wouldn't be hanging out with my friends with my parents."

Of course, at the same time adults represent a fast-growing social media user population (Lenhart et al., 2010b). As parents integrate into this new landscape for information, they must negotiate the communicative boundaries that exist with children. Wrote one student, "My parents are so ridiculous. If I didn't accept their friend requests it would have been a big issue. I had to. I just ignore them. She [my mother] comments on my pictures and I just sigh." Tensions build in the family communications because of the way students see the sites—not as public spaces per se, but rather as private social spaces for large peer audiences. "I don't want them seeing my stuff," wrote one participant, "but they get so sad asking why I don't add them so I just do."

Negotiating family relationships gets to the core of some of the emerging disconnects noticed in social media use by young people today. Because it was born as a social outlet, reserved for young people, they conceptualize the space as just that. But as social media continue to integrate into all communication and information arenas, those boundaries are collapsing. Employers now regularly scan the social media profiles of perspective employees, to see how they use these tools. Families now increasingly use social networks to facilitate their own many-to-many communication platforms, and newborns are given public identities before they can eat solid foods.

Instead of seeing social networks as drivers of enhanced communication, shared experiences, and expression, in the discussions students saw social networks as reserved for them and their friends, and that were strictly for types of content and communication that aren't for family, employers and so on. Digital media culture has moved networks far beyond this sacred space, and young people will increasingly need to realize this if they are to utilize networks for more diverse purposes. Starting with mom and dad seems to be a good place.

~ Talking Civic Life

The final part of the small group discussions explored social media use for news, democracy, and participation in public life. Students began by candidly expressing "hating news" because "it's so negative and it's always the same thing" or not being "a news person." In this way, news is a tricky word to discuss in the context of social media and young people. Most thought of news in rather traditional ways, like something their parents watched in front of a television every night at 6 p.m. Once they were pushed to think about their news habits not in the context of traditional media and their parents, but through their own daily media use, a different picture emerged.

The survey data reported that students were relying on social media platforms for most of their personal and public information consumption. The small group discussions reinforced the trends. A majority of the students mentioned their social networks as places where they find most of their information, and specifically through word-of-mouth, aggregators, and feeds. The following sample quotations shows the shift in the news-gathering habits of young people:

- "I hear things through my friends—word-of-mouth, or on Facebook, or *Yahoo*."
- "Word-of-mouth, or the *Daily Show*. And different homepages like Google and *Yahoo*."
- "Facebook, Twitter. I rely on my friends to provide whatever information with their updates."
- "I have *i*Google that collects feeds from random news outlets."
- "My *Yahoo* homepage that shows me the *New York Times*, AP, NPR, etc."

Few students mentioned going to specific news sites, even fewer mentioned television[18] or newspapers. Once the participants divulged their own news habits, the discussion shifted to the impact that social media has on the news process. The discussions here revealed a dichotomous view of news in digital spaces. Students acknowledged the abundance of information available in real time and for a seemingly endless array of issues, events, and ideas. "News is everywhere and technology has made it easy to find," said one student. "The only drawback is that there is so much that it's tough to retain it all." Echoed another, "Since news is now on-demand, you can gather all relevant information, including things you may have otherwise missed."

Students also acknowledged the role of social media in helping to facilitate a more personalized and diverse flow of information. In parts of the discussions students were quite savvy about understanding the benefits of digital technologies for news flow. One participant mentioned that news had "provided a space for the consumer to have a voice." Others mentioned that now "when something happens…there are more venues for getting the word out." Others agreed that "there are more sources of news out there, and it seems that it has created more of a culture of wanting to be in the know."

Interestingly, they became cynical about the credibility of the content itself. "I do agree that [social networks] have their advantages, but for news it's the worst thing that could have happened," said one student. "You have a whole bunch of people that are considered news [makers] but it's all just opinion. It's dangerous, and spreads misinformation." They lamented the number of "stupid people" in the world and the resulting clutter of information make it harder to discern fact from fiction, and reliable from unreliable content. The quotations below exemplifies the general negative tone of the news discussion:

- "It's killing news in its most basic form of reliability and trust because every time an article gets passed along, it's losing a tiny bit of face and being replaced by opinion. So the story is getting out more—it's spreading—but it's weaker and less credible."
- "I agree that [social media] has helped spread news, but it's kind of like the game telephone because the news gets skewed when it spreads like that so you need to go to a source you yourself find credible to find out exactly what has happened."
- "[Social media] can help because you learn about things so much quicker, but they also hurt because anyone can say what they want but are held to a lesser standard than traditional media outlets."

Why are students apprehensive and negative towards social networks as facilitators of credible content? It seemed that when talking about news they did not connect the opportunity provided for more interactive forms of information gathering and sharing with credibility and accuracy of content. Instead, they reverted back to understandings of news content that beckon a golden past of objectivity. Perhaps, as university students, they are being taught about news and communication models that don't incorporate social media as useful drivers of news content. Perhaps because social media are often seen as distractions for many of their formal experiences (education, family, etc.) they don't see a translation into how these tools can enhance news content in general.

And students were even more vitriolic towards Twitter. A majority of the participants saw little value in a tool they described as "narcissistic," "annoying," "stupid," and "meaningless." In fact, only the very few heavy social media users and self-proclaimed news junkies saw value in Twitter as an efficient aggregator of news and information. Most simply interpreted it in a very limited way, "It's stupid," claimed one participant, "I don't need to know what you're doing so frequently, and you don't need to know what I'm doing so frequently." "It annoys me," said another, "because it's an unnecessarily constant updates of what people are doing. It's useless." And finally, "What are you Tweeting about? Okay, your cat just did something funny. Keep it to yourself." When I asked them about following outlets, causes, and organizations, there was little dialog in the room.

Nevertheless, the small group discussions generally grappled more with the facilitation of news through social media than many of the other topics in the discussions. They were wary of the credibility of news in social networks, but more receptive to what social networks had provided for audiences. Said one student, "[social media] seems to have created more of a culture of wanting to be in the know. It's no longer cool to not know what's going on. So I think it's good because it's making people want to know information. But it's bad because it's also making people lazy by not going out of their way to get credible information." And said another, "...the Internet makes it easier to put lies out into the world just as easily as it is to put truth out there. It goes both ways. It's a venue for truth and untruth." Still other students commented: "I feel a lot more well read than if I didn't have it," "I definitely feel more connected, and more informed," and, "I think you can't b*llsh*t anymore. The Internet provides a place to find the truth."

Based on the survey results, and the skeptical tone with which they saw news in the social media landscape, there seems to be opportunity to inspire young people to be more dynamic and interactive in their news consumption. One student summed up this newfound opportunity:

> I think the Internet has been a huge help because it has provided a space for the consumer to have a voice. Yes, there will be [bad information] posted out there but the Internet makes it so easy and accessible to question and research things. If you're reading an article on nytimes.com, and then you look into the comment section, you need to turn on the BS filter. Ultimately, we've always been fed misinformation by the old methods of news, at least now we have a say in the matter, as well as, easier access to do research.

A Disconnect Emerges

The small group discussions show an emerging disconnect between the use and perceived value of social media for young people. The value of social media was evident in both the survey results and also, in fits and spurts, across many of the small group discussions. This was seemingly lost however, in the social context of these new connective networks. Students valued peer-to-peer communications and the diverse information they provide, but were overtly negative towards the potential of these communities to have real value for news, democracy, and civic life. They admitted spending a lot of time on social networks but were loathe to mention constructive things they were doing with this time. They saw potential for diverse news flow and community engagement but envisioned most of their time as simply social wandering.

Perhaps it is natural to see the time spent surfing in social spaces as little more than just that: surfing. Because these tools have been framed as social spaces where friends *hang out* it was hard for the students in the discussions to mention much more than what they do on a person-to-person level. As the survey data showed, with a greater reliance on these spaces for much of their information habits, there is a clear need to see social networks as more than just spaces for personal missives from friends and family. As long as students value connectivity but don't move beyond connecting as an end, they will not take advantage of the more holistic and dynamic opportunities provided by dynamic social networks. Perception matters.

Social Tethering vs. Social Connectivity

The disconnect between use and value that was apparent in this study can be explained through the phenomenon of tethering, made popular by

MIT scholar Sherry Turkle. In Turkle's (2008; 2005; 2004) work on social technologies and their relationship to humans, she describes tethering as the increasing dependence on technology to facilitate self-worth, community, and communication. Turkle (2008) writes, "our new intimacy with machines compels us to speak of a new state of the self, itself…a new place for the situation of a tethered self" (p. 1). She sees the growing dependence on digital technologies, specifically the "smart" phone, as an act of self-establishment, where youth, through their devices, "turn other persons into 'self-objects' to shore up their fragile sense of self" (p. 128).

The disconnect in this study stems somewhat from the idea that young citizens are "always there" (Urry, 2007), and that they're tethering places themselves at the center of the mediated equation (Goggin, 2009; Srivastava, 2005). The students in this study felt such a strong need to be present that it subsumed their perception of their social networks as much more than self-serving tools they use to feel a sense of belonging. Turkle (2008) explains that "the mores of tethering support group demands: among urban teens, it is common for friends to expect that their peers will stay available by cell or instant message" (p. 126). The need to be available, and to know that others are, had such a strong connection for the students in this study; no matter how much they were self-deprecating about the impact of this need on their daily lives, they simply could not turn the technology off or see it in a wider light.

Tethering deviates from connectivity in how we understand "connecting" with others. Students were constantly checking in on others' profiles on their own terms, and with little dialog, interaction or interpersonal presence. Checking in on friends or maintaining distant contact connotes a need to preserve some sense of inherent belonging. In *Alone Together: Why We Expect More From Technology and Less From Each Other*, Turkle paints a picture of the burden these new technologies place on young people as they grow to be independent and contributing citizens:

> [For young people] computers and mobile devices offer communities when families are absent. In this context, it is not surprising to find troubling patterns of connection and disconnection: teenagers who will only "speak" online, who rigorously avoid face-to-face encounters, who are in text contact with their parents fifteen or twenty times a day, who deem even a telephone call "too much" exposure and say that they will "text, not talk." (p. 270)

Indeed, using other peoples profiles, updates, tweets and posts to shore up a sense of self in this study went a long way in justifying the abundant use of social media technologies—and without an obligation to see these tools as more than simply connecting, gazing or peering. Like the human urge to look at the car crash on the side of the road, or tune into the most disdainful, interesting, or provocative human actions, social media provide a window to gaze at a world of peers-friends, acquaintances and family—that we can use to place ourselves in a space of comfort, or of need, or want.

The disconnect that results is one where the tethering is mistaken for connectivity. Students appreciate being connected and use social media to facilitate most of their daily information and communication needs. At the same time, however, they don't see the value in this because they only see the use of social media through a very self-centered silo. The result is that as more and more information and communication habits migrate to social and mobile technologies, the perception of them remains primarily as tools for social pleasure, connection, and little else.

Bridging the Disconnect?

Building digital and media literacy competencies in youth and young citizens can help embrace these tools for the wider access and engagement they can bring to communities, and can help to discern the difference between tethering and connectivity. Youth may have the capacity to use these tools for differing reasons when certain social or civic circumstances call for them, (think Kony) but in the context of daily life, how they use these tools to engage meaningfully cannot only benefit their sense of self-worth but also their sense of place and community. Hobbs (2010) writes of the new knowledge that young people need to achieve this heightened sense of meaningful contribution, noting "such ubiquitous and easy access to so many information and entertainment choices requires that people acquire new knowledge and skills in order to make wise and responsible decisions" (p. 16).

Part Three of this book offers a starting point for discussions into media literacy as the bridge to building digital media competencies in young people today, aimed at building their sense of self through social and civic connectivity. The exploration, so far, has shown that the potential for heightened engagement in daily life is at the ready, and this engagement is evident in response to large-scale civic and social movements. However, in the context of daily life, there is a disconnect in the value of these tools to facilitate social and civic engagement in a digital media culture. Developing these skills, from a young age, is imperative. The last part of this book advocates for those frameworks as essential for the cultivation of an inclusive, active, and engaged citizenry.

· PART THREE ·

A FRAMEWORK FOR MEDIA
LITERACY & THE EMERGING CITIZEN

· 6 ·

MEDIA LITERACY EDUCATION
IN DIGITAL CULTURE: BRIDGING
THE DISCONNECT

The future of digital culture—yours, mine, and ours—depends on how well we learn to use the media that have infiltrated, amplified, distracted, enriched, and complicated our lives. How you employ a search engine, stream video from your phonecam, or update your Facebook status matters to you and everyone, because the ways people use new media in the first years of an emerging communication regime can influence the way those media end up being used and misused for decades to come.

— Howard Rheingold, *Net Smart*, 1

Learning how to effectively use digital media, as Rheingold notes, plays a significant role in the ways new technologies are utilized in society. The question, then, is not whether or not these technologies are enhancing or dumbing down our culture, but rather how we can learn to use them in smart and meaningful ways. At the outset of *Net Smart: Learning To Thrive Online* Rheingold (2012) posits, "Instead of confining my exploration to whether or not Google is making us stupid, Facebook is commoditizing our privacy, or Twitter is chopping our attention into microslices (all good questions), I've been asking myself and others how to use social media intelligently, humanely, and above all mindfully" (p. 1).

Many of the explorations into what these technologies do to us are reactive—they ask about impact during or after we engage with a technology—and not proactive; studying how we can better use these technologies to increase our sense of place and purpose in the world. Learning to use social media intelligently is something that many places of education have yet to introduce or formally integrate into their curricula. Of course this is no easy task. Burdened by both rapid technological advancement and slow bureaucratic responses, many educators are hampered by less than envious positions of managing outcomes that often fail to keep pace with the rapid growth of digital media outside of the school. As a result, a disconnect has emerged between social media use and perception detailed in Part Two of this book. A myriad of factors contribute to this disconnect [beyond the *cynical chic* disposition of college students, and the bandwagon effect that occurs in small group discussions].

First, there remains a stable resistance to use popular social media in professional settings, i.e., the workplace, the classroom. As I noted above, rapid technological advancement and slow education responses often cause a lag in how technologies and tools are appropriated in formal spaces of education. Rheingold (2012) supports this claim in writing, "educational institutions cannot change swiftly and broadly enough to match the pace of change in digital culture..." (p. 252). As a result, what we see are the restricting of popular social technologies from schools. Gutierrez & Tyner (2012) write that, in an age of increasing global societies and connective networks, "...it could be said that the education sector is an anachronism in its own time as it continues to prepare students for a society that no longer exists (p. 2). Works by Alvermann et al. (1999), Knobel & Lankshear (2010), and Jenkins et al. (2013) offer pathways for applying popular technologies and participatory learning models in formal and informal educational settings. While such initiatives are growing, they remain on the periphery of public education.

Second, these tools and technologies were born as "social" amplifiers, with little effort made to see them as anything more. From "social," literally being in the title of this umbrella of media technologies, to how these technologies are marketed, they are positioned for social connectivity—and specifically towards youth. This is problematic for both how the tools are presented to young people, and also for how young people are taught about the tools' purposes and uses. Again Rheingold (2012) notes: "...the emerging digital divide is between those who know how to use social media for individual advantage and collective action, and those who do not" (p. 252). This challenge seems formidable. The possible "dangers" around Internet safety, inappropriate content, and cyberbullying are far more predominant and tangible issues than thinking about participatory culture, collaborative inquiry, and connected learning (see Byron, 2010; Mills, 2010; Slonje et al., 2008; Smith et al., 2008). In their work, Losh & Jenkins (2012) note the problematic position of limiting student access to media. They argue for the need to open education to the new dynamic platforms that digital media offer instead of limiting access on the grounds of its "danger" to youth. The misuse and hacking of school-issued iPads given to students in Los Angeles as part of a deal between the public school district and Apple speak exactly to this point.[19]

Third, because these tools predominately facilitate peer-to-peer communication, sharing, and interactivity, they are disrupting traditional top-down silos for information flow, while at the same time integrating many different types and forms of content into single streams. This makes it difficult to teach how to discern certain types of information from others. Kendall & McDougal (2012) note the challenges that exist in implementing the right approaches towards education about digital tools in a rapidly evolving digital media culture. Without the relevant educational approaches young people will be hard-pressed to use social networks in any ways not socially motivated.

I don't believe that the students I spoke to for this book are naïve or unknowledgeable about digital media's potential for engagement in democratic life. Rather, I think that the relative newness of these tools and the lack of any structured learning around or about them has created a disconnect between how young people envision digital tools and how they use them. Below I propose a series of connectors that can help reframe social media platforms as more holistic and inclusive tools for daily civic life. The connectors are *small tweaks* to bridge the emerging divide between how we use social media in daily life and how we are (not) learning to use it in formal and informal education. First, however, I want briefly to explore some advancements in the study of digital media and learning that will help place the proposed "connectors" in meaningful and relevant contexts.

Digital Media [Literacy] and Learning

In his introduction to *Net Smart*, Rheingold (2012) sets a foundation of inquiry that positions the future value of social media in the hands of citizens:

> The mindful use of digital media doesn't happen automatically. Thinking about what you are doing and why you are doing it instead of going through the motions is fundamental to the definition of mindful, whether you are deciding to follow someone on Twitter, shutting the lid of your laptop in class, looking up from your BlackBerry

in a meeting, or consciously deciding which links *not* to click. Although educational institutions have been slow to incorporate digital literacies, practical know-how is available to those who figure out how to find it. This know-how, from the art of growing social capital in virtual communities to the craft of cultivating wiki collaboration, might determine whether life online will drive us to distraction, or augment and broaden our minds. (pp. 1–2)

These seemingly small decisions we make on a daily basis—from clicking links to re-tweeting and posting updates—end up defining what our public voice looks and sounds like. Who we follow and support, on a small level, will end up dictating whose voices are heard the loudest and the farthest. Just like viewers drive the popularity of morning news shows, sitcoms, and films, online all the choices we make dictate which peers and public figures are most heard. Therefore, "...knowing how to make use of online tools without being overloaded with too much information is, like it or not, an essential ingredient to personal success in the twenty-first century" (Rheingold, 2012, p. 2).

Beyond personal success, there lie opportunities for more collaborative and public gainfulness from digital technologies. The social potential of these tools, Rheingold (2012) notes, is what may dictate their ultimate fate as vibrant beneficial platforms for social and civic progress: "I see a bigger social issue at work, in addition to personal empowerment: if we combine our individual efforts wisely, enough of the right know-how could add up to a more thoughtful society as well as enhance those individuals who master digital network skills" (p. 2). Because new social platforms embody a culture of participation, the digital and media literacy competencies needed to competently navigate these spaces can be the difference between being deceived and critically evaluating content and between collaborative production and wasting time.

In 2006, the MacArthur Foundation spearheaded a digital media and learning movement to "drive positive change in American education that builds on the new modes of learning observed among young people using digital media and related tools" (MacArthur). This movement has supported a wide scope of research that outline digital media and learning assessment (Schwartz & Arena, 2013), youth and social networking forums and learning spaces (Fields & Grimes, 2012), and the expansion of dynamic learning cultures in a participatory age (Riley & Literat, 2012; Middaugh, 2012; Kligler-Vilenchik & Shresthova, 2012; Williamson, 2013). Two particular areas in this movement—*connected learning* and *participatory politics*—relate specifically to media literacy and young people, and shed light on possible responses to the disconnect evident in this book.

Connected Learning

The *Connected Learning*[20] movement aims to build a more social, interactive, and embedded learning culture. Ito et al. (2012) position the movement as "seek[ing] to leverage the potential of digital media to expand access to learning that is socially embedded, interest-driven, and oriented toward educational, economic, or political opportunity." They base connected learning on evidence that "the most resilient, adaptive, and effective learning involves individual interest as well as social support to overcome adversity and provide recognition." The ability to *connect* learning with interests and a sense of personal and social responsibility is at the center of the connected learning movement. Growing gaps in educational attainment and opportunity present significant barriers to learning for adolescents today, one of which mirrors the disconnect found in Part Two of this book:

> Young people are immersed in a media ecology that is increasingly commercialized and that elevates the importance of informed, individual choice. Established institutions, norms, and practices for guiding young people's access to information and learning are being confronted by always-on social communication and abundant media and information. (Ito et al., 2012)

To respond to this confrontation, connected learning is positioned at the nexus of *academics, interests, and peer culture*. The connected learning movement aims to embrace a vibrant digital media landscape and savvy media users to build more equal, collaborative, and experiential learning experiences.

This approach to learning seems long overdue. The real value of the movement is in its locating of learning environments and initiatives that are blending passions and peers in spaces of engagement. The digital tools that are used to connect these peers become conduits for collaborative learning, and not simply what youth do when they are "away" from the classroom.

Participatory Politics

The MacArthur-supported Research Network on Youth and Participatory Politics[21] conducted one of the largest surveys on youth and political behavior to date. Cohen and Kahne (2012) define participatory politics as "interactive, peer-based acts through which individuals and groups seek to exert both voice and influence on issues of public concern. Importantly, these acts are not guided by deference to elites or formal institutions." (p. vi). The report is rich with data that explore the civic lives of young people, and also the role of digital media in their public participation. Their findings point to a more inclusive role for youth in participatory culture: "Participatory politics are an important avenue to provide young people with a level of voice and control not often seen in the realm of institutional politics." (p. x). Cohen and Kahne (2012) advance five key takeaways that show a clear relationship between digital and participatory media and civic engagement:

1. Large proportions of young people across racial and ethnic groups have access to the Internet and use online social media regularly to stay connected to their family and friends and pursue interests and hobbies.
2. Participatory politics are an important dimension of politics.
3. Interest-driven online activities appear to lay a foundation for engagement in participatory politics through the development of "digital social capital."
4. New media have the potential to facilitate an equitable distribution of political participation among young people from different racial and ethnic groups.
5. Many youth get news through participatory channels but believe they would benefit from learning how to judge the credibility of what they find online. (pp. vii–x)

These five points depict a youth population that, like the connected learning movement, is using personal interests, digital technologies, and peers to facilitate their participation in daily political life. Cohen and Kahne (2012) explore the role of traditional metrics for political participation (voting, volunteering, etc.) for this population, but find a much more pressing need to "support youth in formal and information educational settings that strengthen their ability and desire to produce media that is informed, persuasive, and distributed effectively" (p. xi).

In their list of implications, Cohen and Kahne (2012) single out the need for media literacy, "Youth must learn how to judge the credibility of online information and find divergent views on varied issues" (p. xi). As political opinions, advertisements, and advocacy campaigns integrate further into our social networks, young people must be able to make sense of the wide array of messages they consume at increasingly fast speeds. Media literacy education is one of the core outcomes advanced to better connect personal interests and social media use to public identity and participatory politics.

These two examples offer valuable insights into the learning environments that are increasingly relevant to youth in digital culture. They are important to this book because they offer outcomes that place peers, interests, and activism at the root of young people and engagement today.

A host of other studies have explored how learning environments are incorporating media literacy practices in places of formal education. Collectively these studies begin to show where and how teaching digital and media literacy are most useful and best located. There is broad agreement that focusing on meaning, evaluation, and interpretation of media messages better suits the learning styles of youth than does gathering and memorizing information (Franzoni et al., 2008; Hobbs, 2011; Kiili et al., 2008; Kraidy, 2002; Lindgren & McDaniel, 2012). Digital storytelling is also found to enhance students' learning ability, collaborative skills, and critical inquiry (Peppler & Kafai, 2007; Watson & Pecchioni, 2011). Critical media literacy learning outcomes have also been advocated as core mechanisms for transformative learning (Tisdell, 2008; Taylor, 2000).

The discussion on digital media and learning is a needed one in the United States and around the world today. The expansion of learning to incorporate digital media technologies and collaborative platforms offers much opportunity for future generations. Of course, as Rheingold notes, it's not the technologies or the tools that will define how we use these spaces. Rather, what will define the value of these tools is how we as citizens learn to use them to enhance our personal lives and society at large. To bridge the disconnect I explored in Part Two of this book, I want to offer a series of *connectors* that can be approached in formal and informal spaces of education to help reenvision social media tools in more vibrant and purposeful ways.

Connectors

The figure below (see Figure 6.1) recommends four *connectors* to help bridge the divide between how young people use social tools and technologies, and how they perceive their place and role in daily life. In the left part of the figure we see the dominant perceptions that students conveyed about the role of social media in their daily lives. Overwhelmingly, students saw their time spent with social media sites as wasteful, an unhealthy pleasure, a strictly social outlet where they mostly "stalked" or "creeped" on peers, and platforms where they could not stop seeking connections.

The right circle presents many of the opportunities that the social networks provide, as seen in the survey of student social media use on a daily basis. Peer-to-peer connectivity was central to the facilitation of information and communication. A sense of community played a large role in why they engaged with peers and family. The ability to express political and social ideas and opinions was central to their use of social networks. And finally, their sense of connectedness to the world, through news, entertainment, shopping, and other daily behaviors increasingly found relevance on social networks.

The space in between these circles represents the chasm where uses and perceptions did not add up. This space is where media literacy competencies come into play. To enable a more inclusive, purposeful, and value-driven identification for young people with social media tools and platforms, the four proposed "connectors" can bridge more purposeful and value-driven uses and behaviors within social media spaces.

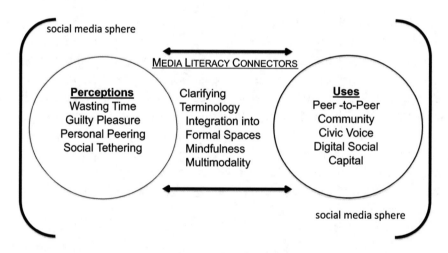

Figure 6.1. Media Literacy Connectors.
Source: Author

The media literacy connectors are positioned to shift the perception of social media from personal time-wasting tools to more vibrant spaces for expression, community, and voice. As we look forward to more human-integrated digital technologies (like Glasses), the need to effectively use digital tools for our information and communication needs becomes that much more important.

Media literacy education, in this context, must expand its role to build critical competencies that connect traditional modes of inquiry with new digital and mobile spaces. In a 2010 report to the Federal Communications Commission titled, *Empowering Parents and Protecting Children in an Evolving Media Landscape* Hobbs, Hope Culver and Mendoza wrote:

> Media literacy includes both the ability to *critically analyze media* and the *ability to create media messages in many forms*. Traditionally, media literacy educators have emphasized exploration of news, advertising, entertainment and popular culture. (Hobbs, 2008). Now educators are exploring how media literacy concepts and pedagogy apply to digital technologies and online social media. (p. 2)

To explore the constructs of media messages—news, advertising, entertainment, and so—in digital spaces, we need first to better define how these spaces treat such information, and what that means for our relationship with that information. The media literacy connectors here provide a starting point towards re-orienting this relationship in the context of integrated social media spaces.

Clarifying Terminology

The first proposed "connector" advocates for the clarification of terminology on social networks. The lenient use of the terms *news feed, friend, follower* is influencing how youth conceive information flow and peer-to-peer sharing on social networks. More clarity about what these terms mean in the context of our digital and physical identities can help build more constructive approaches to navigating and contextualizing social media spaces. Students should not only be able to differentiate between what news feeds mean on Facebook versus an aggregator on Google news, Reuters, or the Associated Press, but also what advantages and disadvantages Facebook Friends pose in terms of interactivity, communication, and personal relationships.

Youth should be able to discern what "follower" means in the context of their social identities. When they "friend" someone, what type of connotation does that have for them and the person they "friended?" How does the term "news feed" shape the discernment and understanding of current events versus personal opinion? The idea that we are "commenting" on YouTube videos while we sit alone in front of the computer changes the notion of audience, anonymity, and public expression.

In *A Handbook for Media Literacy*, Silverblatt et al. (2009) note "A primary objective of the ideological approach [to media literacy], then, is to move beyond the description of a media production into a discussion of the values implicit within the presentation, as well as whose interests are served by such ideas (p. 5). To build a strong functional identity about how we perceive social networks, we must clarify the terms associated with these spaces. Defining these terms can help to provide greater structure for the functions and uses of the tools themselves (see boyd, 2006; and boyd & Ellison, 2007), and the content that flows through them.

Integration into Formal Spaces

Along with a clear understanding of terms, the purposeful integration of social media tools into the classroom, workplace, and home, can help position social media in more inclusive civic contexts. Rey Junco has conducted extensive research into how social media impacts the college classroom, and has found that multitasking in class—particularly with Facebook—is negatively associated with GPA (see Junco, 2012a; 2012b; 2012c; Junco & Cotten, 2012). At the same time, his research specifically with Twitter and learning management systems shows that with proper design, implementation, and oversight, social media tools can be made more purposeful to students' learning outcomes (see Junco et al., 2012a, 2012b; Junco et al., 2011; Junco & Cotten, 2010).

Integration into formal spaces does not mean simply allowing tools and platforms to be used without any direction, scope, or vision. However, it does start by challenging the all too common "put it away" culture that exists in most formal settings, and moving towards a more planned approach to using social technologies in formal spaces. In the workplace, tools like Yammer, Wiggio, and Diigo are seen as healthy social alternatives to Facebook and Twitter. Schools are also using suite of educational technologies to build in more opportunities for collaborative engagement both in and out of the classroom.

A host of new resources exists that explore the more formal integration of social technologies into the classroom. In *Toys to Tools* Kolb (2008) offers some insightful ways to build mobile phones into structured learning opportunities. In *Teaching with Tools Kids Really Use*, Brooks-Young (2010) argues for a wide integration of web and mobile technologies across the school system. Beyond these examples, a host of texts explore the integration of social and mobile technologies in formal classroom settings. (See Baker, 2012; Davis, 2009; Hoeschmann & Poyntz, 2012; Prensky, 2010; Solomon & Schrum, 2007.)

With proper design and implementation, teachers and students can see social tools in more purposeful contexts. Like Junco found, if left to their own devices, students may not learn as much from them as we would hope. But if nudged to use them in more meaningful ways, young people have a better chance to realize the potential that they hold.

Mindfulness

This recommended connector supports exercising mindfulness to develop greater attention to using social media spaces as integrated information hubs. Rheingold and others focus on the development of metacognition for learning in digital culture. Rheingold (2012) writes: "The word metacognition means the act of thinking about thinking and more; *metacognitive strategies* enable people to apply what they have learned about attention control to new learning tasks" (p. 65). Rheingold cites a host of studies (see Livingstone, n.d.; Hall, 1999; Lehrer, 2009) that discuss how to build metacognition through meditation techniques. He cites work that shows that students who practiced metacognition had higher GPAs, more self-control of their attention, and could allocate attention in more strategic ways.

In the context of this study, we can apply mindfulness to the ways in which our attention can get lost in the depths of social media. Anecdotally, we all have experienced the power of social media to seduce us into staring at screens, reading about friends, or often forgetting why we visited a site in the first place. There is a known tendency for distraction in social networks (Carr, 2011; Wood et al., 2012; Junco, 2012a, 2012b, 2012c). Finding ways to build more mindful awareness about how we use social media, for what purpose, and to what end can help strengthen the end results of our experiences with them (Rosen, 2012). I'm not going so far (yet) to think that meditation should be a fundamental part of all curricula, but a focus on mindfulness when it comes to self-awareness about our online behavior can nudge young people to be more diligent, useful, and inclusive with the time they spend online.

How might this happen? Structuring learning opportunities for students to use social media to find spaces for civic voices—advocacy, outreach, community organizing, social movements, open data sources, and innovation—is a start. Also having students analyze where they find information, how it can be used to support or lead action-based causes, or simply spread awareness about issues. It's also valuable to have young people go "offline" (Moeller et al., 2010; 2011) for a day or two to notice how and where information habits shift and change when not faced with constant information streaming throughout their day. Another way to promote mindfulness is to have students map their social media activity, to explore the diversity of their networks, how much they "communicate" in real time, and the type of content they are engaging with. This can happen in the context of a specific network, or through a tool: like a tablet or mobile phone.

These quick examples all strive to build more self-reflective and mindful approaches to engagement with technology. Rheingold (2012) advocates for a host of "motivations, perspectives, and heuristics (mental tricks)" (p. 68) that humans can employ to better build and maintain attention and direction in their daily lives. If we apply this to digital media use we may be able to direct and focus our attention to more meaningful and valuable experiences, or at the very least *reframe our understanding of these tools from attention diverting to community enabling.*

Multimodality

The last connector is the notion of multimodality. A host of scholarship has combined the notion of multimodality with digital and media literacies. Lim et al. (2011) stress the more active consumer as a perquisite for multimodal proficiency in digital culture "This proliferation of user-generated content compounds the subjectivity of the information, which they create as each different mode offers the potential for different representational and communicational action by their users" (Kress, 2003, p. 5) (p. 174).

In this study, students reported a clear propensity to create and share content, ideas, opinions, links, and creations with their online communities. They did so with little hesitation. In a sharing culture there is room for interpretation and subjectivity. Part of the disconnect I found stemmed from the reliance on peers to facilitate information flow but the lack of value the students associated with was the content they received. This comes from a view of credibility couched in traditional top-down information flow. Even if peers were sharing links from reputable sources, they weren't readily acknowledged, or they were lost in the sea of personal missives and opinions that surrounded the content. Developing multimodal competencies (Kellner, 2002; Kress, 2003; Jewitt & Kress, 2003) can help students navigate the complex landscape for meaning creation, shared narratives, and peer-sourced content. Again, Lim et al. (2011) write:

> Accompanying the proliferation of multimodal representation in today's media landscape have been shifts in how meanings are created and understood (Jewitt & Kress

2003; Lankshear & Knobel 2003). With the widespread deployment of different modalities, media and materials, each with its own logic and affordances, media consumers' meaning-making processes are getting more complex than ever. (p. 175)

As young people are utilizing digital skills and practices to broaden their repertoire of social and civic communication, media literacy education cannot stop at the critical analysis of messages. It must include the ability to navigate a complex and multifaceted digital media terrain in both "receptive and expressive modes" (Lim et al., 2011). This entails the ability to discern types of content, modes of information delivery and reception, savvy sharing, expression and reception skills, and the need to see value in vibrant peer-to-peer networks. Multimodality, in this context, is media literacy for integrated information platforms.

Towards a Model for Media Literacy and the Emerging Citizen

This chapter advocates for a learning culture that better bridges the current divides between young peoples' perception and use of digital media for social and civic engagement in daily life. In response to the dizzying array of new technologies and connective platforms that appear seemingly every month or two, educators must work to provide relevant and holistic responses. These responses can live in classrooms—and hopefully will—but should also be seen as competencies learned through the context of daily life, work, and play.

Media literacy education is positioned to provide a stable and wide infrastructure to help promote both critical inquiry and critical expression as foundations for learning how to flourish in digital spaces. In their FCC Report, Hobbs, Hope Culver & Mendoza (2010) advance the following arguments for media literacy as a necessary educational movement for the future of civic society:

- With available access to the widest array of information resources in the history of the world, people today need sophisticated skills and competencies involving the ability to *find information, comprehend it, and use it to solve problems*. The growth of the knowledge economy is dependent upon workers who have these skills. (Kinzer and Leander, 2003)
- Media literacy supports the development of life skills including leadership, ethics, accountability, adaptability, personal productivity, personal responsibility, self-direction, and social responsibility. These competencies are associated with the *ethical use of information and communications technology*. (Buckingham, 2003)

- With more types of popular culture and entertainment media available at their fingertips, people need the ability to *make responsible leisure-time choices that meet their needs and reflect their values*. This is especially important since some media experiences may be offensive and degrading to the human spirit, in direct opposition to values of the family, church, and community. (Behrman, 2006)
- The ability to identify message purpose, target audience, point of view, and other features of visual, print, sound, and digital 'texts' enables people to *critically analyze and evaluate the quality* of both information and entertainment in their cultural environment. (Livingstone, 2008)
- To fully participate in contemporary society, people need to be able to *create and produce their own messages*, using print, visual, digital, sound, and online social media. Participating actively in self-governance is a vital part of citizenship in a democracy. (Hobbs, Hope Culver, & Mendoza, 2010, pp. 12–13)

In reality, the fundamentals of critical inquiry have not changed much. Hobbs, Hope Culver, and Mendoza point out that finding and comprehending information, using information competently and ethically, evaluating the quality of information, and being able to create messages in our own voice are core to media competency regardless of the medium, technology, or platform. However, in a ubiquitous digital culture, media literacy frameworks need to be applicable in a wide variety of contexts, beyond just classrooms. They must be activated and scalable, and they must be for all. Rheingold (2012), after acknowledging the barriers involved with change in formal education systems, notes "…but the good news is that knowledge and know-how can spread through online networks as swiftly as well as pervasively as a viral video. And it's up to us to do so" (pp. 252–53).

The next chapter of this book advocates a framework that positions media literacy as a movement for a more engaged, active, and participatory citizenry not confined to a classroom, but for all people to engage with digital media culture in savvy and connective ways.

· 7 ·

THE 5A'S OF MEDIA LITERACY: A NORMATIVE MODEL FOR THE EMERGING CITIZEN

In *Spreadable Media: Creating Value and Meaning in Networked Culture*, Henry Jenkins, Sam Ford, and Joshua Green (2013) explore emerging forms of participatory culture and audience engagement that are at the center of politics, business, and communication in a networked age. They write:

> The growth of networked communication, especially when coupled with the practices of the participatory culture, provides a range of new resources and facilitates new interventions for a variety of groups who have long struggled to have their voice heard. New platforms create openings for social, cultural, economic, legal, and political change and opportunities for diversity and democratization for which it is worth fighting. (p. xiv)

Through a myriad of insightful case studies and examples, Jenkins, Ford, and Green contend that citizens, with a host of connected networks available at their fingertips, can facilitate and sustain the open flow of communication and participatory spaces: often in contrast to the control-minded companies that own and develop the content. The networks that are diversifying the scope of engagement for publics, however, are only as diverse and engaging as those who occupy these networks.

In this chapter, I want to propose a framework that advocates media literacy as the educational movement to help strengthen the emerging networked landscape that Jenkins, Ford, and Green detail. This framework builds on the work of media literacy pioneers who have been exploring and developing models to advance media literacy in classrooms and society in general.[22]

The 5A's of Media Literacy for the Emerging Citizen

ACCESS to media

AWARENESS of authority, context, credibility

ASSESSMENT of how media portray events and issues

APPRECIATION for the diversity of information, dialog, collaboration, and voices online

ACTION to become part of the dialog

Figure 7.1. The 5A's of Media Literacy for the Emerging Citizen.

Origins of the Framework

In the summer of 2007, at the first ever Salzburg Academy on Media and Global Change,[23] 51 students from over 15 countries around the world gathered to build a network for media literacy and global change. Students worked collaboratively to create curricular materials to be disseminated to secondary and higher education institutions around the world. Through the creation of Global media literacy case studies, the participants at the Salzburg Academy entered into cross-cultural dialogue that, at its core, reflects new understandings of media from diverse perspectives. The Academy curriculum is premised on the notion that engagement and participation in civic life requires people to have an awareness of the ways in which media influence cultural ideologies locally and globally. Since its inaugural session in 2007, over 390 students and 60 faculty members have participated from over 35 countries around the world.

In the inaugural years of 2007–08, students and faculty at the Academy struggled to build a media literacy framework that provided common entry points for global cohorts of students. The case studies that students built in international groups all started with a story, and included points for further reading or viewing, exercises, and reflection questions (Mujica, 2012; Shumow & Chatterjee, 2012; Reese, 2012). While the case studies were theoretically sound and grounded in media literacy pedagogy, they lacked a progression that connected from critical inquiry to critical action. The faculty and students undertook a project to identify the core attributes of media literacy for global audiences. The framework needed to respect but not be restrained by borders, cultural differences, or long-held stereotypes and beliefs. We needed a framework for exploring terms, issues, and ideas that could be relatable across cultures and borders, and that could be applied to any issue or event, past or present.

The result was the formation of a new model for media literacy, which emphasizes flexibility, representation, and inclusiveness that has as its specific entry point the concept of the *emerging citizen*. Developed as the "*5A's of Media Literacy*" (Mihailidis, 2009b), the framework aims to provide young citizens with a common structure for media competencies in digital culture.

The 5A's: A Continuum

Access⟶ Awareness⟶ Assessment⟶Appreciation⟶Action

Figure 7.2. The 5A's Continuum.

The 5A's of Media Literacy was developed to assist young citizens in learning to be *aware of their role as global citizens, respect and value diversity, understand how the world works [socially, culturally, politically, economically, technologically, environmentally], participate in and contribute to communities on both a local and global level, act to make the world a more sustainable place,* and *take responsibility for their actions.* (Mihailidis, 2011)

The 5A's were designed to portray media education not in terms of silos (TV, radio, print, Internet) but to reflect a more inclusive approach to media technologies that are converging and increasingly borderless (Mihailidis, 2011). The "5 A's," developed as a continuum—*access* to media, *awareness* of media's power, *assessment* of how media cover international and supranational events and issues, *appreciation* for media's role in creating civil societies, and *action* to encourage better communication across cultural, social, and political divides— approaches critical media inquiry habits on local, national and global levels (Mihailidis, 2009b). They start with an understanding that their democratic society does not exist as currently conceived without access to information, and they conclude with the idea that in today's hypermedia environment, we all have the ability to be active participants in global communities. (Mihailidis, 2011)

Access

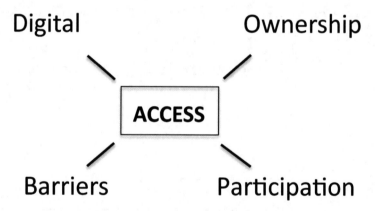

Figure 7.3. The Access Competency.

The most fundamental starting point for media literacy and engaged citizenship is the notion of *Access.* Without access to information, civic society would not exist in its current form. While we can debate the merits of media as facilitators of diverse information (see Boler, 2010; Coleman & Shane, 2012; Hindman, 2009; Schudson, 2008), an expanding digital culture has positioned media as the primary catalyst for information and communication flow in civic society. In the continuum, *Access* connotes two meanings: on the one hand, it concerns access to information—i.e., diverse messages that help to inform, engage, and provide varied viewpoints—and on the other hand, it entails access to technologies—the ability to access tools to facilitate information and communication needs, to share, and to express. While notions of access differ based on age, discipline, and local or national media systems, the concept is bound by a fundamental right to consume a diverse variety of information.

Core Access Questions

- Where does the information originate?
- Who owns the information?
- Who controls access to the information?
- What are the barriers to access?
- What different types of information can be accessed?
- How do different media technologies alter the type of access I have to information?
- How does access differ from national, religious, ethnic, racial, gender, and sexual orientation backgrounds?

These questions provide a starting point for exploring access issues on individual and societal levels. The choices that young people make to access certain information help to define that information's prevalence to society at large. Their actions matter, and it starts with the first click they make on a link every day. Under the access umbrella, I've isolated four specific areas that relate directly to media literacy explorations on how and why access matters.

- The notion of **Ownership** is fundamental to access. The beginnings of all access discussions in media literacy classrooms revolve around who controls the information and how that influences content, distribution, and reception. Access discussions should also incorporate the market vs. public sphere concepts for contemporary media ownership (Bagdikian, 2004; Baker, 2007; Cooper, 2003; Croteau & Hoynes, 2005).
- Investigating **Barriers** to access entails how we find information: the obstacles are to certain mediums or types of information, and how these obstacles influence digital divides (see Norris, 2003; Van Dijk, 2006; Selwyn, 2004), participation gaps, and the ability to consume and/or share diverse information.

- The **Digital** arena acknowledges the role of technology in how we access information, from the tools we use to how these platforms influence the type of information we can find, share, remix, and appropriate.
- Lastly, digital platforms now facilitate how we receive information, but also how actively we to share, comment, express, and **participate**. Participating in collaborative networks stems from the access we have to various spaces, platforms and networks.

Access helps us consider the origins of information: specifically how selecting certain content or technologies over others dictates the social flow of that content, and frames the perspective from which we begin to see an issue or topic evolve. Once access has been approached in full, the 5A's continuum moves to the larger conceptual issues of media's cultural, civic, social, and political impact.

Awareness

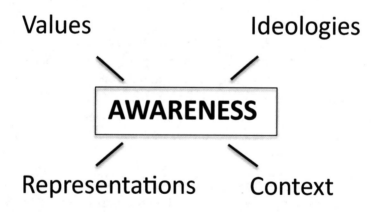

Figure 7.4. The Awareness Competency.

As societies become more interconnected by digital media systems that hold no regard for physical borders or boundaries, media become a central facilitator for dominant discourse of cultural norms around the world. If access is the fundamental entry point for a media literacy framework, awareness is the contextual foundation.

Media literacy emphasizes active inquiry as a cornerstone of its discipline. This inquiry must be accompanied by an acknowledgement of way information is interpreted when consumed away from cultural, social, and geographic familiarity. In this context, to be *aware* of media's power is to understand the perspective from which all media messages are created.

Core Awareness Questions

- What is the meaning of the information provided in larger social & civic contexts?
- What are the larger value systems in which media messages are constructed?
- How can we be aware of the representations media cultivate?
- How do media messages affect values?
- What cultural, political, social, or economic representations are embedded in the information?
- What are the underlying assertions associated with the information?
- What larger ideological positions are presented in this information?
- What are the limitations to understanding culture through media?

These questions are positioned to move the discussion into "big picture" explorations of how media build representations, promote or diffuse stereotypes, and help extend cultural conformity or resistance. Kellner (1995b) notes the potential power of media to define and set cultures for passive audiences:

> For cultural studies, media culture provides the materials for constructing views of the world, behavior, and even identities. Those who uncritically follow the dictates of media culture tend to "mainstream" themselves, conforming to the dominant fashion, values, and behavior.... Television, film, music, and other popular cultural forms are thus often liberal or conservative, or occasionally express more radical or oppositional views. (p. 8)

Awareness promotes a critical understanding of how information works to define cultural norms and social values. The awareness umbrella incorporates four areas that anchor explorations of media's ability to provide context, reflect values, develop ideology, and cultivate representations.

- Exploring **Context** in media messages helps to expose the interrelated set of conditions that develop the meaning of a message. Media literacy education embraces the complexity of media systems to help build contextual understandings of any and all messages.

- Alongside context, **Values** dictate the underlying assertions, points of view, and biases inherent in the messages themselves. Media support, contextualize, and build worldviews that are inherently tied to the origination of the message, and its means for dissemination, reception, and interpretation. Much has been made of the value systems inherent in media messages and structures (see Boyd-Barrett & Newbold, 1995; Bryant & Oliver, 2009; Perse, 2001). Media literacy helps position value formation as part of the critical inquiry process.
- Values help to support **Ideologies**: the integrated assertions and concepts that individuals, groups, or cultures use to build coherent worldviews. Croteau et al. (2011) note that "most media scholars believe that media texts articulate coherent, if shifting, ways of seeing the world. These texts help to define our world and provide models for appropriate behavior and attitudes" (p. 159). Awareness challenges the tendency of mainstream media to reflect dominant social and cultural ideologies by consistent questioning and inquiry.
- **Representations,** lastly, help us acknowledge the inherent positions that all messages take, whether intentional or not. From simple opinions to in-depth political or social content, all messages have inherent goals. Media literate awareness is about identifying the representations in the message—and the audience—that lead to a certain outcome and using them to critically engage with the message and its larger intentions.

Awareness builds from access, and it leads towards the next 'A' in the continuum, which is premised on assessing how messages are constructed to carry a specific message for a specific audience.

Assessment

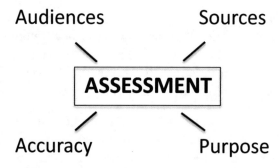

Figure 7.5. The Assessment Competency.

Underneath the larger contexts and value systems attached to media lie the nuts and bolts of how messages are created. Assessment focuses on critical analysis of the scope, point of view, credibility, authority, frame, agenda, angles, and audiences that are associated with specific messages.

Media literacy has long positioned critical analysis as a foundational principle (Sholle & Denski, 1993; Singer & Singer, 1998; Torres & Mercado, 2006). Here, assessment follows access and awareness to deconstruct how messages are specifically positioned to build meaning and target audiences. This includes comparing and contrasting messages, evaluating techniques used to grab attention, and deconstructing the physical attributes of messages to determine how effects are constructed.

Core Assessment Questions

- What is the purpose of the message?
- Who is the intended audience?
- Who is the author of the message?
- What sources are used to advance points in the messages?
- What techniques are used to grab attention?
- What symbols are used to create meaning in the message?
- What is the emotional appeal of the message and how is it triggered?
- How is authority built into the message?
- What information is not included or left out of the message?

Whether deconstructing an advertisement, a political speech, a sports highlight, or a YouTube clip, assessment is the gritty critical analysis that helps unpack the message and its composition from the ground up. This not only includes exploring what's in the message, but also what's been left out of the message. Giving power to audiences to take control of their critical consumption habits elevates the role of the active audience. In a time when critical consumption can easily become critical expression, active assessment is an essential component of media literacy education. The assessment umbrella incorporates the following four areas of specific inquiry:

- In a mass media context, **Audiences** were seen as large, amorphous, singular entities, at the whim of the interests of the message creator. Now, with the power that audiences have to be part of the storytelling process, they take on the role of the prosumer: capable of producing, sharing, and expressing all in the context of consumption (Guerrero & Luengas

Restrepo, 2012; Rennie, 2007; Ritzer et al., 2012). Media literacy assessment incorporates audiences as both passive consumers of content for escape and entertainment, but also as active collaborators in the digital mediasphere.

- In a post-objectivity age, balance, fairness, and **Accuracy** are still fundamental to how media messages are assessed. Accuracy can be explored by verifying sources, searching for balanced viewpoints and exploring the credibility of the information at hand.

- **Symbols** are very important in the critical deconstruction of media texts. What are the codes used to position a message for certain affect? In this context symbols can be physical—music, lighting, angles, text, etc.—or mannerisms—positive messaging, speech style, message framing, emotional appeal, targeted to a certain audience. Media literacy positions symbolism at the center of the producer/consumer relationship. As audience reception is a personal mechanism, individuals are often left to infer symbolism based on their value systems.

- Lastly, critical inquiry into the **Purpose** of the message emerges from critical analysis. Is the intended outcome profit, humor, or to advance a cause? Is it targeted to males or females? Is it positioned to inform, persuade, or both? Media literate individuals must learn to judge media in their own interests and the interests of the audience. Developing purpose in messages is a core attribute of this process.

While still vital to the media literacy process, assessment must now incorporate critical analysis tools for digital technologies. Following the assessment competency, the continuum shifts outward from the message towards appreciation for the wide-ranging role of media in civil society.

Appreciation

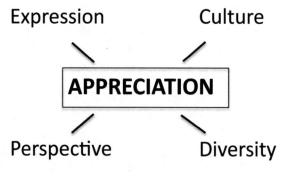

Figure 7.6. The Appreciation Competency.

The diversity of voices in digital media culture provides an opportunity to explore how this new vibrant landscape promotes the development of a healthy civic society. The opportunity has never been greater for citizens to personally tailor their daily information and communication habits. Of course, with this opportunity comes greater responsibility.

Media literacy approaches to appreciation embrace this opportunity to learn about culture, to engage in wide-ranging dialog and discussion, to voice opinions, to embrace civic dialog, and to openly question politicians, community leaders, and media outlets. Appreciation does not create an "us" vs. "them" mentality, pitting media against audience. Rather, it comprises a responsibility to be part of the dialog, and contribute valuably to communities. Media literacy in this context must not only cultivate critical thinking skills, but must also teach about the necessity of vibrant, diverse, and free media in global contexts.

In this regard, appreciation is about embracing the voice we have in a digital culture. It's about creating value for our communities of peers. It is about engaging in dialog that can lead to more diverse and varying viewpoints. At the same time, appreciation is about practicing healthy media diets (Coiro et al., 2008; Goodman, 2003; Kist, 2005; Schooler et al., 2009), that encourage balanced viewpoints, hard and soft news, games and learning, and turning off media when necessary.

Core Appreciation Questions

- In what ways are media beneficial avenues for civil society?
- How does freedom of expression help maintain diversity?
- How can multiple perspectives build a more vibrant media environment?
- How can understanding media lead to more participation?
- How can my voice contribute to more vibrant dialog about issues, events, or hobbies?
- What responsibilities do I have to my family, friends and acquaintances in social media spaces?
- What types of behaviors will help build a more tolerant, diverse, and inclusive media culture?

Finding the connections between messages and their inherent perspectives allows for a fuller understanding of the creator's intentions and motivations. In this way, media can be seen beyond what it does wrong, what it does not do, and what it could do better. Under the appreciation umbrella, the areas of *expression, perspective, culture, and diversity* collectively position the individual as an empowered participant in a vibrant media landscape.

- To be **Expressive** is to be mindful of our voices online. Young citizens today straddle the sensitive line between public and private (boyd, 2009; boyd & Marwick, 2011). This study showed that most people automatically post or share with little thought about where the information goes or who receives it. Media literate expression is about having a voice, respecting others, acknowledging audiences, and mindfully contributing to dialog, whether it's a personal opinion, an experience, or a political statement. Expression can help build imaginative practice with media (Ito, 2005).
- **Perspective** is about being thoughtful in a glutinous and fast-paced media age. With the amount of information that passes through our social feeds, email inboxes, and homepages, we are constantly making valuations with little reflection. Perspective is about stopping to consider not only the content of what we are consuming and sharing, but also the time we spend with media and the value that we derive from this engagement.
- One of the largest assumed benefits of digital **Culture** is the ability to extend our voices beyond borders and beyond divides. We are also now open to a wider amount of culturally diverse information than ever before. While Zuckerman (2013; 2010) has disputed the notion of this opening up as leading to a more diverse information diet, the opportunity presents itself nevertheless. While recognizing that cultures define media institutions and reflect the content they publish, consume, and share, appreciation breeds sensitivity to others and a more tolerant disposition towards media systems.
- Lastly, appreciation is about **Diversity.** In a connected world, where nationalities are tied together through global economic and political policy, we have no choice but to engage with the cultures that we increasingly rely on for a majority of our goods and services. Media literacy must focus on diversity as a window to appreciating the various types of content available. Challenging our own long-held stereotypes can build more tolerance, patience, and understanding for how media portray others and ourselves.

Appreciation, in the 5A's framework, emphasizes the opportunities new media provide for enhanced dialogue and cultural appreciation. Media literacy education that teaches to constantly seek the associations between media and culture can embrace the political, economic, and societal diversities that individuals bring to media messages. Harnessing an appreciation of our place and role in the media landscape leads to the final 'A' in the continuum: action. Here media literacy teaches us to channel our heightened competencies into activist and engaged outcomes to cultivate a more inclusive and diverse society.

Action

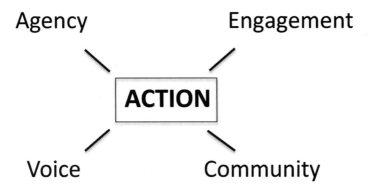

Figure 7.7. The Action Competency.

The final 'A' in the media literacy continuum is **Action.** The growing avenues for active participation in dialog have supported new means for media production and activism across local and global spaces. Media literacy has often assumed, with little evidence, that enhanced critical thinking will lead to civic awareness and engaged participation in civil society. Past research I have conducted shows that if students are learning critical thinking skills without application to the real world or an actionable agenda, they are left to encounter cynical and defeatist propositions (Mihailidis, 2009a).

In a vast media landscape, it's often difficult to envision ways to make our voices meaningful. And certainly the time and effort this may take is far beyond what we normally want to spend. Action, in this sense, is about using our voices to help build a stronger community, stronger contributions to political and social dialog, and engagement in daily life. This starts with knowing that our actions have consequences, and that every link we share, every update we post, and every story we read is shaping the media landscape in new ways. Media literate action connects our critical analysis to the real world.

Core Action Questions

- How can I use media to have a voice?
- How and where can I participate in the creation of meaningful dialog?
- Who are the communities that I connect with, and what role do I have in those communities?
- What new digital avenues can I use to be active and engaged?
- How can I contribute to tolerance, diversity, and discourse in digital media culture?
- Where are my actions beneficial, and detrimental, to my local communities?
- How can I act to help better issues I care about, inform others on my positions, and engage in more valuable dialog?

Action does not necessitate protesting in the streets, commenting on every video watched, or hosting a blog. It could mean advocating, endorsing, or supporting issues that you believe in, petitioning local companies or organizations to raise awareness, sharing relevant information in your peer circles (without being overbearing or alienating), or contributing commentary to causes that you support or refute.

In all media literacy education plans, action is the final question to consider. Finding ways to effectively communicate publicly can help build towards a media literate culture that places value on positive contributions. Four specific areas under the action umbrella support this final part of the media literacy continuum.

- **Community** is at the heart of media literacy activism. Whether community is your local neighborhood, a group of interested gamers online, or a large social advocacy group, thinking externally about the ways in which your media habits can contribute and add value to the community is at the heart of good contributions. Benkler (2005) and Christakis and Fowler (2011) showed us early in this book about the connective power that information networks provide for enhanced community dialog and activism (Shumow 2014).
- Central to communities are the **Voices** of their constituents. Media literacy education must embrace individual and collaborative voices as

the centerpieces of digital media culture. In spaces that are increasingly populated by peers, our voices take on added value and responsibility. Supporting confidence and leadership is central to developing integrity and accountability in our daily media use.

- **Engagement** is a term covered extensively in this book, and somewhat peripherally in media literacy scholarship. Often, there is an assumed point of engagement that materializes from learning critical thinking and analysis skills. However, in a fast-paced digital media age, engagement is fluid and must be stressed as a core competency for being active. What does it mean to "like" something on Facebook, to re-tweet a tweet, promote a YouTube video, or to support a Kickstarter campaign? Engaging in these actions should be reflexive, thoughtful, and purposeful.
- Lastly, media literacy action is about **Agency**: the capability to hold ourselves accountable for our actions, to be responsible for our behavior in digital spaces, and to be mindful and respectful of others. We also must be made aware of the connection between our actions, expressions, and values to the larger world, and our place in it. Agency allows us to move forward with a sense of purpose, using our media tools to help us contribute to the betterment of civic society, and to engage as citizens in a digital media culture. Hobbs (2011a) notes that "when students' ideas and thoughts move towards specific and concrete forms of social action, it can be energizing for young people and adults alike" (pp. 18–19).

Genuine civic action comes from enabling voices and ideas to engage where they feel best positioned to make positive contributions and changes to the world.

Applying the 5A's

The 5A's framework is not meant to be a prescriptive framework. I haven't attached lesson plans for K-12 classrooms or the university. Beyond the few examples I provide below, I don't prescribe ways it can be used in the home, and I don't think there is a singular mechanism for applying the 5A's in afterschool programs, places of work, or any other space of formal or informal learning. Much like our digital media culture today, the 5A's should be used, abused, remixed, re-appropriated, shifted, shaped, and spun by any educator, advocate, scholar, parent, or policy maker who wants to implement real media literacy priorities in their space.

The 5A's represent a scalable model for media literacy education that can be implemented in primary, secondary or higher education. **Teachers** can approach the 5A's in the context of media history, cultural criticism, pop culture, television studies, advertising, gender studies, or children and media. **Lesson plans** can be built around these concepts, or they can be used as reflective and analytical questions that push discussions of media effects into new spaces. In the **home**, parents and caretakers should think about this model in the context of their children's use of media content and platforms. In the **policy arena,** digital citizenship, Internet safety, and cyber bullying can utilize the 5A's model as a public advocacy framework for building safe and practical media use guidelines for communities. **Libraries** and **museums** can use the 5A's to help their patrons better engage with public spaces. **Social advocacy organizations**, campaigning for causes large and small, can build their messaging strategies with the 5A's in mind. There is no one prescriptive use for the 5A's model introduced here: it's open for folks to bend it and apply it in a way that best suits their needs. That said, let me offer two topic-driven examples that place this framework into more workable and applicable contexts. These are only abbreviated overviews of how the 5A's apply to issues across the media spectrum. They can and should be expanded in depth, breadth, and complexity as they are adopted for formal and informal learning spaces.

The Boston Marathon Bombings: Truth, Speculation and Everything in Between

The tragic events that occurred on April 15, 2013, when home-made bombs exploded near the finish line of the Boston Marathon in the Back Bay of Boston, MA, continue to provide a somber and important case of the public's increasing role in the response to acts of terror. The 5A's can provide a very sound way to build understanding and a framework for a large and messy topic.

Issues of *access* necessarily revolve around asking how students learned about the incident: where did they access information from? How did they follow the ongoing events during the week of the manhunt for the bombing suspects? What are the benefits and possible risks associated with accessing information from certain outlets over others. Were there any barriers to accessing information about the incident? There exists a host of rich information on how the incident was covered, and examples of how collaborative networks were utilized to help in the organization of information, and to aid the runners to safety and security. At the same time, access must discuss some of the potential inaccuracies associated with citizen-driven platforms for sharing information and opinion. Using rich examples to ask students to ponder how they accessed information and opinion on the incident, can help them reflect on how this shaped their understanding and opinion of the issue itself.

The *awareness* competency involves students exploring the larger value-positions and cultural contexts embedded in the information. What are the frames that media are using to depict the bombings? Are they attaching ethnic, religious, or political values to the information? As audiences, how do we attribute meaning to the values and ideologies? Why was one of the accused bombers seen in a sympathetic light? And the other in a more responsible and demonized context? Was it the representations of them as older and younger brother? Or was it the boxer image and strict religious observations of the older brother, coupled with the slacker and stoner narrative of the younger brother? And how did media use these narratives to create a story around the brothers, the incidents, and the victims? Awareness of how media provide narrative and ideological context to the brothers can help to unpack the often complex media landscape that exists, and how audiences often bring their own narrative and representative frameworks to the table.

The *assessment* competency unpacks specific messages, to see how the construction of the messages themselves build a collective narrative of the issue at hand. We could, for example, take the controversial *Rolling Stone* cover of the younger brother of the accused bombers, Dzhokhar Tsarnaev, and the highly public debate that ensued. In a media literacy classroom, we would ask the purpose of the message, who it was aimed at, what techniques were used to gain attention, was there an emotional appeal, and was anything omitted or left out of the message. These questions can build a critical framework for understanding the motivations of the creators of the cover, and why debate ensued. We could use the assessment competency to also explore news coverage or the Reddit community space that shared endless images, stories, and opinions.

As we move through the 5A's, *appreciation* asks us to consider how, in the context of the tragic events around the bombing at the Boston Marathon, we can value the diverse viewpoints in helping to provide a more full understanding of the issue at hand. But exploring the different ways that citizens came together to offer their help, organizing through social media platforms, to help the runners and those interested, to offer solace, and even try to provide necessary information to the authorities in the days that followed the marathon. At the same time, we must acknowledge that a more open media landscape necessitates more responsibility for citizens to their communities both online and off. *Appreciation* asks that media literate citizens ask how their behaviors will contribute to more informed, aware, tolerant and participatory dialog about the bombings. How can our voices provide solace and insight, and a platform to help heal. Lastly, appreciation details how our behaviors can help lead us to a more inclusive media culture that helps all constituents hear and understand the issue at hand.

The final "A," *action*, asks us to consider what action we are taking to have a voice and contribute to meaningful dialog around the tragedies of the Boston Marathon. In this competency, students are asked to reflect on their own communities and the role that we have in contributing to the dialog, in helping those in need, and in holding the media accountable to provide, fair, balanced, and critical discourse. How can our actions, from tweeting our opinions, to sharing information about the victims, the suspects, and the city benefit our local communities? And how could they be detrimental? Most importantly, action aims to connect the 5A's, to understanding how the media work to present issues, and how we can act to help advance issues we care about, inform others, and engage in collaborate dialog. This allows complex and emotionally charged issues to be analyzed and discussed in a coherent and ordered way.

The next example I offer shows how the 5A's can also be applied to a lighter medium, the music video, but one that is charged with important cultural issues.

Blurred Lines: Remix Culture to Combat Controversial Narratives

Released on March 26, 2013, *Blurred Lines*, the catchy single by Canadian-American recording artist Robin Thicke and featuring American rapper T.I. and producer and signer Pharrell, quickly became the biggest hit song of the summer. The song features sexually suggestive lyrics and a provocative video that features three female models scantily dressed and interacting with the three recording artists. As the song gained popularity, it became increasingly controversial because of its lyrical and visual depiction of females and sexuality. Then, soon after, an explicit version of the video was released that featured the females topless and in suggestive positions around the males. Of course, this only added to the dialog about the intent of the video. With a trove of public opinion circulating, and responses by the filmmaker and Thicke himself, the 5A's provide a structured approach to the song, the video, and the issues that underlie the message. There are many different ways to interpret and analyze the video. This framework should help to explore these various readings of the video and allow for a critical deconstruction of the text.

Access, in the context of *Blurred Lines*, asks students to consider where they watched the video, how many versions of the video they watched, and where they located different narratives about or on the video. Educators could ask classrooms to find as many different opinions as possible about the video, and identify who created the messages, who owns the information, and how available are these messages to the general public.

The *Blurred Lines* song offers a rich opportunity to discuss what this information—which many easily dismiss as just another "pop song"—means for how we think about gender, relationships, sexual identity, and interactions between males and females today. There are many different ways to understand the messaging as it relates to the position of the males—dressed and upright—and the females, with less clothing and less direct presence in the video. And further, awareness asks about the explicit version of the video, its intentions, aims, representation, and appropriateness. The video offers the chance to engage with the idea of representations as mainstreaming normative culture, reinforcing dominant stereotypes, and contributing to existing value systems that we may or may not condone.

Assessment allows us to deconstruct how the larger values and representations found in the video are put together through the construction of the video itself. From the choice to shoot in black and white, to the scenes involving large props, animals, and actors strutting across the stage, a close analysis of the video can show how the intentions of the message are created. From wide angle shots and lighting to the choice of dress and use of a hashtag, assessing this video helps us understand how the effects were created, and more importantly what's included—and omitted—from the message. Only with a deep critical reading of the text can we understand its impression on us, and how that impression is constructed.

In the context of appreciation, we are able to take our critical reading of the text, and explore the somewhat more murky ideas of where a popular hit video may contribute to our society. When a catchy song grabs the attention of so many people, there is clearly a benefit that it carries. We enjoy the beat, we dance and sing along in public and in our homes, and we carry a nice cognitive dissonance in being able to separate the enjoyment we get from listening with the controversial lyrics and posturing of the video itself. While this dissonance is entirely justifiable, appreciation allows us to situate our enjoyment of the text in a way that helps us acknowledge the opportunity a text like this has to bring us together to discuss some of the issues evoked through the text. Without, of course, draining all the enjoyment we may take from the song. We must, however, do so by engaging in the important conversations that may help us be more aware of what we are promoting each time we listen to the song or watch the video.

Finally, action asks listeners of *Blurred Lines* to think about their responsibility to the popularity of the song, and the issues it promotes. Each time the song gets another listen, or view, the dictates of the message grow in popularity, and consequently, reach. What ways can we use the song to engage in more active dialog that promotes our views on the song, or that helps us build a way to possibly enjoy the song in a smart and aware manner? Action may also be turning the video off, or finding mechanisms to share your voice about the video. Perhaps starting an awareness campaign in the classroom, or helping to share information about the conversation around the video to social networks. Just like most cultural texts, it is hard to pin down an absolute verdict on the *Blurred Lines* song and video. But it is less difficult to find ways to add to the dialog, and encourage more discussion about the texts within and beyond our social spaces.

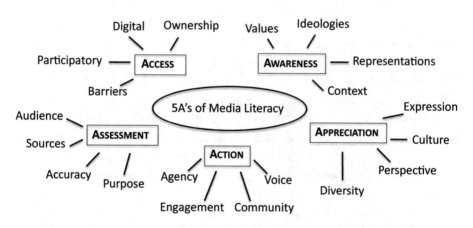

Figure 7.8. The 5A's Ecosystem.

...

These two examples provide a way to envision the 5A's as they apply to real world issues that are presented to us through media. For the emerging citizen, the 5A's can arm young people with the necessary tools and skills to approach a media centric world with savvy, confidence, and mindfulness. I teach this over an entire semester, building media literacy competencies alongside students, as we navigate these principles in detailed, interactive, and collaborative ways (see Appendix E).

The last map shows how the sub-areas of the 5A's form an ecosystem for media literacy and engaged citizenship (see Figure 7.8). This ecosystem is inclusive and reflects competencies citizens can use to enhance their daily lives. Pick pieces from it that you want to highlight in certain areas and ignore those that don't make sense. The point is that the media literacy ecosystem matters, and it should be inclusive, representative, and aligned with the needs of educators, parents, curators, policy makers, and any who find it useful.

Why the 5A's Are Important for Young Citizens

In 1958, Gunnar Myrdal, Swedish economist and social welfare architect, penned words that resonate with relevance to this day:

> Progress has to rely on education. The individual must be made to know the social facts more accurately, including his own true interests and the ideals he holds on a deeper level of his sphere of valuations...I am quite aware that this prescription is nothing less and nothing more than the age-old liberal faith that "knowledge will make us free." (p. 81)

Myrdal's words, in the context of media literacy, reinforce the need for individuals to learn about information in a way that enables them to question the messages that inform their everyday life choices. Media literacy education possesses the capability to help citizens actively understand the role of information in their community and the necessary existence of media for civic society. It also involves the capacity to have a voice and to be expressive, mindful, and thoughtful in this digital age.

The 5A's of media literacy present a guide for thinking about the new social and digital spaces that will demand more of our time and attention. And they help organize the media landscape in a way that *begins with human rights and ends with human actions*. This makes media not some amorphous machine that continues to direct messages at us, but a diverse ecosystem that consists of values, behaviors, contexts, responsibilities, views, points of view, agendas, frames, and on and on. Somewhere in this space, we contribute our own content, ideas, and opinions.

Media provide us a lifetime of resources for knowledge, entertainment, education, and interest that collectively help shape value systems, ideologies, and representations. Now more than ever, we need mechanisms to help us navigate this landscape and to facilitate our own sense of self along the way. *Access, Awareness, Assessment, Appreciation,* and *Action* provide a framework for our media engagement no matter what the topic is, what we think about it, or where we sit in the world. Media literacy grounds this framework, and if young people are armed with the critical skills and dispositions to become more expressive, engaged and active, then digital culture stands to be more vibrant, diverse, and inclusive than ever before.

· CONCLUSION ·

MEDIA LITERACY & CIVIC LIFE
IN DIGITAL CULTURE

Because democracy depends on citizenship, the emphasis then was to think about how to constitute a competent and virtuous citizen body. That led directly, in almost every one of the founders' minds, to the connection between citizenship and education.

— Benjamin Barber, 2002, p. 22

The framers of the Constitution of the United States firmly believed that in order for democracy to thrive, citizens must be well educated. "I know of no safe repository of the ultimate power of society but people. And if we think them not enlightened enough, the remedy is not to take the power from them, but to inform them by education," wrote Thomas Jefferson in a letter to William Jarvis in 1820.

Plato feared that written communication "will create forgetfulness in the learners' souls, because they will not use their memories; they will trust to the external written characters and not remember of themselves" (p. 46). Plato's anxiety is one that continues to be voiced today. How will we form memory, build knowledge, and reach truth if we are no longer forced to remember in an age where information is at our fingertips? Ong, in *Orality and Literacy* (1982) bemoans the threats from technological advancement on the human mind but notes that "we have to die to continue living" (p. 15).

Orality, to Plato and Ong, plays a central role in the maintenance of justice and truth, of knowledge, expression, and tolerance. Plato emphasized education as a core element of building intellect to help awaken all individuals: "Then education is the craft concerned with doing this very thing, this turning around" (Plato). Marshall McLuhan evoked Socrates and Plato's dialog on orality and literacy in his discussion of technological progress and the global village, to "champion contemporary communication technology as a means of enabling social cohesion and global peace" (Thevenin, 2012, p. 62).

Educating citizens has been a dominant response to technological determinism—the notion that technology dictates the development of its social organization and cultural values—for some time. Neil Postman brought determinism into the spotlight with his now famous thesis that, "Our politics, religion, news, athletics, education and commerce have been transformed into congenial adjuncts of show business, largely without protest or even much popular notice. The result is that we are a people on the verge of amusing ourselves to death" (pp. 3–4). Postman believed that the television "attacked" literary and oral culture, and that it was dumbing down society to levels of grave concern. The corruption of society by mass culture was also the formal point of study for a host of media effects traditions, most notably the work of the Frankfurt School, whose main scholars advanced a Marxist proposition for the subsuming of culture by large corporations with few moral obligations to society. These mechanisms were seen by the Frankfurt School as destroying the ability for humans to think critically and progress culturally (see Horkheimer, 1937; Horkheimer & Adorno, 1967). Herbert Schiller's study of mass media as a political economy extended the theories of cultural hegemony and technological determinism put forth by the Frankfurt School, Postman, and others (see Schiller, 1975, 1991, 1995).

These scholarly pursuits represent responses to an unprecedented growth of mass communication industries. The rapid development of the television as a home entertainment medium created a need to understand the role of mass media in culture and society. At the same time, it brought about a need to explore what responses society could take. Plato, Ong, Postman, McLuhan, the Frankfurt School, and a host of others, believed that education was the path to counter an increasingly corporate, imperialistic, and entertainment-riddled society.

Media literacy education was born from a need to find pathways to understand, and to a degree, confront, the dominant media industries of the 21ˢᵗ century. The ideas in this book, and of other contemporary scholars in media education, stand on the shoulders of Plato, McLuhan, and the host of scholarship trying to explore how society can facilitate adequate educational and civic responses to digital culture. They have at their base a unified mission to advance the plight of the citizen through education. The latest advancements in digital technologies are placing a new emphasis on the need to educate citizens for lives of digital competence. Writes Hobbs (2010):

> When people have digital and media literacy competencies, they recognize personal, corporate and political agendas and are empowered to speak out on behalf of the missing voices and omitted perspectives in our communities. By identifying and attempting to solve problems, people use their powerful voices and their rights under the law to improve the world around them. (p. 17)

Empowering citizens to speak out, solve problems and use their voices in effective ways is a prerequisite for engaged citizenship in digital culture. This transcends critical thinking as an end to a means for media literacy education. Media literacy today is as much about critical expression for civic engagement as it is about critical thinking for individual betterment.

Educating Citizens vs. Educating Consumers

> As a society becomes more enlightened, it realizes that it is responsible not to transmit and conserve the whole of its existing achievements, but only such as make for a better future society. The school is its chief agency for the accomplishment of this end. (Dewey, 1938, p. 24)

John Dewey believed that progress and democracy rest upon the education of citizens for lives of active political and civic participation. "The devotion of democracy to education is a familiar fact," wrote Dewey (1938, p. 101) in *Democracy and Education*. Dewey argued that learning must be attached to experience, so that learners can apply their educational experiences to their own sense of place in the world. Education, in this context, was to Dewey about building the individual competencies in citizens to come to their own conclusions, to apply their own value systems to the larger political struggles of the day, and to be active in the application of learning to the world around them.

Contemporaries have built on Dewey's advancement of the active learner, notably Paulo Freire, who positioned education as an emancipatory movement for citizens. In *Pedagogy of the Oppressed*, Freire passionately advocates for education as a means of giving voice to the voiceless and challenging hegemonic agendas that are dictated by oppressors. Wrote Freire (1970):

> Education as the practice of freedom—as opposed to education as the practice of domination—denies that man is abstract, isolated, independent, and unattached to the world; it also denies that the world exists as a reality apart from people. Authentic reflection considers neither abstract man nor the world without people, but people in their relations with the world. (p. 81)

The ideas of Dewey and Freire position education as an active civic pursuit. No longer is the rote retention of knowledge enough. Learning must have an emancipatory agenda. It must be about action and engagement: about building confidence, awareness, and tolerance in learners. Media literacy education, as I have advocated throughout this book, has no choice but to embrace this perspective. Thevenin (2012) argues that by "building on recent efforts to emphasize media educations potential to encourage informed, engaged citizenship, we can envision and implement activist-oriented media literacy initiatives in an effort to confront injustice and promote positive social change" (p. 68).

To implement "activist-oriented initiatives," media literacy must move the silo of the *critical consumer*. Using the "consumption" context is problematic on two fronts. First, it signifies a corporatized, capitalist frame for media education. This places learning in a model that minimizes media's complexities and messiness. Media literacy is about much more than consuming messages: it's about sharing, expression, revolution, and exploration. Second, a consumption frame is a one-way model, promoting intake and little else. Consumer ideologies do little to connect to political participation or civic engagement. They do not advocate for participation, expression, voice, or inclusion on public dialog.

Today, we exist in a more immersive media culture than ever before. Relatively, the fast-paced technological changes we see today are similar to what Plato, Ong, McLuhan, Postman, and others experienced in their time. What ties these changes together is the innate human disposition to share stories. Jenkins, Ford and Green write in *Spreadable Media* (2013) that "...while new tools have proliferated the means by which people can circulate material, word-of-mouth recommendations and the sharing of media content are impulses that have long driven how people interact with each other" (pp. 2–3).

Storytelling, in the context of this technological revolution, is not limited to those with a printing press, to those who can afford to own the operations to make information public, or to those who stand on a soapbox. Today, storytelling happens throughout every hour of every day or every year. It happens through the myriad of portable devices that are with us at all times of the day and night. Storytelling today is collaborative. Citizens tell stories. Parents tell stories. Friends tell stories. Families tell stories. Co-workers tell stories. Consumers *do not* tell stories. Media literacy education for the emerging citizen is about building expressive competencies in young people. Media literate citizens tell stories about politics, communities, friends, issues, or any ideas they are passionate about.

I introduced a series of conflating circles in chapter two, which I titled the *nexus of digital media culture and citizenship*. I want to show this again, to emphasize the importance of digital storytelling for media literacy education today. The tools that are collapsing the boundaries between the citizen and the media are putting a greater emphasis on citizens to engage in the active expression of ideas.

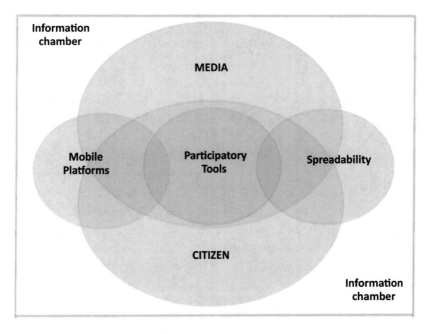

Figure 9.1. The Nexus of Digital Media Culture and Citizenship.
Source: Mihailidis, P. (2012): News Literacy: *Global Perspectives for the Newsroom and the Classroom*. NY: Peter Lang.

This book has argued continuously that media literacy teaches critical inquiry and critical expression to build stronger relationships between citizens, institutions, and communities. In digital culture, connecting media and civic voice is especially important. At the outset of this book I proposed two questions to frame my arguments for media literacy as a core civic competency:

1. *How can media literacy enable core competencies for value-driven, diverse and robust digital media use?*
2. *How can media literacy enable a more civic-minded participatory culture?*

The answer to the first question is a matter of perception. It doesn't take wholesale changes in how we regulate technologies, or how we implement them in the home and school. Rather, it's about positioning young citizens' everyday use as more integrated into all facets of daily life. We covered a host of examples throughout this book (and you can see more in the Appendixes) that show how social media tools are used to advance social, civic, and political causes. If we teach youth to use social media tools for more than just socializing, perhaps they will re-imagine the use of these tools for larger and more inclusive purposes. That's a lofty goal, but media literacy is where it has to start. The connectors proposed in Chapter six are one way to move towards this outcome.

If media literacy can reframe how we perceive and use social media in daily life, then the hope is that the second question is answered organically and naturally by the new civic behaviors of young citizens. This may be wishful thinking, but like Howard Rheingold mentions at the outset of *Net Smart*, it's "the way that people use new media in the first years of an emerging communication regime [that] can influence the way those media end up being used and misused for decades to come." (p. 1). I strongly believe in the dictates of people to drive the shape, form, reach, and value of any new technology. They can do that organically, or be assisted by education that supports new thought around how to use technology. In *ReWire: Digital Cosmopolitans in the Age of Connection*, Ethan Zuckerman nods to Rheingold's techno-optimism, when he writes:

> If we want a world that values diversity of perspective over the certainty of a singular belief, a world where many voices balance a privileged few, where many points of view complicate issues and push us towards novel solutions, we need to build that world. (p. 233)

I want to conclude by offering four concepts that position media literacy as the key movement to support new forms of engaged citizenship today and in the future.

Media Literacy Is about Agency

Throughout this book I have argued that young people have more opportunities to engage in public dialog than ever before. We've looked at this phenomenon both in the context of large-scale civic coordination and everyday public communication. From a media literacy perspective this is an issue of *agency*: both on the individual and societal levels. Individual agency is about helping young people gain the knowledge, confidence, and responsibility to see how their personal behaviors help drive public discourse. Social agency is about connecting personal behaviors to a network of peers, family, friends, and acquaintances. The ecosystems for our choices are intertwined within large and diverse groups who are connected to other large and diverse groups, and on and on. The notion of agency places the media literate individual at the center of a more connected, responsible, and diverse landscape. Giving youth the confidence to personally and publicly extend their values, opinions, and ideas into comfortable and uncomfortable spaces can help guide public debate into more insightful and meaningful spaces.

Media Literacy Is about Limitations

We have talked a lot about media literacy as a movement movement that is premised on giving voice through teaching and learning how to critically think and critically express. However, studies show that we seek and find information that suits our existing beliefs, (see Manjoo, 2008) and that digital media companies are hyper-tailoring information to us based on our past searches, sites visited, comments made, and general Internet activity (see Pariser, 2011; Vaidhyanathan, 2012). This presents a potentially problematic information vacuum for the uncritical citizen. If we are not made to see all sides of an issue, and to realize the limitations we have in accepting or fully comprehending ideas and positions we fundamentally disagree with, we will continue to contribute to the increasingly polarizing state of politics in the United States. Media literacy can help young people realize how limited we are in our information consumption capabilities. Media literacy can help people move beyond comfort zones to engage with dissenting voices and find common ground on local, national, or global issues. Acknowledging these limitations is an important step to more diverse and open dialog.

Media Literacy Is about Participation

I have advocated throughout this book for participatory culture as central to a truly media literate citizenry. Participatory culture is a more complex topic than this book has time to explain. However, in the context of media literacy, participation is about accountability. The students whom I spoke to about their social media behaviors generally absconded their responsibility to audiences online. They didn't respond to participation in a context beyond self-driven updates, posts, or comments. Participatory culture is about finding ways to thoughtfully add voice and perspective to whatever personal or public ideas, causes, or interests we support. In *Spreadable Media*, Jenkins, Ford and Green (2013) discuss the relative struggle of understanding what participation means in digital culture:

> Contemporary culture is becoming more participatory, especially compared with earlier media ecologies primarily reliant on traditional mass media. However, not everyone is allowed to participate, not everyone is able to participate, not everyone wants to participate, and not everyone who participates does so on equal terms...In some cases, networked publics are tapping this expanded communication capacity to create a more diverse culture—challenging entrenched institutions, expanding economic opportunities, and even, in the case of religious media, perhaps saving our souls. Others are simply using it to get on with the business of their everyday lives. (p. 298)

Regardless of the complications noted by Jenkins et al., media literate citizens acknowledge their participation as contributing to a public arena, offering something to an active audience, and advancing an agenda in some way, shape, or form. Participatory culture acknowledges that media literate audiences will also play a role in the conferral of our participation or the rejection of an idea. Whether or not it is about fan communities, a startup business, or on social networks, responsible participation is central to a more vibrant media landscape.

Media Literacy Is about "Us"

Lastly, media literacy is about change. It's about political, economic, social, and cultural progress. It's about challenging dominant hegemonic powers.

Without an activist orientation, media literacy will continue to educate people without a real outcome in mind. By activist I don't mean the need to revolt, scream, yell, or march. Rather, in a civically minded participatory culture, there needs to be a strong understanding of shared outcomes. Is it more responsible advertising? More of all these things? No advertising? Fewer political advertisements? Less female exploitation? Whatever the intended outcome, media literacy is about using education to help, in the smallest or largest ways, reform. The 5A's model in this book ends with action: action taken to make the world a better place. How that happens is up to each individual, but that lofty goal has to be the aim of media literacy education, or else we will always follow the dictates of those few in control.

The Emerging Media Literate Citizen

There is no escaping the reality that we have evolved into a society in which electronic information represents the substrate of much of daily life. It is a natural outcome of our having advanced past the mechanical age. And just as our addition to the benefits of the internal combustion engine led us to such demand for fossil fuels as we could no longer support, so, too, has our dependence on our mobile smart phones, touchpads, laptops, and other devices delivered us to a moment when our demand for bandwidth—the new black gold—is insatiable. (Tim Wu, *The Master Switch*, p. 319)

I began this book by writing that we live between worlds. I think a lot about the life that I lead in my community, in my neighborhood, at my university, and with my family. I often wonder how this life is translated in digital culture. I see my students struggling to stay away from their phones as they buzz throughout the classroom. I see myself struggling to stay away from my mobile devices at family functions, sitting around with the neighbors, or even on my way to the office.

This dependence, as Tim Wu states in *The Master Switch*, is indeed insatiable. With each new technology comes new uses and abuses that dictate technology's value to society. We are indeed in the middle of a time of fast-paced technological change. Unlike the television or radio, which were large but fairly uniform in their implementation and use, the Internet has spawned a paradigm shift arguably as influential as the alphabet and printing press.

In times of rapid change, it's easy to become enamored with tools and technologies, and lose sight of the people that are dictating their uses and defining their value. Society tends to focus on how digital tools are influencing civic revolt, or how they are being used to make money (for us or off of us) with new marketing and advertising gimmicks. Less often do we focus on how to help integrate these tools into our social, political, and civic systems. And even less are we introducing new frameworks and models for education.

I proposed the 5A's of media literacy as a way to connect critical analysis and critical expression in digital culture. On a continuum, these present logical entry and exit points for thinking about our relationship to media. Ideally (and unrealistically) I envision the "A's" as automated response mechanisms that emerge when we confront new information. I see them popping up, like knee reflexes, when we are reading an article, watching a YouTube clip, or sharing a link. I hope they help us provide more reflection for our own media use and for the media we share, whether for work or pleasure.

My explorations around emerging citizenship and media literacy show why media literacy is more vital now for the continuation of civic democracy than arguably at any point in the past. I also think media literacy is bigger than a classroom endeavor. Public education cannot be expected to respond in a timely and efficient manner to the rate of technological progress we've seen so far in the 21st century. Perhaps we are at the beginning of a wholesale change in the way we organize teaching and learning for a digital culture. As education systems take time to respond and change, I continue to believe that citizens are becoming more savvy, sophisticated, and expressive through social media channels. I also think a concerted effort for media literacy competencies developed in public and private schools, in the home, in after-school programs, and in general, will help to build even more diverse and purposeful uses every day.

The students that we read about in this book were all very cognizant of their ability to have a voice. They perceived social media as at the center of their daily information and communication needs. Many discussed using social media to find information about passions, hobbies, or interests they were passionate about or to facilitate conversations about current events, whether pop culture or global politics. There are many signs that a digital culture is indeed unfolding with many avenues for engaged participatory behavior. At the same time, few saw any real tangible value for social media. Facebook was for peering at friends. Twitter was for finding out about celebrities. *Instagram* was for pictures of yourself. YouTube was for wasting time watching silly videos. I think this is a problem of framing. I think media literacy education, specifically the 5A's framework I've proposed above, offers a way to see these tools, and all the tools that will soon follow, as more than simply social outlets. If indeed we have a perception problem, new tools are not going to solve it, nor are youth that have been told these tools are social outlets and little else.

John Dewey (1916) wrote in *Democracy and Education*, "People live in a community by virtue of the things they have in common; and communication is the way in which they come to possess things in common" (p. 4). Media literacy education is necessary to enable people to participate in civic societies that are increasingly mediated. Only an educated, informed, and literate citizenry, will protect and advance the dictates of tolerant and diverse democracy in the digital age. While no single educational movement, or literacy, will be able to solve problems of oppression, inequality, and suppression, the struggle for balance will be a struggle for the ability to have a voice. Individuals and societies that don't utilize the opportunities of a digital media culture will be left out of the emerging global society.

Media literacy is a path for emerging citizens to thrive in a digital culture—leading an active, engaged, and participatory generation.

· APPENDIX A ·

SOCIAL ADVOCACY CAMPAIGNS, MISSIONS & CAUSES USING DIGITAL NETWORKS

The following list is an arbitrary portrait of nineteen social advocacy campaigns, movements and organizations that are utilizing collaborative technologies, engaged communities, and digital literacy to advance their cause. Whether through for – profit mechanisms, volunteers, or marketing campaigns, these examples provide a collective look at how movements around the world are utilizing digital tools for advancing civic and social missions. Their communities are asked to be part of their agendas, and utilize interactive platforms and missions to advance their work. The more media literate the communities they engage with, the more successful, responsive and truly inclusive these initiative can be. That's what I argue in chapter 3 of this book, and throughout.

This list is by no means exhaustive or inclusive. There are literally thousands of examples that could be included here. These are a few that my students and I have come across, and find relevant, meaningful, enjoyable, and fun.

Lastly, some of these examples are detailed in more depth than others. These are examples that I wanted to spotlight for their involvement of crowds, interactive technologies, and collaborative ideas.

Avaaz

http://www.avaaz.org/en/index.php
Meaning "language" in several European and Asian languages, Avaaz has become *the* place for starting petitions and actions for just about any cause. Avaaz has the reach necessary to be heard in just about any issue, and has several success stories to show. The webpage mainly gathers petitions, but unique qualifier is that they focus on current issues to show politicians that people demand a certain outcome. To date over 23 million petitions have been registered through Avaaz.

Better World Books

http://www.Betterworldbooks.org
Since 2002, Better World Books has donated over 9.5 million books to libraries around the world, raised 15 million dollars for literacy research and outreach, and donated over 11 million books to places of need. Their model is one where they hold book drives to gather and resell books, which then provides support to fund literacy projects and book giving around the world, with a specific focus in Africa. This pro-social mission has been an outright success.

Carrotmob

http://www.carrotmob.org
Carrotmob, since 2003, has been working to incentivize businesses to become more sustainable and conscious of their practices in local communities. Carrotmob founder Brent Schulkin began to explore how groups could influence change by not simply yelling and marching, but by actively engaging the business community in change for the better. The basic premise of Carrotmob is that a local business partners with the Carrotmob, who then works with their community to set up a buying day at that organization. If it were a hardware store, for example, they would post notice that on a certain Saturday people should come to the store and be ready to purchase a certain amount of goods. Those goods can be kept by consumers in some cases, but will be donated to local communities or organizations helping those in need. The hardware store, in agreement with Carrotmob, must invest a certain portion of its hefty take from the sale, to make its business

more sustainable. This could involve investing in making the building LEED certified, investing in new infrastructure, more sustainable energy, or the like. In the end, the business profits and becomes more sustainable at the same time. And the community profits by donating to those in need and helping support the betterment of a business. It's a win-win situation. Carrotmobs have been launched around the world and have involved a host of different businesses. They rely on crowds of invested citizens to first pledge their support online and then employ collective action to help support business and community needs at the same time.

Causes

http://www.causes.com/
Causes.com lets people start their own causes for change. Their impressive track record includes: supporting the first cancer research paper to be funded by small-dollar donors and the funding of public protests in the Amazonian rainforest. The webpage allows people to donate directly to a cause, or sign a petition. To date over 153 million people have supported over 1 billion actions taken in 142 countries, which combine crowd funding and petition activism.

Change

http://www.change.org/
Change is another petition-based webpage that offers a platform for people to gather signatures to promote social causes. Users launch campaigns of their own on a host of issues and engage communities of interested people to help support their initiatives.

Charitywater.org

http://www.charitywater.org/
Charity Water lets people start their own fundraisers by pledging to different activities, and leveraging their social network. Charity Water also lets people pledge their birthday gifts to the organization. With a 100% guarantee for all dollars donated to the company, Charity Water provides a map and GPS tracking coordinates to let donators track each dollar they give to the organization.

Citizens Connect

http://www.cityofboston.gov/DoIT/apps/citizensconnect.asp
Citizens Connect, launched in 2011 by the City of Boston's Department of
Innovation and Technology and the Mayor's Office of New Urban Mechan-
ics, aims to eliminate barriers between citizens and their local constituents
by "empower[ing] residents to be the City's eyes and ears." This mobile app,
quite simply, allows residents of the city of Boston to send photos, messages, or
texts to the city about any issues they see that need to be addressed. Whether
they are street signs in need of repair, potholes, malfunctioning street lights,
or any other issue that the public wants to communicate to the city, instead
of looking for a number to call, and waiting on the phone, they simply can
open Citizens Connect and send the image with a note on the location, or
they can allow the app to offer the location automatically. This prototype
allows a more open and direct capacity for citizens to have a say in local issues
of concern, or positive things they want to point out. The city received over
20,000 messages in its first roll out of the app in 2012, and plans to expand
with an incentivized platform for citizens to earn badges, points, and rewards
from the city for constant engagement around local civic issues. A tool like
this exemplifies the new ease with which citizens can participate in daily civic
life. They need the tools (smartphone) of course, but after that, their default
capacity to take part in this process can be seamless and meaningful and help
improve urban infrastructure for entire neighborhoods.

Citizinvestor

http://www.citizinvestor.com/
Citizinvestor uses unfunded and low-prioritized governmental projects, and
lets citizens directly fund the projects they find the most important. The funds
will only be used if a project reaches 100% funding and can be started instantly.
If it doesn't achieve the goal the funders will have their money returned.

Dumb Ways To Die

http://dumbwaystodie.com/
This campaign for the Australian Metro services uses a very sleek design, a fun
and catchy tune, and some smart humor to spread safety awareness for public

transportation. Through a witty song and interactive site that shows unrelated "dumb ways to die," the campaign engages in safe public behavior, while at the same time creating content that was shared by millions around the world. Supported by a flashy interactive web page, the video has gone viral and the song can be bought at iTunes.

Dove Evolution / Real Beauty Campaigns

http://www.dove.us/social-mission/campaign-for-real-beauty.aspx
http://realbeautysketches.dove.us/
The Dove brand, in 2006, launched their *Real Beauty* campaign with a *Dove Evolution* advertisement that went viral, to the tune of over 20 million views. This video launched a social advocacy campaign that led to much debate, controversy, and remixing of the ad itself. The controversy stems from Dove being owned by Procter & Gamble, the same company that owns and operates the Axe Brand, which aggressively targets youth with hypersexual content. In 2012, Dove released its *Sketches* ad, also a very successful advertisement promoting a discussion on the idea of beauty, self-esteem, and media. Despite their controversial nature, these ads were very successful in building a coherent discussion around the role of media to engage in messages of beauty and representations. If nothing else, the Dove campaigns created many avenues for media literacy discussions to take place in schools and homes around the world.

Global Voices

http://www.globalvoicesonline.org
Launched in 2005 by Rebecca McKinnon and Ethan Zuckerman at Harvard's Berkman Center for the Internet and Society, Global Voices is an international community of citizen bloggers who share content and tell stories about the issues that are impacting and defining their local communities. Consisting of volunteer writers and part-time editors, Global Voices offers a threefold mission:

- Call attention to the most interesting conversations and perspectives emerging from citizens' media around the world by linking to text, photos, podcasts, video and other forms of grassroots citizens' media.
- Facilitate the emergence of new citizens' voices through training, online tutorials, and publicizing the ways in which open-source and

free tools can be used safely by people around the world to express themselves.

- Advocate for freedom of expression around the world and protect the rights of citizen journalists to report on events and opinions without fear of censorship or persecution. (http://globalvoicesonline.org/about/)

To date, the global voices project has gathered tens of thousands of posts from thousands around the world. Members drive content, collaborate on work, and host forums for innovative idea and information sharing. Not only can this space enhance more participation and contribution into the site, but also more readership and trust in the diverse voices that do contribute.

Gumelection 2012

http://gumelection.com/
Gumelection was a street art project launched with the intention to promote public voting while at the same time keeping the streets a little cleaner. Gumelections involve people printing posters to hang in public that ask citizens to discard their gum to the side they like less. In 2012, anyone could download a premade poster featuring Obama and Romney from the Gumelection web site, take it out in the street and hang it up at a wall. The poster encouraged passers by to put their gum on the face of the candidate they liked less. Placing gum on one of the candidates can be seen as a mental process of remembering to vote, and of course prevent gum from falling on the streets. A simple but genius idea, Gumelection hosted a series of campaigns that garnered notoriety and success for their public art statements.

Kickstarter

http://www.kickstarter.com
Launched in 2009, Kickstarter is an open-platform fundraising space for artists, musicians, designers, and other creative entrepreneurs to post and pitch ideas, and ask for support from the crowd to help bring their projects to life. Since their launch, more than 3.7 million people have pledged over $554 million, funding more than 38,000 creative projects. Kickstarter boasts an impressive 44% success-rate for all projects uploaded to the site. What's most impressive about this space, is that Kickstarter asks for no creative or financial stake or control in the projects that are posted to the space, and 100% of the projects are by

the community, for the community, with no strings attached. If pledges reach their goal and exceed it, it's in good faith that they will meet the extra demand for their product. Backing projects on Kickstarter removes the bureaucratic layers that exist in creative pursuits. The crowd literally funds what they value and want to see come to fruition. Because donations are placed in the hands of the creators entirely, they believe in the process of creation and creativity as a metric for the exchange of goods and ideas. Oscar-nominated films, award-winning musicians, open-sourced classical music projects, collaboratively written books, smart watches, minimalist wallets, and other creative products have become vastly successful through Kickstarter. More recently, however, is the growing capacity of Kickstarter as a collaborative tool for civic engagement. In the last year, the Kickstarter community has supported: journalists to report in dozens of countries on six continents, reporting large, investigative stories; sustainable urban design projects around the world aimed at building smarter, safer, and greener urban spaces; a safecast tool that helps volunteers gather and distribute data on radiation levels in Japan in the wake of the Fukushima Daiichi Nuclear Plant meltdown; and an air quality egg, which lets citizens trace and transmit air quality data in their local neighborhoods. Requiring trust, collaboration and a belief in the value of these creative ideas is a leap for society, and one that media literate crowds will demand more and more of.

1 In 4 Women

http://www.1in4women.com/
The 1 in 4 Women campaign, launched as a partnership between Refuge and Avon, aims to teach people to speak about domestic violence and gain support through a community. Through the use of an interactive campaign, viewers are able to choose how they would respond to a conversation where domestic abuse is the issue. Interactivity comes into play with each video ending in a question about what the viewer would say to a person who is experiencing domestic abuse.

Radi-Aid – Africa for Norway

http://www.africafornorway.no/
Radi-Aid is a satirical campaign that advocates for non profit organizations to stop using only pictures of poverty in Africa. They raise the question of how

others would think of Norway if the only thing they would get to see would be a movie about all the negatives about Norway. In this faux campaign Africans are collecting radiators to ship to Norway. The idea behind the campaign is to spark debate and make people think critically about how the presentation of countries in non-profit causes often stigmatizes and stereotypes the population of a country. The campaign started with a Live-Aid type of music video on and was furthered with a satirical debate in Norway's biggest newspaper *Aftenposten*.

Save The Troy Library Book Burning Campaign

http://www.criticalcommons.org/Members/MCIMR/clips/save-the-troy-library-adventures-in-reverse
In 2011, the Public Library in Troy, Minnesota, was facing a tough battle to save its life. With a diminishing budget, and a vote upcoming on funding for the library, the local Tea Party affiliates near Troy launched a campaign against the library, citing raised taxes as the main reason to not support the library. In response, the Troy Library hired the Leo Burnett Agency to help reposition the discussion of a library's worth to the community. The resulting "book burning" campaign successfully reframed the local debate from taxes to the importance of the library for the community. The final vote was a landslide victory for the Troy Library. The campaign itself, smart and witty, helped launch discussions about the tension between public relations and advocacy organizations, and the value of engaging communities around their interests through a diversity of viewpoints.

Thunderclap

https://www.thunderclap.it/
Thunderclap allows people to create and promote causes for community engagement. When a cause has reached a certain number of supporters the webpage will send out the same message on all of the Facebook and Twitter accounts of everyone who has signed up, making it easier for it to be recognized since many are seeing the same thing at the same time.

Tom's Shoes

http://www.toms.com

While the company has come under questioning around exactly where their products end up, Tom's has been overwhelmingly successful in launching a business with a strong social advocacy mission to help provide shoes to children in need. Their model is quite simple: for every pair of Tom's shoes bought, the company donates one pair to a needy person in Africa. This advocacy mission has brought millions of shoes to youth throughout Africa, while at the same time leading the sustainable business concept.

Ushahidi

http://www.ushahidi.com

This platform, now one of the most well-known for civic activism and community work, was born in 2008 in response to the post-election violence in Kenya. A simple mapping tool was built and offered for mobile users to help track where violence was occurring in Nairobi and throughout the country. This allowed for citizens to avoid dangerous zones, and also for emergency relief and peace-keeping troops to help stabilize the violence. Since, Ushahidi has become a global organization devoted to information collection, visualization, and interactive mapping. They provide infrastructure, strategy and community portals for helping to monitor elections, map local shows or campaigns, and assist in the development and deployment of causes local and global. In addition to its work in Kenya, Ushahidi has helped to track the reconstruction process in Haiti, to track election fraud in Bulgaria, environmental conditions in Indonesia, Women's Tech movements in Africa, and a host of other local and global initiatives. Of course, these platforms and data gathering initiatives are dependent upon crowds and networks of local citizens to help gather, aggregate, and appropriate content from which Ushahidi can build its interactive platforms for certain initiatives. It goes without saying that this not only requires active and inclusive participation by citizens, but moreover of knowledgeable and invested citizens working towards a unified goal or outcome.

· APPENDIX B ·

STUDY METHODOLOGY & PARTICIPANT SAMPLE

The survey employed for this book emerged from a study conducted to better understand how young citizens use social media in their daily lives, and how they perceive its value for them personally and publically. The following two general research questions were posed in 2011, when the study was launched:

RQ1–How do university students conceive of social media's role in their daily information and communication use?
RQ2–How do university students conceive of social media's role in civic life?

To explore these questions, 873 students across 9 universities on the East Coast of the United States participated in an extensive survey questionnaire. The universities were selected through existing contacts of the researchers, and those contacts were asked to disseminate a 67-question survey to their classes during the 2011 academic spring semester. Following the completion of the survey questionnaire, eight focus groups were conducted with 71 participants. Participants were offered a small payment and food to join a 60–90-minute focus group session exploring the themes of the survey. To ensure uniformity of the data, research participation was contingent on undergraduate status, and confidentiality was guaranteed.

Survey Questionnaire

The survey questionnaire was developed to assess social media habits across six categories: news, politics, relationships, entertainment, education, and privacy. The survey was developed, pretested, and refined in the context of a special topics course in Social Media and Participatory Culture, taught in the fall of 2010 at Hofstra University. After extensive primary and secondary research into relevant literature and comparable studies, the survey was built with categories that together reflect a broad framework for main uses of social media today. (1) *News* questions asked about information-consumption habits through social media; (2) *politics* asked questions about local and national politics, elections, voting, and volunteering; (3) *privacy* explored information, expression and identity concerns online, and the willingness to share personal information online; (4) *entertainment* explored student social network use for games, shopping, music, movies, and leisure activities in general; (5) *education* posed questions about social media use in class, with the class, and the effectiveness of social media for education in general; and finally (6) *relationship* questions investigated how social media has or has not affected communication between family, friendships, and significant others.

Approximately eight questions were devoted to each survey category. Initial versions of the survey contained upwards of 12–15 questions, which were narrowed down after pretests, and survey revisions. The survey was administered in the spring semester of 2011, through faculty contacts at nine universities in the eastern part of the United States. The faculty were provided a link to the survey and asked to distribute as widely as possible in their universities. Most began with their courses, and extrapolated to larger bodies if possible. This limits the true randomization of the survey, but with the diverse range of faculty and institutions represented, and the relative diversity of the sample as a whole, the survey did provide valuable insights and generalizations.

Small Group Discussions

After the survey questionnaire was administered, eight focus group discussions were conducted at four of the nine participating universities: Hofstra University, Brooklyn College, Temple University, and the University of Maryland. Students were offered a small fee and refreshments to participate in the

60-minute session, by random selection after they opted to sign up for the sessions. In total 71 students participated in the sessions.

A protocol was developed to complement the survey, specifically exploring student dispositions towards social media and the influence in their lives across the survey categories. The sessions were moderated by the author of the study, and were designed to be as free, open, and interactive as possible. The dialog was loosely structured, with guidance provided at points to maintain boundaries for the discussions. It was not important to cover all of the category areas as it was to find main themes and dispositions of how students perceived social media's role in their daily lives. With over 400 minutes of recorded dialog, the sessions provided depth, reflection, and insight into the data collected through the survey.

The sessions were taped and transcribed by graduate research assistants at Emerson College. A coding protocol was developed by the researchers to locate themes around student dispositions towards the six categories explored in the survey. The graduate research assistants coded the transcriptions for these themes, and from there the data was extrapolated to explore general student dispositions towards social media as a personal, social, and civic platform. The resulting themes were compared to the survey data to find general patterns in the overall study. The large number of participants allowed for vibrant and diverse conversations to take place, resulting in insightful dialog around how social media are influencing students' views on community, society, and democracy.

· APPENDIX C ·

SOCIAL MEDIA HABITS SURVEY

Instructions

This survey inquires about your social media habits. Completing the survey will take approximately 25 minutes. All results and analysis will remain absolutely confidential and anonymous. Thanks for taking the time to answer the survey in full. If you have any comments/questions about the survey, there is space at the end to do so.

BACKGROUND / DEMOGRAPHIC

1. What is your class standing: Freshman   Sophomore   Junior   Senior

2. What is your gender: Male   Female

3. What is your ethnicity:
> African American/Black
> Biracial/Multiracial
> White Americans/European Americans/Caucasians
> Hispanic/Latino/Latina
> Asian American/Pacific Islander

Native American/American Indian
Arab American
Other

4. Parents level of education:

Mother	*Father*
NONE	NONE
Some High School	Some High School
Completed High School	Completed High School
Completed Undergraduate University Degree	Completed Undergraduate Degree
Completed Graduate Degree (Masters/PhD)	Completed Graduate Degree

5. What is your college major?
   What is the state/country where most of your previous education occurred?

6. Have you ever voted before?
   Yes _____   No _____

7. Do you belong to any volunteer organizations?
   Yes _____   No _____

8. On average, how many hours per day do you spend on the Internet?
   0–2   3–4   5–6   7–8   more than 8

9. On average, how many hours per day do you spend on social media sites (Facebook, Twitter, etc.)?
   0–2   3–4   5–6   7–8   more than 8

10. Overall, how would you classify your media use in general?
    Light
    Medium
    Heavy

PART I – NEWS

11. How much time per day do you spend reading/watching news on the Internet?
    Less than 1 _____ 1–2 hours _____ 3–4 hours _____ more than 4 hours _____ I don't get news online _____

12. On an average day, are you more likely to:
Read news in print _____ Listen to news on the radio _____ Watch news on TV _____ Watch/read news online _____ Do all of these equally _____ Do none of these _____

13. Which of the following sites do you get your news from (select all that apply)?
Facebook _____ Twitter _____ Tumblr _____ Digg _____ MyS-pace _____ CNN iReport _____ Wikipedia _____ None of these _____ Other (please specify) _____

14. Do you ever visit *blogs* for news?
Yes _____ No _____

15. If yes to the previous question, how many *blogs* on average do you visit regularly for news?
0–3 _____ 4–7 _____ 8–10 _____ more than 10 _____

16. Do you have a news application on your phone?
Yes _____ No _____
If Yes, please list here _____

17. When looking for news do you (select all that apply):
Visit a specific online news site (i.e., NYTimes, CNN) _____
Google it _____
Go to Facebook _____
Search Twitter _____
Call Family members/friends _____
Pick up a newspaper _____
Turn on the TV _____
None of these _____
Other (please specify below) _____

PART II – FRIENDS & COMMUNITY

18. How have social media affected your friendships?
I feel closer with my friends because of social media _____
It hasn't changed my friendships at all _____
I feel further apart from my friends because of social media _____

Because of social media:
I feel like I have more friends _____
I feel like I have less friends _____
It hasn't changed the number of friends I have _____

19. Do you spend more time talking to friends online or in person?
More time online _____ More time in person _____ About the same _____

20. Are you friends with your parent(s) on Facebook?
Yes _____ No _____

21. Put the following in order of usage when communicating with your family
(1 most often, 7 least often):
Talking on the Phone _____
Facebook _____
e-mail _____
Text Messaging _____
Writing Letters _____
Skype _____
Face-to-Face _____

22. Are you involved in any clubs/organizations that regularly meet face-to-face?
Yes _____ No _____
If yes, list here _____
Have you ever met face to face with anyone you met online?
Yes _____ No _____
Have you ever dated online?
Yes, I still do _____ On occasion _____ I've tried it, but it's not for me
_____ Never have _____

23. In general, how do you prefer to communicate with friends & family?
Nothing beats talking in person _____
Texting and occasionally talking on the phone _____
Using social media is the best way to communicate _____

PART III – POLITICS & DEMOCRACY

24. I get my information about politics from:

Facebook	Often ____	Sometimes ____	Rarely ____	Never ____
Twitter	Often ____	Sometimes ____	Rarely ____	Never ____

Blogs	Often ____	Sometimes ____	Rarely ____	Never ____
Online News Sites	Often ____	Sometimes ____	Rarely ____	Never ____
Email	Often ____	Sometimes ____	Rarely ____	Never ____
TV	Often ____	Sometimes ____	Rarely ____	Never ____
Newspapers	Often ____	Sometimes ____	Rarely ____	Never ____
Word of Mouth	Often ____	Sometimes ____	Rarely ____	Never ____

25. Social media is the primary means of communicating with others about politics.
Strongly Agree _____ Somewhat Agree _____ Somewhat Disagree _____ Strongly Disagree _____

26. I use social media to actively voice my opinions about things going on in the world.
Often _____ Sometimes _____ Rarely _____ Never _____

27. I follow political figures on Twitter?
Yes _____ No _____

28. I belong to a political and/or news group/fanpage on Facebook
Yes, several _____ Only one or two _____ None, I don't use Facebook for that _____

29. Did you vote in the 2008 Presidential election?
Yes _____ No _____

30. Overall, I think social media have:
Made me more aware of politics _____ Made me less aware of politics _____ Not changed my political awareness at all _____

PART IV – EDUCATION

31. How many of your classes use social media for educational purposes?
None _____ 1 _____ 2 _____ 3 _____ 4 _____ All of them _____

32. How often do you use homework assistance sites like sparknotes and freetranslation ?
Often _____ Sometimes _____ Rarely _____ Never _____

33. How many of your classes use assignment submission software, like turnitin?

    None _____ 1 _____ 2 _____ 3 _____ 4 _____ All of them _____

34. How many of your teachers use blackboard or a similar classroom technology to post syllabi and assignments online?

    None _____ 1 _____ 2 _____ 3 _____ 4 _____ All of them _____

35. How often do you use Wikipedia for research?

    Often _____ Sometimes _____ Rarely _____ Never _____

36. Which of the following Internet sites do you use for conducting primary research (check all that apply)?

    Google _____
    Yahoo _____
    Bing _____
    YouTube _____
    Blogs _____
    Encyclopedia.com _____
    Diigo _____
    Other (please specify) _____

37. How often are you deterred from reading passages that look lengthy?

    Always _____ Sometimes _____ Rarely _____ Never _____

38. Social Media have made:

    Classes more interesting
    Strongly Agree _____ Somewhat Agree _____ Somewhat Disagree _____
    Strongly Disagree _____
    Classes easier
    Strongly Agree _____ Somewhat Agree _____ Somewhat Disagree _____
    Strongly Disagree _____
    Learning fun
    Strongly Agree _____ Somewhat Agree _____ Somewhat Disagree _____
    Strongly Disagree _____
    It easier to waste time in class
    Strongly Agree _____ Somewhat Agree _____ Somewhat Disagree _____
    Strongly Disagree _____

Teachers out of touch with students
Strongly Agree _____ Somewhat Agree _____ Somewhat Disagree _____
Strongly Disagree _____
Learning more dynamic
Strongly Agree _____ Somewhat Agree _____ Somewhat Disagree _____
Strongly Disagree _____
No difference in the classroom at all
Strongly Agree _____ Somewhat Agree _____ Somewhat Disagree _____
Strongly Disagree _____

39. Have you ever taken a course entirely online?
    Yes _____ No _____

PART V – LEISURE & ENTERTAINMENT

How often do you:
40. Shop online
    Often _____ Sometimes _____ Rarely _____ Never _____

41. Shop with your mobile phone
    Often _____ Sometimes _____ Rarely _____ Never _____

42. Watch TV shows online for free
    Often _____ Sometimes _____ Rarely _____ Never _____

43. Download and share music for free
    Often _____ Sometimes _____ Rarely _____ Never _____

44. Purchase music from iTunes (or similar platform)
    Often _____ Sometimes _____ Rarely _____ Never _____

45. Purchase CDs
    Often _____ Sometimes _____ Rarely _____ Never _____

46. Download movies from the Internet for free
    Often _____ Sometimes _____ Rarely _____ Never _____

47. Read peer reviews of movies/shows to determine if you will watch them
    Often _____ Sometimes _____ Rarely _____ Never _____

48. Do you trust sharing personal information (credit cards) with online merchants?
Yes _____ Only with major retailers _____ No, but I share it anyway _____ I don't share personal information online _____

49. When was the last time you left your house to rent a movie?
Within the last week _____ Within the last month _____ It's been months _____ I can't remember it's been so long _____

I spend my free time:
50. On Social Media sites
Very likely ____ Somewhat likely ____ Not very likely ____ Rarely ____ Never ____

51. Browsing the Internet
Very likely _____ Somewhat likely _____ Not very likely _____ Rarely _____ Never _____

52. Watching TV
Very likely _____ Somewhat likely _____ Not very likely _____ Rarely _____ Never _____

53. Playing online games
Very likely _____ Somewhat likely _____ Not very likely _____ Rarely _____ Never _____

54. Hanging around with friends
Very likely _____ Somewhat likely _____ Not very likely _____ Rarely _____ Never _____

55. Reading
Very likely _____ Somewhat likely _____ Not very likely _____ Rarely _____ Never _____

56. Away from media altogether
Very likely _____ Somewhat likely _____ Not very likely _____ Rarely _____ Never _____

57. Other (please specify) _____

PART VI – PRIVACY & EXPRESSION

58. How concerned are you about your privacy online?
    Very concerned _____ Somewhat concerned _____ Not really concerned _____ I don't think about it at all _____

59. Do you feel that the social media sites you use do a good job of protecting your privacy?
    Yes, they do a very good job _____ Somewhat _____ Not all _____ I don't really know _____ I don't really care _____

60. Do you free that you have control over your online identity?
    Yes, complete control _____ For the most part _____ Not really _____ I have no idea about all the information out there about me, and I don't care _____

61. Are you concerned that your online identity will have an influence on your future career?
    Very _____ Somewhat _____ Not at all _____

62. I read the privacy policies of the social networking sites I belong to?
    Always _____ Sometimes _____ Rarely _____ Never _____

63. How much personal information do you make public on Facebook?
    Everything _____ Most information, but I keep some private _____ Only a bit of my information is public _____ None _____

64. When using the following media, do you use your real name or a fake profile?
Email	Real name _____	Fake name _____	Never used it _____
Blog	Real name _____	Fake name _____	Never used it _____
Facebook	Real name _____	Fake name _____	Never used it _____
Twitter	Real name _____	Fake name _____	Never used it _____
SMS (cell)	Real name _____	Fake name _____	Never used it _____
Online Chat	Real name _____	Fake name _____	Never used it _____

65. Do you know anyone who has experienced a safety issue as a direct result of his or her social media use?
    Yes _____ No _____

66. If Yes, what was the issue _____

PART VII – CONCLUSION

67. In the space below please fill out any additional comments, suggestions, reflections on social media and your life.

Thanks for taking the survey, all questions can be directed to:

· APPENDIX D ·

SMALL GROUP DISCUSSION PROTOCOL

Opening

Thank you for participating in this discussion. The point of this session is to have an open and free dialog about the role of social media in our lives. Specifically, we'll explore four topics:

RQ1: *How is social media changing our lives in the 21st century?*
RQ2: *How have social media changed how we communicate with friends, family, etc.?*
RQ3: *How have social media changed our information consumption and sharing habits?*
RQ4: *How have social media influenced civic society and democracy today?*

Introduction

- Discuss what social media means for this study

Part I (15–20 min) – Social Media's Role In Your Life

- How many hours a day do you spend with Social media?
- What is the main thing you do on Social Networks?
- How big a role do you think Social Media have in your life?
- What the most positive/negative influences of Social Media in general? In your life specifically?

Part II (15–20 Minutes) – Friends & Family

- Are all your family members on Facebook? Are you Facebook friends with your family?
- How do you think Facebook has influenced your family relationships? Do you feel it has made you closer? Not changed anything?
- Are there examples of times when you have entered into an awkward family situation because of Social Media?
- Do you think Social Media have made you closer with your friends?
- Has Facebook eliminated the need for face-to-face interaction?
- What about relationships? What have social media done to those?

Part III (15–20 Minutes) – News, Citizenship, And Democracy

- How have social media influenced news?
- Do you think social media have helped or hurt news? How about democracy?
- What do you think social media, like Facebook, will do to politics in the future?

Part IV (15–20 Minutes) – Privacy, Expression, Society

- Do you feel like your identity is secure online?
- Do you think social media are going to have an influence on your career?
- Are you comfortable with all the public sharing that happens with personal information? Why or why not?

Closing

- How much longer will social media be around? Why? What's next?

Anything anyone would like to add at all, that we haven't discussed? Any Questions?

Thanks!

· APPENDIX E ·

5A'S MEDIA LITERACY
SYLLABUS EXCERPT

This syllabus was excerpted from a Spring 2011 course taught at Hofstra University, in Hempstead, NY. The readings may be somewhat dated in this respect, but the cohesion of topics and progression of the course reflect the 5A's model presented in this book.

Course Outline, Readings, Assignments

Week	Topic	Reading	Assignments
#1	Introductions / Course Overview / Love-Hate Media		
#2	My Identity / My Media Profile	*Watch: Ethan Zuckerman, Global Voices* Gillmor, Principles for a New Media Literacy	*My Identity / My Media Profile Part I*

Week	Topic	Reading	Assignments
#3	The Core Principles of Media Literacy: The 5A's	• Mihailidis, 5A's Handout • Mihailidis, Beyond Cynicism • True Enough – Intro, 1	Reading Contribution
#4	ACCESS Can you own information?	Media Ownership Handouts	Reading Contribution
#5	ACCESS **Regulators vs. Deregulators Debate**	True Enough – 2–4	**ACCESS – Time Stamp**
#6	AWARENESS Bias, Context, Values....and Loose Change	True Enough – 5–6, Epilogue	Reading Contribution
#7	**FILM SPOTLIGHT #1 Control Room**	*Film: Control Room*	**Film Discussion**
#8	AWARENESS Comparing Global Images – Katrina vs. Tsunami vs. Haiti	*none*	**AWARENESS - Forgotten Worlds Image Essay**
#9	ASSESSMENT News and Journalism in a Digital Age	Tuned Out, 1–4	
#10	ASSESSMENT Social Media and Civic Voice **Debate – New Media & New News**	Tuned Out, 5–7	Reading Contribution
#11	APPRECIATION 5 Songs at My Funeral – expression and culture	Here Comes Everybody, Intro, 1–5	**ASSESSMENT – Media Literacy Case Study Presen-tations & Drafts**
#12	**FILM SPOTLIGHT #2 Food, Inc.**	*Film: Food, Inc.* Here Comes Everybody – 6, 7, 8	

Week	Topic	Reading	Assignments
#13	APPRECIATION: What does a Media Literate Person look like?	Here Comes Everybody, 9–11	Reading Contribution
#14	ACTION – PSA Screenings, contest & Q&A	*none*	**Media Literacy PSA Screenings**
#15	ACTION: Looking Forward – The 5A's: A framework for your civic life	*none*	*My Identity, My Media Profile, Part II*

ASSIGMENT SNAPSHOT
ACCESS – Media Time Stamp
AWARENESS – Forgotten Worlds
ASSESSMENT – Case Study
APPRECIATION – PSA
ACTION – Contributions

NOTES

1. Walter Lippmann, in *Public Opinion*, and other works, formed early ideas about weak tie engagement in society. He was pessimistic about the public's ability to engage with complex civic issues, not because of barriers to access, but more because they lacked the inquisitive disposition or care to. He wrote in *Public Opinion*, "The mass of the reading public is not interested in learning and assimilating the results of accurate investigation." Lippmann believed that citizens "were too self-centred to care about public policy except as pertaining to pressing local issues."
2. Of course, the reasons to not cover this murder nationally can be understood through mechanisms for judging newsworthiness. Unfortunately, senseless killings like this happen all too often, and a majority never garners the type of coverage that this case has.
3. The debate outlined by Buckingham here is explained in greater detail in my doctoral dissertation, titled "Beyond Cynicism: How Media Literacy Can Make Students More Engaged Citizens." The following few paragraphs are excerpted and paraphrased from a more detailed exploration.
4. Parts of this section are adapted from Mihailidis' (2008) *Beyond Cynicism: How Media Literacy Can Make Students More Engaged Citizens*. I would also like to thank here Benjamin Thevenin for his artful expression of media literacy and engaged citizenship, which helped form many of the ideas in this section.
5. Taken from the 2006 publication, *Global Trends in Media Education*, by Tony Lavender, Birgitte Tufte, and Dafna Lemish, (Eds.). See references for full citation.

6. These three points were excerpted from Mihailidis & Thevenin (2013) "Media literacy as a core competency for engaged citizenship in participatory democracy," *American Behavioral Scientist*, 57(9), 1611–1622.

7. For an entire book on this topic, see: Henry Jenkins, Sam Ford, and Joshua Green's *Spreadable Media: Creating Value and Meaning in a Networked Culture*. MIT Press, 2013.

8. www.change.org

9. From fivethirtyeight.com: "FiveThirtyEight's mission is to help *New York Times* readers cut through the clutter of this data-rich world. The blog is devoted to rigorous analysis of politics, polling, public affairs, sports, science and culture, largely through statistical means. In addition, FiveThirtyEight provides forecasts of upcoming presidential, Congressional and gubernatorial elections through the use of its proprietary prediction models." FiveThirtyEight was founded by Nate Silver in March 2008, and was licensed by the *Times* in August 2010. It is produced in conjunction with the *Times* graphic and interactive journalists and its team of political editors, correspondents and polling experts." http://fivethirtyeight.blogs.nytimes.com/about-fivethirtyeight/

10. In *Here Comes Everybody*, Shirky explains group dynamics in some length (267–68). He differentiates the relative difference in group size as an influence on their outcomes: "By understanding these two basic constraints of group action—number of people involved and duration of interaction—any given tool, new or familiar, can be analyzed for goodness of fit" (268). In this book I am focusing on the attributes of media literate groups, and so take liberties at exploring the group function through the individual lens, and not for the organizational outcomes and group dynamics. For group dynamics, see books by Howe (2008), Surowiecki (2005), Shirky (2010), and Tapscott and Williams (2006).

11. Jenkins coins the term in his 2006 Book, *Convergence Culture: Where Old and New Media Collide* (p. 134) to discuss the relationship between fans and organizations, citing the Star Wars franchise.

12. The data here and in Chapter Five were published in *Information, Communication, and Society* in a paper titled: "The Civic-Social Media Disconnect: Exploring Perceptions of Social Media for Engagement in the Daily Life of College Students". DOI:10.1080/1369118X.2013.877054

13. See Appendix B for complete methodology and Appendix C for the survey.

14. The participating universities in this study were: Brooklyn College, Drexel University, Florida International University, Hofstra University, Montclair State University, Penn State University, Temple University, the University of Maryland, and Wheelock College.

15. There was a mortality rate in the survey of around 100. So in some questions, that were filled incorrectly or skipped, the number of responses can be in the lower 800s. The overall large number of participants, however, justifies the results of the study, and the mortality rate is therefore insignificant to the points made in the book.

16. For reasons of confidentiality, the names of the student participants are not included in these write-ups. The students were all undergraduates at four universities in the United States: Brooklyn College, Hofstra University, Temple University, and the University of Maryland. The write-ups here incorporate their views holistically and do not personalize or differentiate based on location. Because the conversations were not about specific programs or tools, and structured the same way for each group, there was no inherent reason to differentiate names or separate interview sessions.

17. A few of the small discussion groups took place during the tsunami that ravaged the Japanese coast and caused a nuclear shutdown, and many students talked about the role Facebook played in informing them of this event from a number of different angles.

18. In a few instances, students did mention local television news as a way to find out what was happening in their immediate communities. This was in the context of being in their homes either in the early morning or with parents.

19. See full story, "Students Find Ways To Hack School-Issued iPads Within A Week" at: http://www.npr.org/blogs/alltechconsidered/2013/09/27/226654921/students-find-ways-to-hack-school-issued-ipads-within-a-week

20. See the full *Connected Learning* Manifesto at: http://dmlhub.net/sites/default/files/Connected_Learning_report.pdf And visit their web site at: http://connectedlearning.tv/

21. See full Participatory Politics report at: http://dmlhub.net/sites/default/files/YPP_Survey_Report_FULL%281%29.pdf

22. Two approaches are of particular relevance to the framework I advance below. In 2005, Douglas Kellner and Jeff Share published an article titled "Toward Critical Media Literacy: Core Concepts, Debates, Organizations, and Policy," in which they advance a theoretical model for critical media literacy. The authors build on Kellner's work in multiple literacies and multiculturalism in media culture (see Kellner, 1995a, 1995b, 1998, 2004; Kellner & Share, 2009), to argue that the foundations of media literacy education must be expanded to address culture, citizenship, and democratic participation. Kellner & Share see critical media literacy as "tied to the project of radical democracy and concerned with developing skills that will enhance democratization and participation. It takes a comprehensive approach that would teach critical skills and how to use media as instruments of social communication and change" (p. 372). Kellner and Share advocate for media literacy education creating more open and transparent dialog about politics, race, gender, sex, and ethnicity in our culture. At the same time, they acknowledge the potential problems of pervasive media culture can advance, among them hyperviolence, sexism, homophobia, ethnocentrism, and racism.

In 2010, Hobbs developed five digital and media literacy competencies—*Access, Analyze, Create, Reflect, Act*—that she framed with two overarching questions: "How can educators make use of popular culture, mass media, and digital technologies to help students develop *critical thinking skills?*" and "How do students learn to be responsible and effective communicators with an appreciation of the human condition in all it's complexity?" (p. viii). Hobbs uses this framework to advocate for digital and media literacy that teaches about news and current events in ways that are engaging for students and that stem from a personal interest they have. Hobbs' five-point framework positions media literacy education to meet youth at their starting point and build effective teaching and learning experiences from there. She notes:

> A generational shift in citizenship styles is occurring. Increased mistrust of the media means young people may not believe much of what they hear, see, or read on the news. Many young people are focused on personal, individual expression, not on working collaboratively to make changes in their community. Instead of joining a local political party or running for office, young adults may participate in networks of interest-group communities, base on issues like the environment, jobs, gender equity, democracy in developing nations, or social justice. (p. 149)

Both of these frameworks are readily available, in various forms of publication, and come highly recommended.

23. The Salzburg Academy was born as a project of the Salzburg Global Seminar, a non-profit institution that for almost 70 years has convened imaginative thinkers from different cultures and institutions, organizes problem-focused initiatives, supports leadership development, and engages opinion-makers through active communication networks, all in partnership with leading institutions from around the world and across different sectors of society. The Seminar's mission is to challenge present and future leaders to solve issues of global concern.

REFERENCES

Acquisti, A., & Gross, R. (2006). Imagined communities: Awareness, information sharing, and privacy on the Facebook. In *Privacy enhancing technologies* (pp. 36–58). Springer Berlin Heidelberg.

Adams, D., & Hamm, M. (2001). *Literacy in a multimedia age*. Norwood, MA: Christopher-Gordon.

Allan, S. (2012). "Civic voices: Social media and political protest." In P. Mihailidis (Ed.) *News literacy: Global perspectives for the newsroom and the classroom*. New York: Peter Lang, 23–39.

Allan, S. (2013) *Citizen witnessing: Revisioning journalism in a time of crisis*. Cambridge, England: Polity.

Alvermann, D. E., Moon, J. S., & Hagood, M. C. (1999). *Popular culture in the classroom: Teaching and researching critical media literacy. Literacy studies series*. International Reading Association, Web site: http://www. reading. org.

Alvermann, D. E., & Hagood, M. C. (2000). Critical media literacy: Research, theory, and practice in "New Times." *The Journal of Educational Research*, 93(3), 193–205.

Anderson, S. (2011, April 19). Young people using social media for more than just socializing. *AOL News*. Retrieved: http://www.aolnews.com/2011/04/19/young-people-using-social-media-for-more-than-just-socializing/

Arke, E.T. (2005). Media literacy and critical thinking: Is there a connection? Dissertation, School of Education, Duquesne University, August.

Aufderheide, P., & Firestone, C. M. (1993). *Media literacy: A report of the national leadership conference on media literacy*. Cambridge, UK: Polity Press.

Bagdikian, B. H. (2004). *The new media monopoly: A completely revised and updated edition with seven new chapters*. Boston, MA: Beacon Press.

Baker, C. E. (2007). *Media concentration and democracy*. New York: Cambridge University Press.

Baker, F. W. (2012). *Media literacy in the k-12 classroom*. Eugene, OR: International Society for Technology in Education.

Barabasi, A. L. (2003). *Linked - How everything else is connected to everything else and what it means for business, science, and everyday life*. New York: Penguin Group.

Barber, B. (2002). The educated student: Global citizen or global consumer? *Liberal Education*, Spring: 22–29.

Barber, B. (2007). *Consumed: How markets corrupt children, infantilize adults, and swallow citizens whole*. New York: Norton.

Barnes, S. B. (2006). A privacy paradox: Social networking in the United States. *First Monday*, 11(9), 11–15.

Bartlett, J., & Miller, C. (2011). Truth, Lies and the Internet: A report into young people's digital fluency. *Demos*. Retrieved: http://www.demos.co.uk/files/Truth_web.pdf

Beer, D., & Burrows, R. (2010). Consumption, prosumption and participatory web cultures: An introduction. *Journal of Consumer Culture*, 10(1), 3–12.

Behrman, E. H. (2006). Teaching about language, power, and text: A review of classroom practices that support critical literacy. *Journal of Adolescent & Adult Literacy*, 49, 490–499.

Benjamin, W. (2008). *The work of art in the age of mechanical reproduction*. New York: Penguin.

Benkler, Y. (2005). *The wealth of networks: How social networks transform markets and freedom*. New Haven, CT: Yale University Press.

Benkler, Y., & Nissenbaum, H. (2006), Commons-based peer production and virtue. *Journal of Political Philosophy*, 14, 394–419.

Bennett, W. L. (2007). *Changing citizenship in the digital age*. Prepared for OECD/INDIRE conference on millennial learners, March 2007. Retrieved: http://spotlight.macfound.org/resources/Bennett-Changing_Citizenship_in_Digital_Age-OECD.pdf

Bennett, W. L. (2008). "Changing citizenship in the digital age." In W.L. Bennett (Ed.) *Civic life online: Learning how digital media can engage youth*. The John D. and Catherine T. MacArthur Foundation Series on Digital Media and Learning. Cambridge, MA: MIT Press, 1–24.

Bennett, W. L., & Segerberg, A. (2011). Digital media and the personalization of collective action: Social technology and the organization of protests against the global economic crisis. *Information, Communication & Society*, 14, 770–799.

Bennett, W. L., & Segerberg, A. (2012). The logic of connective action. *Information, Communication & Society*, 15(5), 739–768.

Bennett, W. L., & Wells, C. (2009). Civic engagement: Bridging differences to build a field of civic learning. *International Journal of Learning and Media*, 1/3, 1–10.

Bennett, W. L., Wells, C., & Freelon, D. (2010) "Civic media: The generational shift from mainstream news to digital networks." In L. Sherrod, J. Torney-Purta & C. Flanagan (Eds.) *The handbook of youth engagement*. New York: Wiley, 393–424.

Bennett, W. L., Wells, C., & Freelon, D. (2011) Communicating civic engagement: Contrasting models of citizenship in the youth web sphere. *Journal of Communication* 61, 835–856.

Berman, M. G., Jonides, J., & Kaplan, S. (2008). The cognitive benefits of interacting with nature. *Psychological Science*, 19(12), 1207–1212.

Bilton, N. (2010, May 12). The price of Facebook privacy? Start clicking. Retrieved: http://www.nytimes.com/2010/05/13/technology/personaltech…

Bimber, B. (1998). The Internet and political transformation: Populism, community and accelerated pluralism. *Polity*, 3, 133–160.

Bimber, B. (2000). The study of information technology and civic engagement. *Political Communication*, 17(4), 329–333.

Bimber, B. (2001). Information and political engagement in America: The search for effects of information technology at the individual level. *Political Research Quarterly*, 54, 53–67.

Boler, M. (Ed.). (2010). *Digital media and democracy: Tactics in hard times*. Cambridge, MA: MIT Press.

Botsman, R., & Rodgers, R. (2010). *What's mine is yours: The rise of collaborative consumption*. New York: Harper Business.

boyd, d.m. (2006). Friends, friendsters, and myspace top 8: Writing community into being on social network sites. *First Monday*, 11(12).

boyd, d.m. (2009). Why youth (heart) social network sites: The role of networked publics in teenage social life. *Social Science Research Network*. Retrieved: http://papers.ssrn.com/sol3/papers.cfm?abstract_id=1518924

boyd, d.m. (2010). "Facebook and radical transparency." danah boyd. Apophenia. http://www.zephoria.org/thoughts/archives/2010/05/14/facebook-and-radical-transparency-a-rant.html (May 24).

boyd, d.m., & Ellison, N. B. (2007). Social network sites: Definition, history, and scholarship. *Journal of Computer-Mediated Communication*, 13: 210–230.

boyd, d.m., & Marwick, A. (2011). Social privacy in networked publics: Teens' attitudes, practices, and strategies. *Social Science Research Network*. Retrieved: https://papers.ssrn.com/sol3/papers.cfm?abstract_id=1925128

Boyd-Barrett, O., & Newbold, C. (1995). *Approaches to media: A reader*. New York: Hodder Arnold.

Brabham, D. C. (2008). Crowdsourcing as a model for problem solving an introduction and cases. *Convergence: The International Journal of Research Into New Media Technologies*, 14(1), 75–90.

Brasel, S.A., & Gips, J. (2011). Media multitasking behavior: Concurrent television and computer usage. *Cyberpsychology, Behavior, and Social Networking* 14(9), 527–534.

Brooks Young, S. (2010). *Teaching with the tools kids really use: Learning with web and mobile technologies*. Thousand Oaks, CA: Corwin.

Brownell, G., & Brownell, N. (2003). Media literacy and technology in a media-saturated democracy. Refereed proceeding from *The National Social Science Perspectives Journal*. El Cajon, CA: National Social Science Association.

Bryant, J., & Oliver, M. B. (2009). *Media effects: Advances in theory and research* (Vol. 10). New York: Taylor & Francis.

Buckingham, D. (1993). *The making of citizens: Young people, news, and politics*. London: Routledge.

Buckingham, D. (1994). *Children talking television: The making of television literacy*. London: Falmer.

Buckingham, D. (2003). *Media education: Literacy, learning and contemporary culture*. Cambridge, UK: Polity Press.

Buckingham, D. (2005). Will media education ever escape the effects debate? *Telemedium: The Journal of Media Literacy* 52(3) (summer): 17–21.

Buckingham, D. (2007). *Beyond technology: Children's learning in the age of digital culture.* Cambridge, UK: Polity.

Buckingham, D. (Ed.). (2008). *Youth, identity, and digital media.* Cambridge, MA: MIT Press.

Burke, M., Marlow, C., & Lento, T. (2010, April). Social network activity and social well-being. In *Proceedings of the 28th international conference on human factors in computing systems.* ACM, 1909–1912.

Byron, T. (2010, January). Do we have safer children in a digital world? A review of progress since the 2008 Byron Review. *The Byron Review.*

Carducci, R., & Rhoads, R. A. (2005). Of minds and media: Teaching critical citizenship to the plugged-in generation. *About Campus* (November-December): 2–9.

Carr, N. (2011). *The shallows: What the Internet is doing to our brains.* New York: W. W. Norton and Company.

Castells, M. (2012). *Networks of outrage and hope: Social movements in the Internet age.* Cambridge, UK: Polity Press.

Center for Media Literacy (ND). *Aspen Institute report of the national leadership conference on media literacy:* Washington, DC. Retrieved: http://www.medialit.org/reading_room/article582.html

Chadwick, A., & Howard, P. N. (Eds.). (2010). *Routledge handbook of Internet politics.* London: Taylor & Francis.

Change.org (ND) About. Retrieved: http://www.change.org/about

Christ, W. G. (2004). Assessment, media literacy standards, and higher education. *American Behavioral Scientist* 48(1): 92–96.

Christ, W. G. (Ed.). (2006). *Assessing media education: A resources handbook for educators and administrators.* Mahwah, NJ: Lawrence Erlbaum Associates.

Christ, W. G., & Potter, W. J. (1998). Media literacy, media education, and the academy. *Journal of Communication* 48(1): 5–15.

Christakis, N. A., & Fowler, J. (2011). *Connected – How your friends' friends' friends affect everything you feel, think, and do.* New York: Back Bay Books.

Clapp, W. C., Rubens, M. T., Sabharwal, J., & Gazzaley, A. (2011). Deficit in switching between functional brain networks underlies the impact of multitasking on working memory in older adults. *Proceedings of the National Academy of Sciences,* 108(17), 7212–7217.

Clarke, J., Hall, S., Jefferson, T., Roberts, B. (1976). "Subcultures, Cultures and Class." In S. Hall & T. Jefferson (Eds.) *Resistance through rituals.* London: Routledge.

Cohen, C., & Kahne, J. (2012). Participatory politics: New media and youth political action. *MacArthur Research Network on Youth and Participatory Politics.* Available: http://dmlhub.net/sites/default/files/YPP_Survey_Report_FULL%281%29.pdf

Coiro, J., Knobel, M., Lankshear, C., & Leu, D. J. (2008). *Handbook of research on new literacies.* London: Routledge.

Coleman, S., & Price, V. (2012). "Democracy, distance and reach: The new media landscape." In S. Coleman & P. Shane (Eds.) *Connecting democracy: Online consultation and the flow of political communication,* (23–43). Cambridge, MA: MIT Press.

Coleman, S., & Shane, P. (Eds.). (2012). *Connecting democracy: Online consultation and the flow of political communication*. Cambridge, MA: MIT Press.

Cooper, M. (2003). *Media ownership and democracy in the digital information age*. Stanford, CA: Center for Internet and Society.

Center for the Internet and Society, Stanford Law School, cyberlaw. Available: http://Stanford. edu/blogs/cooper/archives/mediabooke

Courts, P. L. (1998). *Multicultural literacies: Dialect, discourses, and diversity*. New York: Peter Lang.

Croteau, D., & Hoynes, W. (2005). *The business of media: Corporate media and the public interest*. Sage Publications, Incorporated.

Croteau, D., Hoynes, W., & Milan, S. (2011). *Media/society: Industries, images, and audiences*. Thousand Oaks, CA: Sage.

Dahlgren, P. (2003). Reconfiguring civic culture in the new media milieu. In J. Corner & D. Pels (Eds.) *Media and the restyling of politics: Consumerism, celebrity, and cynicism*, London: SAGE Publications Ltd, 151–170.

Dahlgren, P. (2006). Doing citizenship: The culture origins of civic agency in the public sphere. *European Journal of Cultural Studies, 9(3)*, 267–286.

Dahlgren, P. (Ed.). (2007). *Young citizens and new media: Learning democratic engagement*. London: Routledge.

Dahlgren, P. (2009). *Media and political engagement: Citizens, communication and democracy*. Cambridge, UK: Cambridge University Press.

Dahlgren, P. (2012). Young citizens and political participation online media and civic cultures, *Taiwan Journal of Democracy, 7(2)*, 11–25.

Dalton, R. (2009). *The good citizen: How a younger generation is reshaping American politics*. Washington, DC: CQ Press.

Davis, B. G. (2009). *Tools for teaching*. New York: Jossey-Bass.

De Abreu, B. S. (2007). *Teaching media literacy: A how-to-do-it manual and CD-ROM* (No. 156). Chicago: Neal Schuman.

De Abreu, B. (2011). *Media literacy, social networks, and the web 2.0 environment for the k-12 educator*. New York: Peter Lang.

De Abreu, B., & Mihailidis, P. (Eds.). (2014). *Media literacy education in action: Theoretical and pedagogical perspectives*. London: Routledge.

Dean, J. (2005). Communicative capitalism: Circulation and the foreclosure of politics. *Cultural Politics, 1(1)*, 101–137.

Delli Carpini, M. X. (2000). Gen.com: Youth, civic engagement, and the new information environment. *Political Communication, 17(4)*, 341–349.

Deuze, M. (2006). Participation, remediation, bricolage: Considering principal components of a digital culture. *The Information Society, 22(2)*, 63–75.

Dewey, J. (1916). *Democracy and education*. New York: Free Press.

Dewey, J. (1927a/1954). *The public and its problems*. Chicago: Swallow.

Dewey, J. (1938). *Experience and education*. New York: Collier Books.

Duhigg, C. (2013). *The power of habit: Why we do what we do, and how to change.* New York: Random House.

Dunne, Á. (2011). Young people's use of online social networking sites: A uses and gratifications perspective. *Journal of Research in Interactive Marketing* 4(1) (ND): ProQuest Central (SRU). 10 Nov.

Earl, J., Hurwitz, H.M., Mesinas, A.M., Tolan, M., & Arlotti, A. (2013). This protest will be tweeted. *Information, Communication, and Society,* 16(4), 459–478.

Eliasoph, N. (1990). Political culture and the presentation of a political 'self', *Theory and Society,* 19(3), 465–94.

Ellison, N.B., Steinfield, C. & Lampe, C. (2007) The benefits of Facebook 'friends': Exploring the relationship between college students' use of online social networks and social capital. *Journal of Computer-Mediated Communication* 12: 1143–1168.

Ellison, N.B., Steinfield, C., & Lampe, C. (2010). Connection strategies: Social capital implications of Facebook-enabled communication practices, *New Media & Society,* 13(6), 873–892.

Erstad, O., Gilje, O., & de Lange, T. (2007). Re mixing multimodal resources: Multiliteracies and digital production in Norwegian media education, *Learning, Media and Technology,* 32/2, 183–198.

Feuerstein, M. (1999). Media literacy in support of critical thinking. *Journal of Educational Media,* 24(1), 43–54.

Fields, D., & Grimes, S. (2012). Kids online: A new research agenda for understanding social networking forums. *Digital Media and Learning Research Hub,* Fall. Available: http://dml-hub.net/sites/default/files/jgcc_kidsonline.pdf

Franzoni, A. L., Assar, S., Defude, B., & Rojas, J. (2008, July). Student learning styles adaptation method based on teaching strategies and electronic media. In *Advanced Learning Technologies, 2008. ICALT'08. Eighth IEEE International Conference,* 778–782.

Frechette, J.D. (2002). *Developing media literacy in cyberspace: Pedagogy and critical learning for the twenty-first-century classroom.* Westport, CT: Praeger.

Freire, P. (1970). *Pedagogy of the oppressed.* New York: Seabury Press.

Fowler, J., & Christakis, N. (2010). Cooperative behavior cascades in human social networks. *Proceedings of the National Academy of Sciences,* 107/12, 5334–5338.

Gaines, E. (2010). *Media literacy and semiotics.* New York: Palgrave.

Gamson, W.A. (1992). *Talking politics.* Cambridge, UK: Cambridge University Press.

Garrett, R. K. (2006). Protest in an information society: A review of literature on social movements and new ICTs. *Information Communication and Society,* 9(2), 202–224.

Gil de Zúñiga, H., Jung, N., & Valenzuela, S. (2012). Social media use for news and individuals' social capital, civic engagement and political participation. *Journal of Computer-Mediated Communication,* 17(3), 319–336.

Gladwell, M. (2010). Small change. *New Yorker,* 4, 108–111.

Global Voices. (ND). About global voices. Retrieved: http://globalvoicesonline.org/about/

Goggin, G. (2009). Adapting the mobile phone: The iPhone and its consumption. *Continuum.* 23/2, 231–244.

Goodman, S. (2003). *Teaching youth media: A critical guide to literacy, video production & social change* (Vol. 36). New York: Teachers College Press.

Gordon, E. (2013). Beyond participation: Designing for the civic web. *Journal of Digital and Media Literacy*, 1(1).

Granovetter, M. S. (1973). The strength of weak ties. *American Journal of Sociology*, 78(6), 1360–1380.

Guerrero, M., & Luengas Restrepo, M. (2012). Media literate "prodiences": Binding the knot of news content and production for an open society. In P. Mihailidis (Ed.) *News literacy: Global perspectives for the newsroom and the classroom*. New York: Peter Lang, 41–62.

Gutiérrez, A., & Tyner, K. (2012). Media education, media literacy and digital competence Educación para los medios, alfabetización mediática y competencia digital, 4–7.

Habermas, J. (1989). *The structural transformation of the public sphere*. Cambridge, MA: MIT Press.

Hall, P. (1999). The effect of meditation on the academic performance of African American college students, *Journal of Black Studies*, 29(3), January, 408–415.

Hall, S. (1980). "Encoding/decoding." In S. Hall, D. Hobson, A. Lowe & P. Willis (Eds.) *Culture, media, language*. London: Hutchinson.

Hall, S., & Whannel, P. (1964). *The popular arts*. London: Hutchinson.

Harfoush, R. (2009). *Yes we did!: An inside look at how social media built the Obama brand*. New Riders Press.

Hargittai, E. (2005). Survey measures of web-oriented digital literacy. *Social Science Computer Review*, 23, 371–379.

Hartley-Brewer, E. (2009). *Making friends: A guide to understanding and nurturing your child's friendships*. Cambridge, MA: De Capo Press.

Haythornthwaite, C. (2005). Social networks and Internet connectivity effects. *Information, Communication & Society* 8: 125–147.

Heins, M., & Cho, C. (2003). Media literacy: An alternative to censorship, second edition. *The Free Policy Expression Project*. Retrieved: http://www.fepproject.org/policyreports/medialiteracy2d.html#112

Hindman, M. (2009). *The myth of digital democracy*. Princeton, NJ: Princeton University Press.

Hobbs, R. (1998). The seven great debates in the media literacy movement. *Journal of Communication*, 48(1), 6–32.

Hobbs, R. (2007). *Reading the media: Media literacy in high school English*. New York: Teachers College Press.

Hobbs, R. (2008). "Debates and challenges facing new literacies in the 21st century." In S. Livingstone & K. Drotner (Eds.) *International handbook of children, media, and culture*. Thousand Oaks, CA: Sage, 1–38.

Hobbs, R. (2010). *"Digital and media literacy: A plan of action,"* A white paper on the digital and media literacy recommendations of the knight commission on the information needs of communities in a democracy. Washington DC: The Aspen Institute.

Hobbs, R. (2011a). *Digital and media literacy: Connecting culture and classroom*. Thousand Oaks, CA: Corwin Press.

Hobbs, R. (2011b). Empowering learners with digital and media literacy. *Knowledge Quest*, 39(5), 12–17.

Hobbs, R., & Frost, R. (2003). Measuring the acquisition of media-literacy skills. *Reading Research Quarterly* 38(3), July/August/September, 330–355.

Hobbs, R., & Cooper Moore, D. (2013). *Discovering media literacy: Teaching digital media and popular culture in elementary school*. Thousand Oaks, CA: Corwin Press.

Hobbs, R., Hope Culver, S., & Mendoza, K. (2010). *Empowering parents and protecting children in an evolving media landscape*. A report for the Federal Communications Commission. February 1.

Hoechsmann, M., & Poyntz, S. R. (2012). *Media literacies: A critical introduction*. New York: Wiley-Blackwell.

Hoggart, R. (1959). *The uses of literacy*. London: Chatto & Windus.

Horkheimer, M. (1937). "Traditional and critical theory." In M. Horkheimer (Ed.) *Critical theory: Selected essays*. New York: Continuum.

Horkheimer, M., & Adorno, T. (1967). *Dialectic of enlightenment: Philosophical fragments*. Stanford, CA: Stanford University Press.

Howe, J. (2008). *Crowdsourcing: Why the power of the crowd is driving the future of business*. New York: Three Rivers Press.

Ito, M. (2005)."Technologies of the childhood imagination: Yugioh, media mixes and everyday cultural production." In J. Karaganis & N. Jeremijenko (Eds.) *Network/Netplay: Structures of participation in digital culture*. Durham, NC: Duke University Press.

Ito, M. (2009). *Living and learning with new media: Summary of findings from the digital youth project*. Cambridge, MA: MIT Press.

Ito, M., Gutiérrez, K., Livingston, S., Penuel, B., Rhodes, J., Salen, K., Schor, J., Sefton-Green, J., & Watkins, S.C. (2012). *Connected learning: An agenda for research and design*. A research synthesis report of the Connected Learning Research Network http://dmlhub. net/sites/default/files/ConnectedLearning_summary_0.pdf

Jacobs, L.R., Cook, F.L., & Delli Carpini, M.X. (2009). *Talking together: Public deliberation and political participation in America*. Chicago: University of Chicago Press.

Jefferson, T. (1820). To William C. Jarvis. Charlottesville, Va.: Thomas Jefferson Foundation. Retrieved on 18 December 2007 at: http://etext.virginia.edu/jefferson/quotations/jeff0350. htm

Jenkins, H. (2006a). *Convergence culture: Where old and new media collide*. New York: NYU Press.

Jenkins, H. (2006b). Confronting the challenges of a participatory culture (part seven). Retrieved: http://henryjenkins.org/2006/10/confronting_the_challenges_of_6.html

Jenkins, H. (2012). *Textual poachers: Television fans and participatory culture*. London: Routledge.

Jenkins, H., Purushotma, R., Weigel, M., Clinton, K., & Robinson, A.J. (2009). Confronting the challenges of participatory culture: Media education for the 21st century, *A Report for the MacArthur Foundation*, Cambridge, MA: MIT Press.

Jenkins, H., & Thorburn, D. (Eds.). (2004). *Democracy and new media*. Cambridge, MA: MIT Press.

Jenkins, H., Ford, S., & Green, J. (2013). *Spreadable media: Creating value and meaning in a networked culture*. New York: New York University Press.

Jerit, J., Barabas, J., & Bolsen, T. (2006). Citizens, knowledge, and the information environment. *American Journal of Political Science* 50(2), 266–282.

Jewitt, C., & Kress, G. (2003) *Multimodal literacy*, New York: Peter Lang.

Jhally, S., & Lewis, J. (1998). The struggle over media literacy. *Journal of Communication* 48(2): 109–121.

Johnson, P. (2012). *Habermas: Rescuing the public sphere*. London: Routledge.

Jolls, T., & Thoman, L. (2005). About CML: *Center for media literacy*. Retrieved: http://www.medialit.org/about-cml

Jones, C., Ramanau, R., Cross, S., & Healing, G. (2010). Net generation or digital natives: Is there a distinct new generation entering university? *Computers & Education*, 54(3), 722–732.

Junco, R. (2012a). In-class multitasking and academic performance. *Computers in Human Behavior*, 28(6), 2236–2243.

Junco, R. (2012b). Too much face and not enough books: The relationship between multiple indices of Facebook use and academic performance. *Computers in Human Behavior*, 28(1), 187–198.

Junco, R. (2012c). The relationship between frequency of Facebook use, participation in Facebook activities, and student engagement. *Computers & Education*, 58(1), 162–171.

Junco, R. (2013a). I spy: Seeing what students really do online. *Learning, Media and Technology*, 1–15.

Junco, R. (2013b). Comparing actual and self-reported measures of Facebook use. *Computers in Human Behavior*, 29(3), 626–631.

Junco, R., & Cotten, S. R. (2010). Perceived academic effects of instant messaging use. *Computers & Education*, 56, 370–378.

Junco, R., & Cotten, S. (2012). No A 4 U: The relationship between multitasking and academic performance. *Computers & Education*, 59(2), 505–514.

Junco, R., Heiberger, G., & Loken, E. (2011). The effect of Twitter on college student engagement and grades. *Journal of Computer Assisted Learning*, 27(2), 119–132.

Junco, R., Elavsky, C. M., Heiberger, G. (2012a). Putting Twitter to the test: Assessing outcomes for student collaboration, engagement, and success. *British Journal of Educational Technology*, 1–15.

Kahne, J., Lee, N., & Feezell, J. (2010). The civic and political significance of online participatory cultures among youth transitioning to adulthood. *DML Central Working Paper*. Irvine, CA. Available: http://www.dmlcentral.net

Kahne, J., Lee, N., & Feezell, J.T. (2012). Digital media literacy education and online civic and political participation. *International Journal of Communication*, 6, 1–24.

Kahne, J., Ulman, J., & Middaugh, E. (2011). *Digital opportunities for civic education*. Washington, DC: American Enterprise Institute.

Kaplan, A. M., & Haenlein, M. (2010). Users of the world, unite! The challenges and opportunities of social media. *Business Horizons*, 53(1), 59–68.

Kellner, D. (1995a). *Media culture*. London: Routledge.

Kellner, D. (1995b). "Cultural studies, multiculturalism, and media culture." In G. Dines & J. Humez (Eds.) *Gender, race and class in media*, Thousand Oaks, CA: Sage, 5–17.

Kellner, D. (1998). Multiple literacies and critical pedagogy in a multicultural society, *Educational Theory*, 48(1), 103–122.

Kellner, D. (2002). Technological revolution, multiple literacies, and the restructuring of education. In I. Snyder (Ed.) *Silicon literacies*, London: Routledge, 154 –169.

Kellner, D. (2004). Technological transformation, multiple literacies, and the re-visioning of education, *E-Learning*, 1(1), 9–37.

Kellner, D., & Share, J. (2005). Towards critical media literacy: Core concepts, debates, organizations, and policy. *Discourse: Studies in the Cultural Politics of Education* 26(3), 369–386

Kellner, D., & Share, J. (2007a). "Critical media literacy, democracy, and the reconstruction of education." In D. Macedo & S.R. Steinberg (Eds.) *Media literacy: A reader.* New York: Peter Lang, pp. 3–23.

Kellner, D., & Share, J. (2007b). Critical media literacy is not an option. *Learning Inquiry* 1:59–69.

Kellner, D., & Share, J. (2009). "Critical media education and radical democracy," in M. Apple, W. Au & L. Armando Gandin (Eds.) *The Routledge international handbook of critical education.* London: Routledge, 281–295.

Kendall, A., & Mcdougall, J. (2012). Critical media literacy after the media Alfabetización mediática crítica en la postmodernidad. Retrieved: http://www.revistacomunicar.com/pdf/preprint/38/En-02-PRE-13482.pdf

Kennedy, G., Dalgarno, B., Bennett, S., Judd, T., Gray, K., & Chang, R. (2008). "Immigrants and natives: Investigating differences between staff and students' use of technology." In *Hello! Where are you in the landscape of educational technology?* Proceedings ascilite Melbourne 2008. Retrieved: http://www.ascilite.org.au/conferences/melbourne08/procs/kennedy.pdf

Kiili, C., Laurinen, L., & Marttunen, M. (2008). Students evaluating Internet sources: From versatile evaluators to uncritical readers. *Journal of Educational Computing Research*, 39(1), 75–95.

Kinzer, C., & Leander, K. M. (2003). "Reconsidering the technology/language arts divide: Electronic and print-based environments." In D. Flood, D. Lapp, J. R. Squire, & J. M. Jensen (Eds.) *Handbook of research on teaching the English language arts.* Mahwah, NJ: Erlbaum, 546–565.

Kist, W. (2005). *New literacies in action: Teaching and learning in multiple media.* New York: Teachers College Press.

Kligler-Vilenchik, N., & Shresthova, S. (2012). Learning through practice: Participatory culture practices, *Digital Media & Learning Research Hub.* October. Available: http://dmlhub.net/sites/default/files/Learning%20Through%20Practice_Kligler-Shresthova_Oct-2-2012.pdf

Knobel, M., & Lankshear, C. (2010). *DIY media: Creating, sharing and learning with new technologies* (Vol. 44). New York: Peter Lang.

Kolb, L. (2008). Toys to tools: Connecting student cell phones to education. *International Society for Technology in Education.*

Koltay, T. (2011). The media and the literacies: Media literacy, information literacy, digital literacy, *Media Culture Society* 33, 211–221.

Kraidy, U. (2002). Digital media and education: Cognitive impact of information visualization. *Journal of Educational Media*, 27(3), 95–106.

Kress, G. (2003) *Literacy in the new media age.* New York: Routledge.

Kress, G., & van Leeuwen, T. (2001). *Multimodal discourse: The modes and media of contemporary communication.* London: Arnold Publishers.

Kubey, R., & Baker, F. (1999). Has media literacy found a curricular foothold? *Education Week*, 19(9), 56–58.

Kuiper, E., & Volman, M. (2008). "The Web as a source of information for students in K–12 education." In J. Coiro, M. Knobel, C. Lankshear, & D.J. Leu (Eds.) *Handbook of research on new literacies*. Mahwah, NJ: Lawrence Erlbaum Associates, 241–266.

Kumar, R., Novak, J., & Tomkins, A. (2010). "Structure and evolution of online social networks." In P. Yu, J. Han, & C. Faloutsos (Eds.) *Link mining: Models, algorithms, and applications*. New York: Springer, 337–357.

Kurlantzick, J., & Leader, E. (2012, April 8). "How democracies clamped down on the Internet. For the new bad guys in Web freedom, look beyond authoritarian states," *The Boston Globe Company*.

Lakoff, G. (2004). *Don't think of an elephant: Know your values and frame the debate: The essential guide for progressives*. White River Junction, VT: Chelsea Green Publishing.

Lakoff, G. (2008). *The political mind: Why you can't understand 21st-century politics with an 18th-century brain*. New York: Viking.

Lakoff, G., & Wehling, E. (2012). *The little blue book: The essential guide to thinking and talking democratic*. New York: Free Press.

Lankshear, C., & Knobel, M. (2003). *New literacies: Changing knowledge and classroom learning*. London: Open University Press.

Lankshear, C., & Knobel, M. (2006). *New literacies: Changing knowledge in the classroom*. London: Open University Press.

Lasica, J.D. (2008). *Civic engagement on the move: How mobile media can serve the public good*. The Aspen Institute Communication and Society Program Washington, DC.

Lavender, T., Tufte, B., & Lamish, D. (2003). *Global trends in media education: Policies and practices*. Cresskill, NJ: Hampton Press.

Leaning, M. (2009). *Issues in information and media literacy: Criticism, history, and policy*, volume 1. Santa Rosa, CA: Informing Science Press.

Lehrer, J. (2009, May 18). Don't! The secret of self-control. *New Yorker*.

Leman, N. (1998). The good citizen: How our ideals of citizenship are changing. *The Washington Monthly Online* 30/10, Retrieved: http://www.washingtonmonthly.com/books/1998/9810.lemann.citizen.html

Lenhart, A., Ling, R., Campbell, S., & Purcell, K. (2010). Teens and mobile phones. *Pew Internet and American Life Project*, 20.

Lenhart, A., Purcell, K., Smith, A., & Zickuhr, K. (2010a). Social media and mobile Internet use among teens and young adults. *Pew Internet & American Life Project*, 3. Retrieved: http://web.pewinternet.org/~/media/Files/Reports/2010/PIP_Social_Media_and_Young_Adults_Report_Final_with_toplines.pdf

Lenhart, A., Purcell, K., Smith, A., & Zickuhr, K. (2010b). Social media & mobile Internet use among teens and young adults. *Pew Internet & American life project*, Washington, DC, 155–179.

Lessig, L. (2008). *Remix: Making art and commerce thrive in the hybrid economy*. New York: Penguin.

Levy, P. (1997). *Collective intelligence: Mankind's emerging world in cyberspace*. Cambridge, MA: Perseus Books.

Lewis, J. (2006). News and the empowerment of citizens. *European Journal of Cultural Studies* 9(3), 303–319.

Lewis, K., Kaufman, J., & Christakis, N. (2008). The taste for privacy: An analysis of college student privacy settings in an online social network. *Journal of Computer-Mediated Communication, 14*(1), 79–100.

Ligon, E., & Schechter, L. (2012). Motives for sharing in social networks. *Journal of Development Economics,* 99(1), 13–26.

Lim, S. S., Nekmat, E., & Nahar, S. N. (2011). "The implications of multimodality for media literacy." In K. O'Halloran & B. A. Smith (Eds.) *Multimodal studies – Exploring issues and domains.* London: Routledge, 169–183.

Lindgren, R., & McDaniel, R. (2012). Transforming online learning through narrative and student agency. *Educational Technology & Society,* 15(4), 344–355.

Lippmann, W. (1946). *Public opinion.* New Brunswick, NJ: Transaction Publishers.

Lippmann, W. (1962). *A preface to politics.* Rockville, MD: Prometheus Books.

Livingstone, J. (ND). Metacognition: An overview. http://gse.buffalo.edu/fas/shuell/cep564/metacog.htm

Livingstone, S. (2004a). What is media literacy? *Intermedia,* 32(3), 18–20.

Livingstone, S. (2004b). Media Literacy and the Challenge of New Information and Communication Technologies. *The Communication Review,* 7(1), 3–14.

Livingstone, S. (2008). "Converging traditions of research on media and information literacies: Disciplinary, critical, and methodological issues." In J. Coiro, M. Knobel, C. Lankshear, & D. Leu (Eds.) *Handbook of research on new literacies.* New York: Taylor & Francis, 103–132.

Loader, B. (Ed.). (2007). *Young citizens in the digital age: Political engagement, young people and new media.* New York: Routledge.

Lopez, A. (2008). *Mediacology: A multicultural approach to media literacy in the 21ˢᵗ century.* New York: Peter Lang.

Losh, E., & Jenkins, H. (2012). Can public education coexist with participatory culture? *Knowledge Quest,* 41(1), 16–21.

Louis, W.R. (2009). Collective action—and then what? *Journal of Social Issues,* 65(4), 727–748.

Luke, C. (2000). "Cyber-schooling and technological change: Multiliteracies for new times." In B. Cope & M. Kalantzis (Eds.) *Multiliteracies: Literacy learning and the design of social futures.* London: Routledge.

Luke, A., & Freebody, P. (1997). "Shaping the social practices of reading." In S. Muspratt, A. Luke, & P. Freebody (Eds.) Constructing critical literacies: Teaching & learning textual practice. Sydney: Allen & Unwin; and Cresskill, NJ: Hampton Press.

MacArthur Foundation. Rational & Strategy. Chicago, IL. Retrieved: http://www.macfound.org/programs/learning/strategy/

Madden, M., Lenhart, A., Cortesi, S., Gasser, U., Duggan, M., & Smith, A. (2013). Teens, social media and privacy. *Pew Internet & American Life Project.* http://www.pewinternet.org/Reports/2013/Teens-Social-Media-And-Privacy.aspx

Manjoo, F. (2008). *True enough: Learning to live in a post-fact society.* New York: Wiley.

Masterman, L. (1985). *Teaching the media.* London: Routledge.

Masterman, L. (1998). "Forward: The media education revolution." In A. Hart (Ed.) *Teaching the media: International perspectives*. Mahwah, NJ: Lawrence Erlbaum Associates, xi.

Mercea, D. (2013). Probing the implications of Facebook use for the organizational form of social movement organizations. *Information Communication and Society*, 16(8), 1306–1327.

Middaugh, E. (2012). Service & activism in the digital age: Supporting youth engagement in public life. *MacArthur Research Network on Service and Activism in the Digital Age*. Available: http://dmlhub.net/sites/default/files/Service_Activism_Digital_Age.pdf

Mihailidis, P. (2006). Media literacy in journalism/mass communication: Can the United States learn from Sweden? *Journalism and Mass Communication Educator*, 60(4), 416.

Mihailidis, P. (2008). *Beyond cynicism: How media literacy can make students more engaged citizens*. Doctoral Dissertation, University of Maryland College of Journalism.

Mihailidis, P. (2009a). Beyond cynicism: Media education and civic learning outcomes in the university. *International Journal of Media and Learning* 1/3, 1–13.

Mihailidis, P. (2009b). Connecting culture through global media literacy. *Afterimage: The Journal of Media Arts and Cultural Criticism*. 37/2, 37–43.

Mihailidis, P. (2009c). The new civic education: Media literacy and youth empowerment worldwide. *A report for the Center for International Media Assistance at the National Endowment for Democracy*. Washington DC: September. Available: http://cima.ned.org/reports/media-literacy-empowering-youth-worldwide.html

Mihailidis, P. (2011). New civic voices and the emerging media literacy landscape. *Journal of Media Literacy Education*, 3/1, 4–5.

Mihailidis, P. (2012). *News literacy: Global perspectives for the newsroom and the classroom*. New York: Peter Lang.

Mihailidis, P., & Cohen, J. (2013). Exploring Curation as a Core Digital and Media Literacy Competency. *Journal of Interactive Media in Education*, 2, Spring.

Mihailidis, P., & Thevenin, B. (2013). Media literacy as a core competency for engaged citizenship in participatory democracy, *American Behavioral Scientist*, 57(9), 1611–1622.

Mihailidis, P. (2014). The Civic-Social Media Disconnect: Exploring Perceptions of Social Media for Engagement in the Daily Life of College Students. *Information, Communication, & Society*.

Mihailidis, P., Fincham, K., & Cohen, J. (2014). Towards a media literate model for civic identity on social networks: Exploring notions of community, participation, and identity of university students on Facebook. *Atlantic Journal of Communication* (In press).

Mills, E. (2010, June 4). "Scare tactics, blocking sites can be bad for kids." *CNET News*: Retrieved: http://news.cnet.com/8301-27080_3-20006868-245.html

Mindich, D.T.Z. (2005). *Tuned out: Why Americans under 40 don't follow the news*. Oxford, UK: Oxford University Press.

Mitchell, A., (2010). Revealing the digital news experience: For young and old. *Nieman Reports*, 64(2), 27–29.

Mitchell, A. & Rosenstiel, T. (2012). *State of the media 2012*. The Pew Research Center's project for excellence in journalism. Available: http://stateofthemedia.org/2012/mobile-devices-and-news-consumption-some-good-signs-for-journalism/what-facebook-and-Twitter-mean-for-news/

Moeller, S. (2010). *A day without media*. International center for media and the public agenda, University of Maryland College Park. Retrieved: http://withoutmedia.wordpress.com/

Moeller, S. (2011). *The world unplugged*. International center for media and the public agenda, University of Maryland College Park. Retrieved: http://theworldunplugged.wordpress.com/

Monk, A. (2011). What's the big deal with Facebook? A study of the social media use of 1,632 Canadians, *Abacus Data*, January. Retrieved: http://abacusdata.ca/wp-content/uploads/2011/01/Facebook-report-final.pdf

Montgomery, K. (2007). *Generation digital: Politics, commerce, and childhood in the age of the Internet*. Cambridge, MA: MIT Press.

Morozov, E. (2011). *The net delusion: The dark side of Internet freedom*. New York: Penguin Books.

Morozov, E. (2013). *To save everything, click here*. New York: Public Affairs.

Mujica, C. (2012). Creating shared dialog through case study exploration: The global media literacy learning module. In P. Mihailidis (Ed.) *News literacy: Global perspectives for the newsroom and the classroom*. New York: Peter Lang, 97–120.

Myrdal, G. (1958). *Beyond the welfare state*. London: Duckworth.

National Association of Media Literacy Education (NAMLE). (2007)."The core principles of media literacy education in the United States." Retrieved: http://namle.net/publications/core-principles/

Neal, Z. (2012). *The connected city: How networks are shaping the modern metropolis*. New York: Routledge.

Norris, P. (2003). *Digital divide: Civic engagement, information poverty, and the Internet worldwide* (Vol. 40). Cambridge, UK: Cambridge University Press.

Ofcom. (2005). *Media literacy audit. Report on media literacy amongst children*, Office of Communication. London. Retrieved: http://www.ofcom.org.uk/advice/media_literacy/medlitpub/medlitpubrss/children/children.pdf

Ofcom. (2010). *Children's media literacy audit 2010*. London. Retrieved: http://www.stakeholders.ofcom.org.uk/market-data-research/media-literacy-pubs

Ong, W. (1982). *Orality and literacy: The technologizing of the word*. London: Routledge.

Oxstrand, B. (2009). Media literacy education - A discussion about media education in the Western countries, Europe and Sweden. Paper presented at the Nordmedia09 conference in Karlstad University, Sweden, August 13–15.

Papacharissi, Z. (2009). "The virtual sphere 2.0: The Internet, the public sphere and beyond." In A. Chadwick & P. Howard (Eds.) *Handbook of internet politics*, London: Routledge, 230–245.

Papacharissi, Z. (2010). *A private sphere: Democracy in the digital age*. Cambridge, UK: Polity Press.

Papacharissi, Z. (2011). Introduction to themed issue, On convergent supersurfaces and public spheres online. *International Journal of Electronic Governance, 4* (1). 9–17.

Papacharissi, Z., & Mendelson, A. (2008). Toward a new(er) sociability: Uses, gratifications, and social capital on Facebook. Paper presented at the Internet Research conference, Copenhagen, Denmark, October.

Pariser, E. (2011). *The filter bubble: What the Internet is hiding from you*. New York: Penguin.

Peppler, K. A., & Kafai, Y. B. (2007). From supergoo to scratch: Exploring creative digital media production in informal learning. *Learning, Media and Technology, 32*(2), 149–166.

Perse, E. M. (2001). *Media effects and society*. London: Routledge.

Pew Research Center's Project for Excellence in Journalism. (2013). *The state of the news media 2013: An annual report on American journalism*. Retrieved: http://stateofthemedia.org/2013/overview-5/

Plato. "Phaedrus". In V.B. Leitch (Ed.) (2001). *The Norton anthology of theory and criticism*. New York: W.W Norton & Company.

Plato. "The republic". In S.M. Cohen, P. Curd, & C.D.C. Reeve (Eds.) (2005). *Readings in ancient Greek philosophy: From Thales to Aristotle, third edition*. Indianapolis, IN: Hackett Publishing Company, Inc.

Postman, N. (1985). *Amusing ourselves to death: Public discourse in the age of show business*. New York: Penguin.

Potter, W. J. (2010). *Media literacy, 5th edition*. Thousand Oaks, CA: Sage.

Prensky, M. (2001). Digital natives, digital immigrants. *On the Horizon* 9(5), 1–6.

Prensky, M. (2010). *Teaching digital natives: Partnering for real learning*. Thousand Oaks, CA: Corwin.

Putnam, R. (1995). Bowling alone. *Journal of Democracy* 6(1), Retrieved: http://xroads.virginia.edu/~HYPER/DETOC/assoc/bowling.html.

Putnam, R. (2000). *Bowling alone: The collapse and revival of American community*. New York: Simon & Schuster.

Putnam, R. D., Feldstein, L., & Cohen, D. J. (2004). *Better together: Restoring the American community*. New York: Simon and Schuster.

Reese, S. (2012). "Global news literacy: Challenges for the educator." In P. Mihailidis (Ed.) *News literacy: Global perspectives for the newsroom and the* classroom. New York: Peter Lang, 63–80.

Rennie, E. (2007). Community media in the prosumer era. *3C Media Journal of Community, Citizen's and Third Sector Media and Communication*, (3).

Rheingold, H. (2008a). "Using participatory media and public voice to encourage civic engagement." In W. Lance Bennett (Ed.) *Civic life online: Learning how digital media can engage youth*. Cambridge, MA: MIT Press, 97–118.

Rheingold, H. (2008b). "Mobile media and political collective action." In J. Katz (Ed.) *The handbook of mobile communication studies*. Cambridge, MA: MIT Press.

Rheingold, H. (2012). *Net smart: How to thrive online*. Cambridge, MA: MIT Press.

Richtel, A. (2010, August 24). Digital devices deprive brain of needed downtime. *New York Times*. Retrieved: http://www.nytimes.com/2010/08/25/technology/25brain.html?ref=yourbrainoncomputers

Rideout, V.J., Foehr, U.,G., & Roberts, D.F. (2010). *Generation M2: Media in the lives of 8–18 year-olds*. Henry J. Kaiser Family Foundation, Menlo Park, CA.

Riley, E., & Literat, I. (Eds.) (2012). Designing with teachers: Participatory approaches to professional development in education. *USC Annenberg Innovation Lab* http://dmlcentral.net/sites/dmlcentral/files/resource_files/pdworkinggroup-v6-reduced.pdf

Ritzer, G., Dean, P., & Jurgenson, N. (2012). The coming of age of the prosumer. *American Behavioral Scientist, 56*(4), 379–398.

Romer, D., Hall Jamieson, K., & Pasek, J. (2009). Building social capital in young people: The role of mass media and life outlook. *Political Communication*, 26, 65–83.

Rosen, L. (2010). *ReWired: Understanding the igeneration and the way they learn*. New York: Palgrave Macmillan.

Rosen, L. (2012). *iDisorder: Understanding our obsession with technology and overcoming its hold on us*. New York: Palgrave Macmillan.

Rosenbaum, J. (2003). "How media literacy is defined: A review." Paper presented at the *International Communication Association*, San Diego, CA, May 27. Retrieved: http://www.allacademic.com/meta/p112087_index.html.

Sanchez, C.A., Wiley, J., & Goldman, S.R. (2006). "Teaching students to evaluate source reliability during Internet research tasks." In S.A. Barab, K.E. Hay, & D.T. Hickey (Eds.) *Proceedings of the seventh international conference on the learning sciences*. Mahwah, NJ: Lawrence Erlbaum Associates, 662–666.

Schiebe, C., & Rogow, F. (2011). *The teacher's guide to media literacy: Critical thinking in a multimedia world*. Thousand Oaks, CA: Corwin Press.

Schiller, H. (1975). *The mind managers*. Boston, MA: Beacon Press.

Schiller, H. (1991). *Culture, Inc: The corporate takeover of public expression*. Oxford, UK: Oxford University Press.

Schiller, H. (1995). *Information inequality*. London: Routledge.

Schooler, D., Sorsoli, C. L., Kim, J. L., & Tolman, D. L. (2009). Beyond exposure: A person-oriented approach to adolescent media diets. *Journal of Research on Adolescence*, 19(3), 484–508.

Schudson, M. (1998a). Changing concepts of democracy. *MIT Communications Forum*. Retrieved: http://web.mit.edu/comm-forum/papers/schudson.html

Schudson, M. (1998b). *The good citizen: A history of American civic life*. New York: Free Press.

Schudson, M. (1999). Good citizens and bad history: Today's political ideals in historical perspective. Paper presented at conference on *"The Transformation of Civic Life"* Middle Tennessee State University. November 12–13. Retrieved: http://www.mtsu.edu/~seig/paper_m_schudson.html

Schudson, M. (2008). *Why democracies need an unlovable press*. Cambridge, UK: Polity Press.

Schwartz, D., & Arena, D. (2013). Measuring what matters most: Choice-based assessments for the digital age. *MacArthur Foundation Reports on Digital Media and Learning*. Cambridge, MA: MIT Press. Retrieved: http://dmlhub.net/sites/default/files/9780262518376_Measuring_What_Matters_Most_0.pdf

Scull, T. M., & Kupersmidt, J. B. (2011). An Evaluation of a Media Literacy Program Training Workshop for Late Elementary School Teachers. *The Journal of Media Literacy Education*, 2(3), 199.

Selwyn, N. (2004). Reconsidering political and popular understandings of the digital divide. *New Media & Society*, 6(3), 341–362.

Shah, D.V., McLeod, J.M. & Lee, N-J. (2009). Communication competence as a foundation for civic competence: Processes of socialization into citizenship. *Political Communication*, 26, 102–117.

Share, J. (2009). *Media literacy is elementary: Teaching youth to critically read and create media*. New York: Peter Lang.

Sharma, P., Land, S. M., Jordan, R., Swain, J., & Smith, B. K. (2010). Patterns of interaction and everyday knowledge sharing in social network environments. In *Proceedings of the 9th International Conference of the Learning Sciences-Volume 2* (pp. 394–396). International Society of the Learning Sciences, June.

Shirky, C. (2008). *Here comes everybody: The power of organizing without organizations.* New York: Penguin.

Shirky, C. (2010). *Cognitive surplus: How technology makes consumers into collaborators.* New York: Penguin.

Sholle, D., & Denski, S. (1993). Reading and writing the media: Critical media literacy and postmodernism. *Critical literacy: Politics, praxis, and the postmodern,* 297–321.

Shumow, M. (Ed.). (2014). *Mediated communities: Civic voices, empowerment and belonging in the digital era.* New York: Peter Lang (Forthcoming).

Shumow, M., & Chatterjee, S. (2012). "The role of multimedia storytelling in teaching global journalism: A news literacy approach." In P. Mihailidis (Ed.) *News literacy: Global perspectives for the newsroom and the classroom.* New York: Peter Lang, 139–160.

Siegel, D. A. (2009). Social networks and collective action. *American Journal of Political Science, 53*(1), 122–138.

Silverblatt, A. (2001). *Media literacy: Keys to interpreting media messages,* 2nd edition. Westport, CT: Praeger.

Silverblatt, A. (2004). Media as social institution. *American Behavioral Scientist* 48(2), 35–41.

Silverblatt, A., Ferry, J., & Finan, B. (2009). *Approaches to media literacy: A handbook.* Armonk, NY: ME Sharpe Incorporated.

Singer, D. G., & Singer, J. L. (1998). Developing critical viewing skills and media literacy in children. *The Annals of the American Academy of Political and Social Science, 557*(1), 164–179.

Slonje, R., & Smith, P. K. (2008). Cyberbullying: Another main type of bullying? *Scandinavian Journal of Psychology, 49*(2), 147–154.

Small, G., & Vorgan, G. (2008). *iBrain: Surviving the technological alteration of the modern mind.* New York: William Morrow.

Smith, P. K., Mahdavi, J., Carvalho, M., Fisher, S., Russell, S., & Tippett, N. (2008). Cyberbullying: Its nature and impact in secondary school pupils. *Journal of Child Psychology and Psychiatry, 49*(4), 376–385.

Solomon, G., & Schrum, L. (2007). *Web 2.0: New tools, new schools.* ISTE (International Society for Technology in Education.

Srivastava, L. (2005). Mobile phones and the evolution of social behavior. *Behavior & Information Technology, 24*/2, 111–129.

Steinfield, C., Ellison, N.B., & Lampe, C. (2008). Social capital, self-esteem, and use of online social network sites: A longitudinal analysis. *Journal of Applied Developmental Psychology* 29: 434–445.

Stein, L., & Prewett, A. (2009). Media literacy education in the social studies: Teacher perceptions and curricular challenges. *Teacher Education Quarterly, 36*(1), 131–148.

Stout, H. (2010, April 30). Anti-Social Networking? *New York Times.* Retrieved: http://www. nytimes.com/2010/05/02/fashion/02BEST.html?pagewanted=1&emc=eta1&_r=1&

Surowiecki, J. (2005). *The wisdom of crowds.* New York: Anchor Books.

Swiggum, K. (2008). Hyperworlds: The merging of generation "M," information and communication technologies, online safety, and medial literacy. *PNLA Quarterly, 72*(2), 14–18.

Taboada, A., & Guthrie, J. (2006). Contributions of student questioning and prior knowledge to construction of knowledge from reading information text. *Journal of Literacy Research*, 38(1), 1–35.

Tapscott, D., & Williams, A. (2006). *Wikinomics: How mass collaboration changes everything*. New York: Penguin.

Taylor, E. (2000). "Analyzing research on transformative learning theory." In J. Mezirow (Ed.) *Learning as transformation*. San Francisco, CA: Jossey-Bass, 285–328.

Tewksbury, D. (2003). What do Americans really want to know? Tracking the behavior of news readers on the Internet. *Journal of Communication*, 53(4), 694–710.

Tewksbury, D., & Wittenberg, J. (2012). News on the Internet: Information and citizenship in the 21st century. *Oxford Studies in Digital Politics*. Oxford, UK: Oxford University Press.

Thaler, R., & Sunstein, C. (2009). *Nudge: Improving decisions about health, wealth, and happiness*. New York: Penguin.

Thevenin, B. (2012). The re-politicization of media literacy education. *The Journal of Media Literacy Education*, 4(1), 61–69.

Thoman, E., & Jolls, T. (2004). Media literacy: A national priority for a changing world. *American Behavioral Scientist*, 48, 18–29.

Thoman, E., & Jolls, T. (2005). Media literacy education: Lessons from the Center for Media Literacy. *Yearbook of the National Society for the Study of Education*, 104(1), 180–205.

Thorson, K., Driscoll, K., Ekdale, B., Edgerly, S, Gamber Thompson, L., Schrock, L., Swartz, L., Vraga, E.K., & Wells, C. (2013). YouTube, Twitter and the Occupy Movement. *Information, Communication and Society*, 16(3), 421–451.

Tisdell, E. (2008). Critical media literacy and transformative learning. Drawing on pop culture and entertainment media in teaching for media diversity in adult higher education. *Journal of Transformative Education*, 6(1), 48–67.

Tong, S., van Der Heide, B., Langwell, L., & Walther, J. (2008). Too much of a good thing? The relationship between number of friends and interpersonal impressions on Facebook, *Journal of Computer-mediated Communication*, 13(3), 531–49.

Torres, M., & Mercado, M. (2006). The need for critical media literacy in teacher education core curricula. *Educational Studies*, 39(3), 260–282.

Tufekci, Z., & Wilson, C. (2012). Social media and the decision to participate in political protest: Observations from Tahrir Square. *Journal of Communication*, 62(2), 363–379.

Tufte, T., & Enghel, F. (2009). Youth engaging with the world: Media, communication and social change. *The International Clearinghouse on Children, Youth and Media's Yearbook*.

Turkle, S. (2004). Relational artifacts. Final report on proposal to the National Science Foundation. SES 0111-5668.

Turkle, S. (2005). *The second self: Computers and the human spirit*. Cambridge, MA: MIT Press.

Turkle, S. (2008). "Always on/always on you: The tethered self." In J. Katz (Ed.) *Handbook of mobile communication and social change*. Cambridge, MA: MIT Press, 1–21.

Turkle, S. (2012). *Alone together: Why we expect more from technology and less from each other*. New York: Basic Books.

Urry, J. (2007). *Mobilities*. Cambridge, UK: Cambridge University Press.

Vaidhyanathan, S. (2012). *The Googlization of everything:(And why we should worry)*. Berkeley: University of California Press.

Valenzuela, S., Park, N., & Kee, K.F. (2009). Is there social capital in a social network site?: Facebook use and college students' life satisfaction, trust, and participation. *Journal of Computer-Mediated Communication*, 14, 875–901.

Valenzuela, S., Arriagada, A., & Scherman, A. (2012). The social media basis of youth protest behavior: The case of Chile. *Journal of Communication*, 62(2), 299–314.

Van Dijk, J. A. (2006). Digital divide research, achievements and shortcomings. *Poetics*, 34(4), 221–235.

Walgrave, S., Bennett, W. L., Van Laer, J., & Breunig, C. (2011). Multiple engagements and network bridging in contentious politics: Digital media use of protest participants. *Mobilization*, 16(3), 325–349.

Walther, J., van Der Heide, B., Kim, S., Westerman, D., & Tong, S. (2008). The role of friends' appearance and behavior on evaluations of individuals on Facebook: Are we known by the company we keep? *Human Communication Research*, 34(1), 28–49.

Wasko, M. M., & Faraj, S. (2005). Why should I share? Examining social capital and knowledge contribution in electronic networks of practice. *MIS quarterly*, 35–57.

Watkins, S.C. (2009). Got Facebook? Investigating what's social about social media. Retrieved: http://www.newswise.com/articles/social-media-actually-strengthen-social-ties-various-demographics-engage-differently-study-says

Watson, J. A., & Pecchioni, L. L. (2011). Digital natives and digital media in the college classroom: Assignment design and impacts on student learning. *Educational Media International*, 48(4), 307–20.

Wattenberg, M.P. (2007). *Is voting for young people?* Boston, MA: Pearson Education.

Weil, D. K. (1998). *Toward a critical multicultural literacy*. New York: Peter Lang.

Williamson, B. (2013). The future of the curriculum: School knowledge in the digital age. *The John D. and Catherine T. MacArthur Foundation Reports on Digital Media and Learning*. Cambridge, MA: MIT Press. Available: http://dmlhub.net/sites/default/files/The_Future_Of_The_Curriculum.pdf

Wood, E., Zivcakova, L., Gentile, P., Archer, K., De Pasquale, D., & Nosko, A. (2012). Examining the impact of off-task multi-tasking with technology on real-time classroom learning. *Computers & Education*, 58(1), 365–374.

Wu, T. (2010). *The master switch: The rise and fall of information empires*. New York: Knopf.

Zhang, W., Johnson, T. J., Seltzer, T., & Bichard, S. L. (2010). The Revolution will be networked: The influence of social networking sites on political attitudes and behavior. *Social Science Computer Review*, 28(1), 75–92.

Zuckerman, E. (2010). Listening to global voices. *TEDGlobal*.

Zuckerman, E. (2013. *Rewire: Digital cosmpolitans in the age of connection*. New York: W.W. Norton.

Zukin, C., Keeter, S., Andolina, M., Jenkins, K., & Dell Carpini, M. X. (2006). *A new engagement? Political participation, civic life, and the changing American citizen*. Oxford, UK: Oxford University Press.

INDEX

N